THE SECRET GEOMETRY OF WASHINGTON, D.C.

The Integrity and Power
of the Original Design

Nicholas R. Mann

Green Magic

Secret Geometry of Washington D.C. © 2020 by Nicholas Mann.

All rights reserved.
No part of this book may be used or reproduced in any form without written permission of the author, except in the case of quotations in articles and reviews.

Green Magic
53 Brooks Road
Street
Somerset
BA16 0PP
England

www.greenmagicpublishing.com

Typeset by K.DESIGN
Winscombe, Somerset

ISBN 9780995547896

GREEN MAGIC

Contents

Acknowledgements   vi

Introduction   vii

Novus Ordo Seclorum: America and the New Order of the Ages   viii

1. The L'Enfant Plan and Traditional Geometry   1
2. The Creation of the Federal City   25
3. The Power of Place in the Place of Power   38
4. Major Pierre Charles L'Enfant   51
5. The Geometric Order of the Federal City   65
6. The Golden Section   87
7. The Triangle and Other Avenues   108
8. Washington after L'Enfant   133
9. The Washington Monument   148
10. '... That harmony and combination of the different parts with the whole'   155
11. Avenues to the Stars   169
12. References   193

Index   197

Acknowledgements

A great deal of credit must go to those who have delved into the rich and fascinating history of Washington, D.C. and made their work available to others. Without their efforts I would still be in the library. To Pamela Scott, Richard Longstreth, Ralph Ehrenberg, Don Hawkins, Richard W. Stephenson, J. L. Sibley Jennings, Kenneth Bowling, Bob Arnebeck, Silvio Bedini, John Reps, Hans Paul Caemmerer and all the folks at the Historical Society of Washington, D.C., thank you very much indeed. Especial gratitude must go to Dr. Philippa Berry who gave careful scrutiny to the proofs and made many valuable suggestions. The errors, omissions, claims and conclusions do, of course, remain entirely my own. I would also like to thank geometer John Michell for his inspiration in this field of research, architect Max Licher, Grand Archivist Reynold J. Matthews, the Library of Congress, Dr. Maya Sutton, publisher Peter Gotto, the late Mr. John H. Bream and last but not least, the library staff of Harrisburg, Pennsylvania, for their patient efforts on my behalf. It was a privilege for me to be able to conduct this work; I offer this book to the spirit of a great city in the hope that it may be of service to those who participate in its renewal.

Front and back covers show the L'Enfant Plan of 1791 for Washington, D.C.. Annotations to the plan appear in Thomas Jefferson's hand; for example, the cross through the w in 'Potowmac River'.

Introduction

This book shows how a system of number and geometric proportion, employed in the temples and cities of many of the great civilizations of the past, is present in the original design of the United States capital, the City of Washington in the District of Columbia.

As a result of careful observation of natural phenomena, our distant ancestors realised that every form of life, from the earth, the sun and moon, to the trees, the human body and the seashell, demonstrated common geometric proportions. Once recognised, these proportions were gradually developed into ideas and principles that became highly charged with symbolic and spiritual meaning. These principles were employed in the design of the pyramids of Mesoamerica, the temples of India and Indonesia, the mosques of the Middle East, the Forbidden City of China, and the megalithic monuments of prehistory. They provided measures so that ancient calendars could anticipate eclipses, the movement of the stars and planets could be traced over immense periods of time, and navigation over great distances could take place. With these measures, earth and sky could be divided into regions and degrees with precision and number.

This geometrical system became highly conceptualised in the architectural achievements of ancient Egypt. The complexity of the cosmos was reflected in the design of the Egyptian temple. This was the House of the *Netrw*: the 'divine principles' that included law and geometry. The Pythagoreans, who learnt from the Egyptians, believed that the wisdom enshrined within these principles formed the foundation for all right order in the world. They taught that this knowledge should govern and define the activities of humanity through cities and temples modelled upon the measures of the cosmos. Plato, St. John, and other visionaries described the ratios, measures and dimensions of the divine principles as the means by which the ideal city – the Atlantean city of Magnesia, the New Jerusalem, the City of God, the archetypal 'Heavenly City' – either had been or would be established on earth. In these cities every action was or should be an expression of divine law and power.

Over time, the principles of sacred geometry found expression in the cathedrals, palaces and basilicas of medieval Europe and in the philosophy, art and architecture of the Renaissance. But as knowledge of the system was sometimes disapproved of by the prevailing orthodoxy, some of it also became obscured or secret. The Master Masons of the great cathedrals would not have talked openly about the principles ordering their work, since these were not explicitly present in Christian doctrine.

NOVUS ORDO SECLORUM: AMERICA AND THE NEW ORDER OF THE AGES

Many of the first settlers chose to come to America because of restrictions on unorthodox religious views in their native lands. In the New World, situated across the ocean wherein Plato had located his ideal republic, there was the hope that an unrestricted, visionary order could be established. Americans aspired to surpass in wisdom, freedom and excellence the society and culture they had left behind in the Old World. By the end of the 18th century, with independence newly won, self-government achieved, a revolutionary Constitution and a Bill of Rights defined, many Americans felt that this dream was, at last, being fulfilled. Now the search began for a national seat, a capital city, which could symbolically represent and be an architectural expression of the emerging social order of the new world. It is in this context that the motto inscribed on the reverse of the Great Seal of the United States, *Novus Ordo Seclorum*, 'the new order of the ages', assumes its meaning.

In this book, I argue that the original design of the City of Washington, as an expression of emerging American values, was conceived in close accordance with the ancient system which invested proportion, measure and number with symbolic significance. The French architect Pierre Charles L'Enfant, supported by President George Washington and Secretary of State Thomas Jefferson, was the prime mover in envisioning and laying out the capital city of the United States. In his plan of 1791, L'Enfant translated the ideals of the American Federation – newly enshrined in its Constitution and Bill of Rights (which had been passed that same year) – into a design that was shaped by the long-standing principles of sacred geometry. To this day, the city is a fine example of a great underlying design, cloaked in formal and monumental architecture, providing the necessary points of

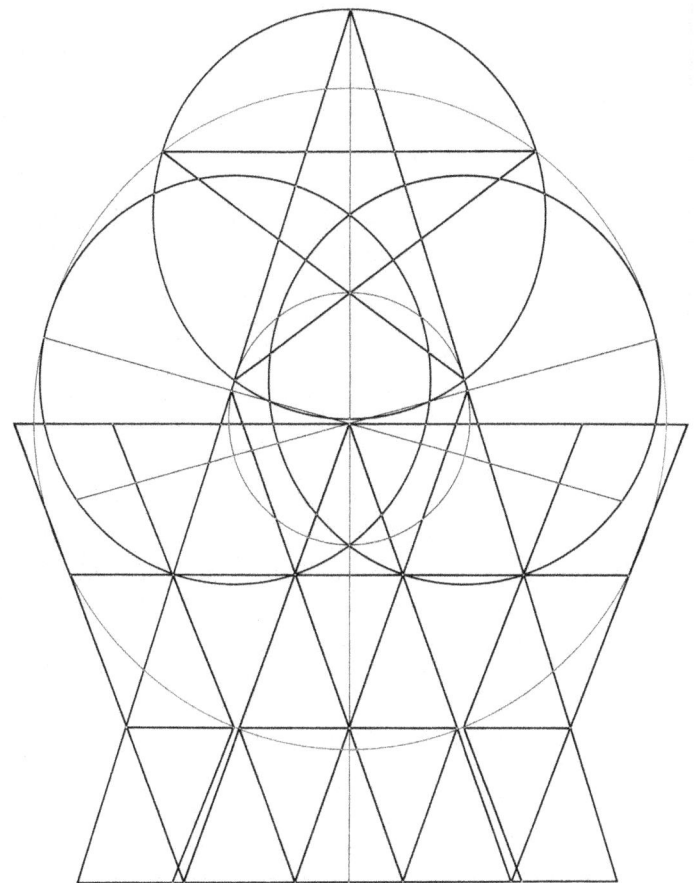

Figure 1. The geometric order in the design of Washington, D.C., as derived from the original plan of 1791 by Major Pierre Charles L'Enfant. Based upon the Golden Section, the pattern determines the placement of important buildings, public squares, diagonal avenues and the grid pattern of the streets. The top of the page looks to the east. The Capitol is in the center. The White House lies on the largest circle, bottom left. The Jefferson Memorial is on the same circle, bottom right. See Figures 17 and 42 for an overlay of this geometry upon the plan of the city.

symbolic focus for a capital city of a great nation. My research revealed, however, that L'Enfant had evidently felt compelled to keep some of his ideas secret – especially their governing geometric principle.

As L'Enfant's design for Washington took shape upon the landscape, it had to integrate symbolic principles with the realities of the new forms of political power. The City of Washington was to be the capital of a democratic and federal republic. The design therefore had to bring together in a practical, rational and secular fabric not only the seat of Congress – the representatives of the people and the States of the Union – but also the offices of the federal government, the seat of the Supreme Court, the house of the President, the monuments and memorials of the nation, and all the commercial and social institutions of the people. It is clear that L'Enfant wanted to define, balance and express these qualities and powers in an appropriate symbolic manner; all authorities are agreed that he succeeded in accomplishing this. This original design for the city was a 'truly grand' and impressive vision. Yet I had to conclude over the course of my research that a series of events, beginning with L'Enfant's own cultural predisposition to privilege a strong central authority, had led to an increasing structural emphasis upon the White House. As a result, the symbolic balance that was intended for the capital of the new republic, as set out in L'Enfant's original design, was first of all not well understood, was secondly incompletely realised, and was finally seriously departed from. The last part of this book describes and analyses the history of this unfortunate deviation from the inspired original design, and it asks: if the symbolism of the capital city was intended to be a true expression of America's heart, its innermost values, what can be done to restore the balance and integrity of the visionary principles that shaped its foundation?

Chapter 1 introduces and outlines the geometrical order of the L'Enfant Plan. Chapters 2 and 3 place the creation of the City of Washington in its political, geographical, historical and mythic contexts. Chapter 4 provides a description of L'Enfant and his work. Chapters 5, 6 and 7 are the core of the book and describe the geometry of the L'Enfant Plan in detail. Chapter 8 describes what subsequently happened both to the plan and to the city. A study of the geometry of the Washington Monument is provided by Chapter 9. Chapter 10 examines L'Enfant's intentions, and discusses the likely extent of involvement in his plan by Freemasons. Chapter 11 draws conclusions and reflects on Washington's future. Sources are provided for each chapter at the end of the book.

1

The L'Enfant Plan and Traditional Geometry

'THE CREATION OF THE WORLD'

According to Professor Mircea Eliade, all traditional architecture attempted to 'repeat the pre-eminent cosmogonic act, the Creation of the world'. These human replications of the act of creation aimed to turn back the clock of time and so restore order to the otherwise chaotic nature of life on earth. Eliade – who spent thirty years as director of the History of Religions Department at the University of Chicago – thought that every act of architecture was a creative act that attempted to bring order into the material elements of the world. Architects and builders observed the patterns and geometric principles within the forms of nature and the heavens, and because they perceived them to originate in the creative realm of the divine, they repeated them in the forms of their buildings, temples and cities upon the earth.

Through careful alignments to the heavens and through the use of pure, simple geometric forms such as the circle, the triangle, the cube, the pyramid and the square, architects believed that the divine order of the New Jerusalem, the City of Revelation, the City of God or some other prototype of the Heavenly City could be realized on earth. The Great Pyramid in Egypt stands as an example of a powerful conceptual simplicity not repeated until very recent times. The Freemasons, whose beliefs were rooted in Egyptian and Judaic architectural traditions, believed that the act of founding the Temple on earth through mathematics and geometry aligned the human world to the celestial; even if its manifest forms could only ever approximate to the pure ratios, numbers and measures of the divine order. The Islamic tradition realised its ideal city in the forms of Mecca and Medina. But standing out above all other forms, it was the 'perfect' ratio of the Golden Section – a proportion found throughout nature that provided architects, artists,

Freemasons, philosophers and mathematicians with an exemplary pattern for restoring the divine, creative order on earth.

In his design for the capital city of the New World, the eighteenth-century architect Major Pierre Charles L'Enfant proved no exception to this long-standing tradition. He took the opportunity to repeat the 'pre-eminent cosmogonic act'; and created a foundation pattern for the City of Washington based upon the Golden Section.

As will be described in this book, L'Enfant followed the pattern of the architectural re-'Creation of the world' by first establishing a new world center, an *axis mundi*, in the site for the US Capitol, the House of Congress. L'Enfant conceived of the Capitol as a primary point of origin in the center of the new country, with one vertical and two horizontal axes passing through it. He established an east–west axis across Washington with the Mall and East Capitol Street, and a north–south axis, that was to function additionally as a new, global, zero-degree meridian, running through North Capitol and South Capitol Streets. As is well known in Freemasonry, this creation of the symbolic definition of the world center and the six directions is the first step in all traditional sacred geometry. Marking the center and the cardinal directions were the first acts in the highly ritualised and geometrical laying out of any temple in classical, Egyptian, Hindu or any other early architectural tradition.

As will be shown in the following pages, the subsequent steps taken by L'Enfant demonstrate that he used the unique proportion of the Golden Section to determine the placement of the city's avenues, the squares, the White House, the Supreme Court, the monuments, the memorials, the streets, the commercial districts, City Hall and the District Courts. Through an elaborate exercise in the pentagonal nature of traditional Golden Section geometry, the French architect created a 'template' – a *Novus Ordo Seclorum* or 'new order of the ages' – for the Capital City of the new American Republic. His imagination fired by the unique opportunity to establish a center and an ideal foundational order for a country the like of which had never been seen before, the evidence clearly shows that L'Enfant followed the practice of ancient architectural tradition. The first Presidents spoke of Washington and its buildings as a manifestation of the 'divine temple' on earth. At its opening in 1800, President Adams saw the new Capitol building as a 'Temple' worthy of the blessing of 'the Supreme Ruler of the Universe'. L'Enfant saw the Golden Section proportions in his design as the perfect means to express the idealistic principles that he had been exposed to throughout his long involvement with the emerging USA and with those individuals behind its foundation from 1776 to 1791.

THE L'ENFANT DESIGN

The diagrams that follow illustrate the geometry that determined the diagonal avenues and focal points of L'Enfant's design for Washington, D.C.. Even though the great size of the principal buildings demanded that the avenues radiated from their entrances rather than through their centers, once these spatial requirements were met the avenues always conformed to the underlying geometric order. The template is informed by fundamental principles employed by architects over millennia; these have traditional, esoteric, but at times quite obvious meanings. The details of this 'L'Enfant Template' are provided in Chapters 5, 6 and 7.

The template begins with the establishment of the center, the Capitol building, as shown in Figure 2. It may be helpful to imagine this stage in relation to a surveyor standing in the center of a level area of sand. The surveyor, like the Capitol building itself, forms a vertical axis that represents a line passing through the center of the earth and pointing upwards into the heavens. Two horizontal lines are drawn by the surveyor through this center, at east–west and north–south. A second person is then introduced to lay out these lines on the sand.

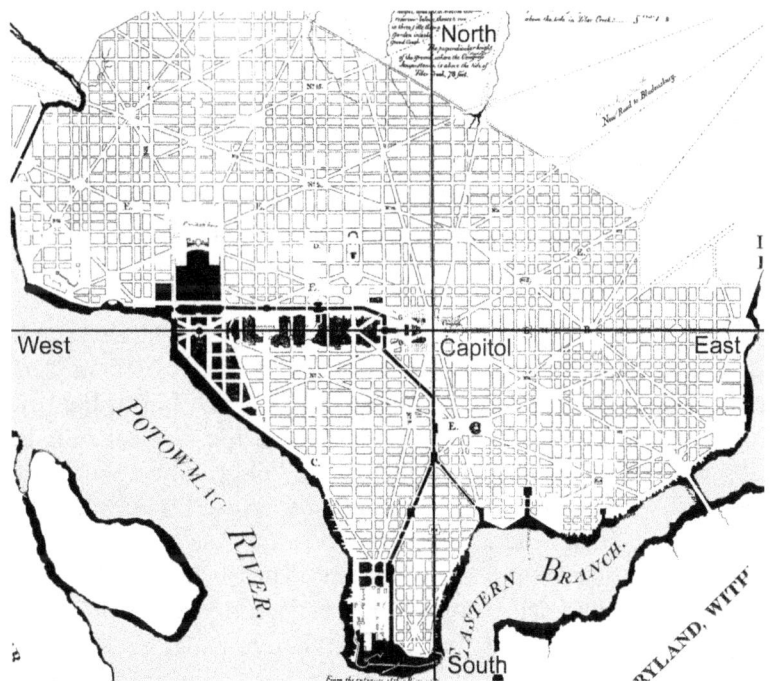

Figure 2.

The Secret Geometry of Washington, D.C.

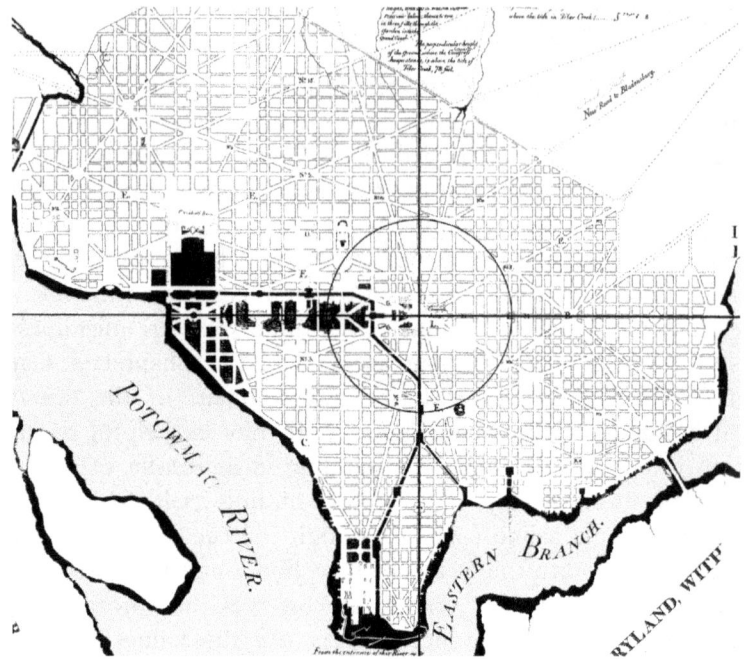

Figure 3.

These lines should be understood as parts of 'great circles' that go around the earth and so are aligned to the earth's center, axis, polar co-ordinates and direction of rotation. In other words, the lines define the relationship of the earth to the sun, the moon and stars; in turn, the lines are defined by these celestial bodies. The two surveyors who worked with L'Enfant, Andrew Ellicott and Benjamin Banneker, established these axes for the City of Washington through their use of astronomy or, in L'Enfant's words, 'celestial observation'.

The next step taken by L'Enfant was to draw a circle around his center point, the Capitol. This is shown in Figure 3 and in detail in Figure 4. The radius of this circle is 0.618 of a mile. This is the distance that each of the avenues radiating out around the Capitol runs before arriving at its first square and principal buildings. The two figures on the sand can create this circle, although of course on a much smaller scale, using two sticks and a piece of cord.

Significant squares on the L'Enfant Plan, including the intended locations of the District Courts, City Hall and the plaza before the Supreme Court, divide this first circle into five equal parts. As shown in Figure 5, the two surveyors on the sand can draw in the lines of a five-pointed star between these points. The easternmost point on the

The L'Enfant Plan and Traditional Geometry

Figure 4.

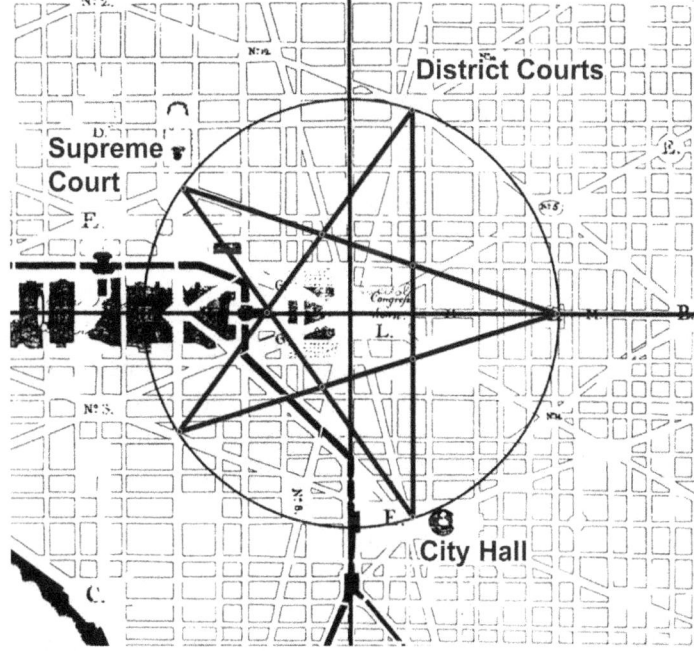

Figure 5.

The Secret Geometry of Washington, D.C.

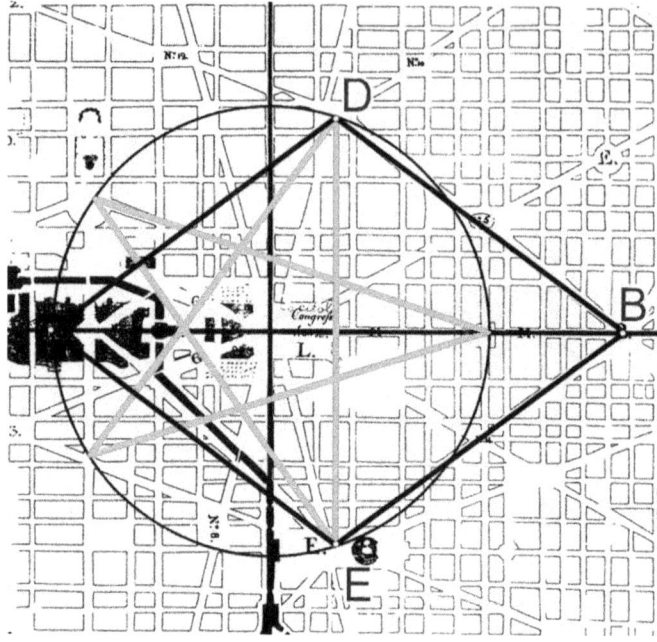

Figure 6.

circumference of the circle was a small square marked 'L' on the plan. This five-fold division of the primary circle will prove to be crucial in determining the orientation of the major avenues of the city.

In Figure 6, lines are run from the westernmost point of this first circle to points D and E of the five-pointed star. Lines of the same length are then extended from D and E to mark a point on the main axis to the east. This key point is a square on the plan that L'Enfant marked with a large 'B'. This principal square was one mile from the center at the Capitol and was the proposed location for a 'Mile or itinerary column'.

There are other ways of arriving at point B once the first circle is divided into five parts. Our two surveyors, for example, could have used their sticks and cord to draw two arcs centered on points D and E. As shown in Figure 7, where the vesica or pointed oval that they have made intersects the east–west axis to the east, they can mark point B. A second primary circle drawn around B, the Mile Column on the L'Enfant Plan, has a radius of exactly one mile. These two circles intersect at D and E, the intended locations for the District Courts and City Hall.

The distance across the primary circle to the center of the second, one-mile circle – the total length of the vesica – is now used to produce the radius of a third circle. Figure 8 shows this third circle

The L'Enfant Plan and Traditional Geometry

Figure 7.

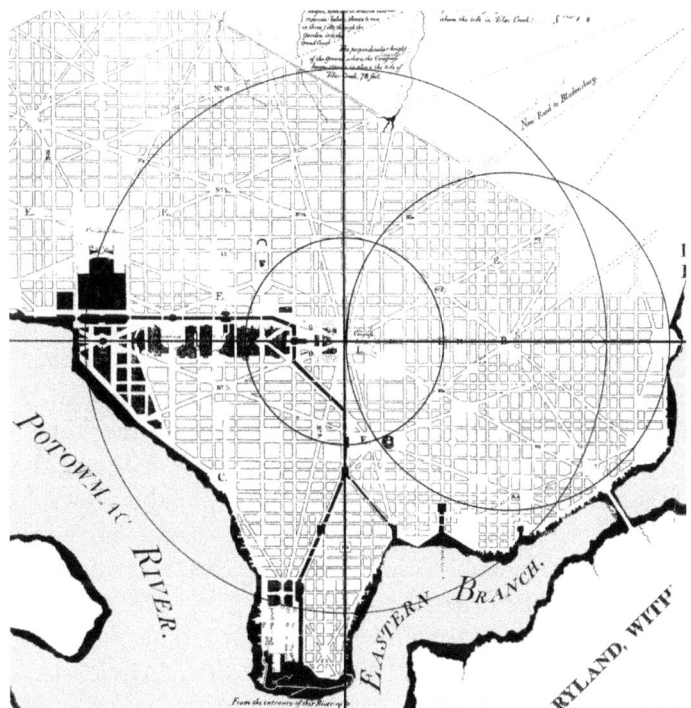

Figure 8.

The Secret Geometry of Washington, D.C.

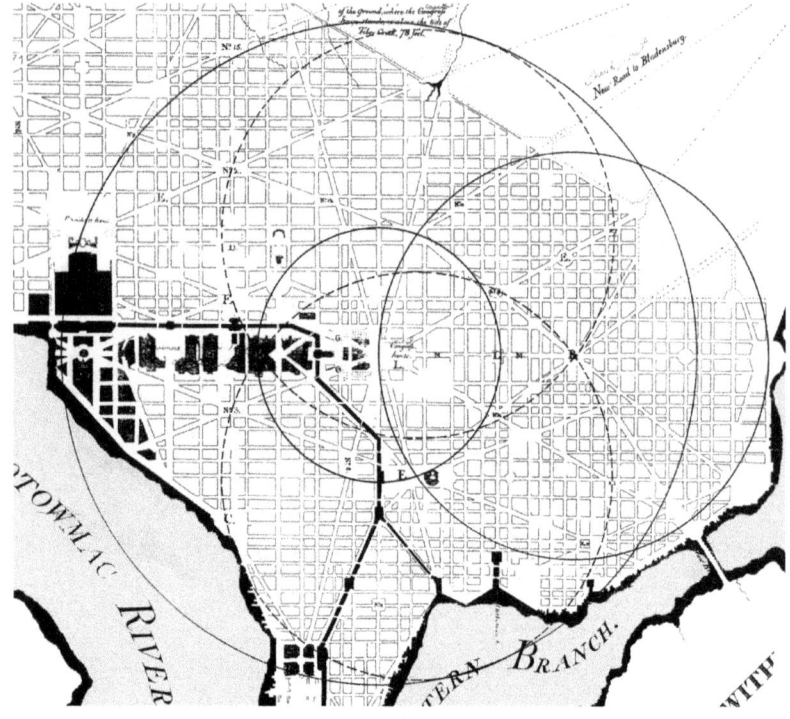

Figure 9.

once again drawn around the plan's center, the Capitol. This third circle is the sum of the radii of the first two circles and therefore has a radius of 1.618 of a mile. This is the distance L'Enfant intended to separate the Capitol and the White House. 1.618 of a mile is in the same ratio to a mile as a mile is to 0.618. This ratio is that of the Golden Section, where the new is to the original as the original is to the whole. Although our imaginary draftsmen on the sand may have used any distance for the radius of their first circle, their three circles are now related through a Golden Section ratio. The center, the axes and the three Golden Section circles provide the key to the fundamental design of the city.

In Figure 9, the draftsmen complete the circles they could have used to determine the center of the second circle to create two 'construction' circles. These will prove to be useful later on, when determining the location of squares and the orientation of avenues.

The first primary circle and the third circle intersect the second circle at points D, E, F and G. Figure 10 shows the second circle, the one-mile radius circle, divided into five equal parts by these points of intersection to form a second five-pointed star. Figure 11 shows an arm of this pentacle

The L'Enfant Plan and Traditional Geometry

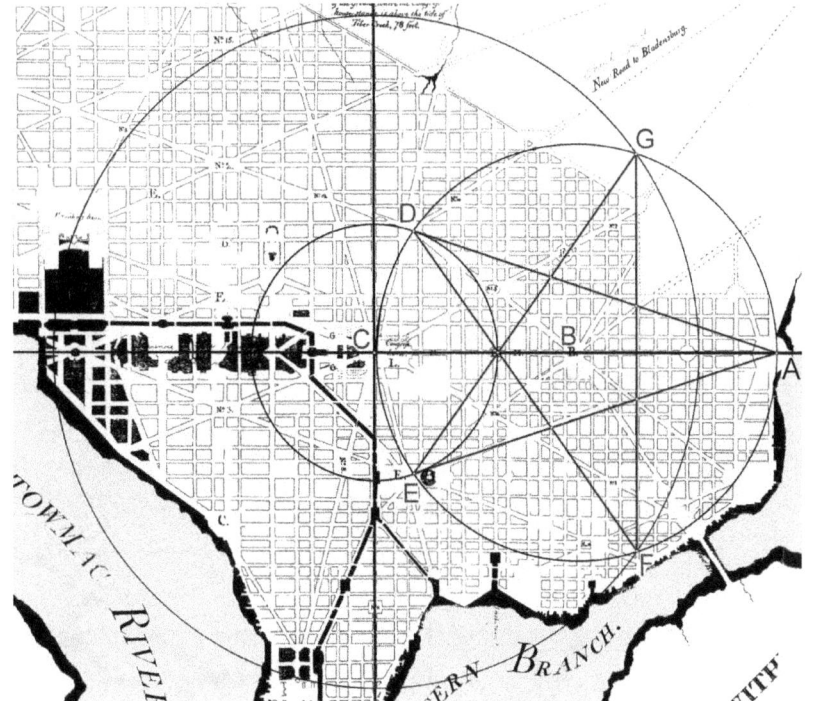

Figure 10.

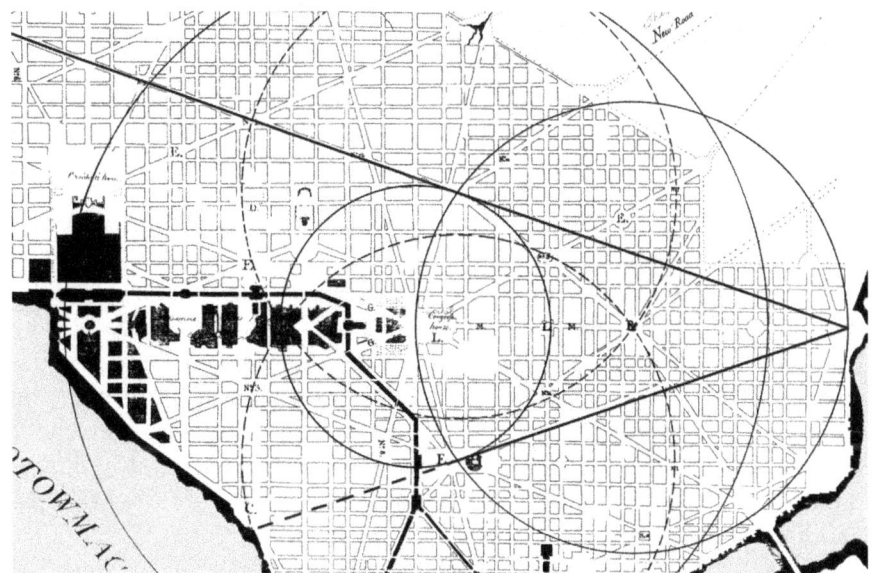

Figure 11.

Figure 12.

extended to provide an all-important orientation for Massachusetts Avenue in the western part of the city.

Our draftsmen now occupy themselves in dividing the largest of the three primary circles into five equal parts. This is shown in Figure 12. The lines of the third pentacle define further significant locations and avenues on the L'Enfant Plan, including a north–south alignment through the intended location for the Supreme Court. If the draftsmen were now to step back and admire all their stars, the result is Figure 13. This is the basic underlying template for the location of the avenues, principal buildings and squares in the City of Washington.

The final drawing of this series, Figure 14, shows the L'Enfant Plan of 1791 superimposed upon a theoretical succession of five-pointed stars.

The L'Enfant Plan and Traditional Geometry

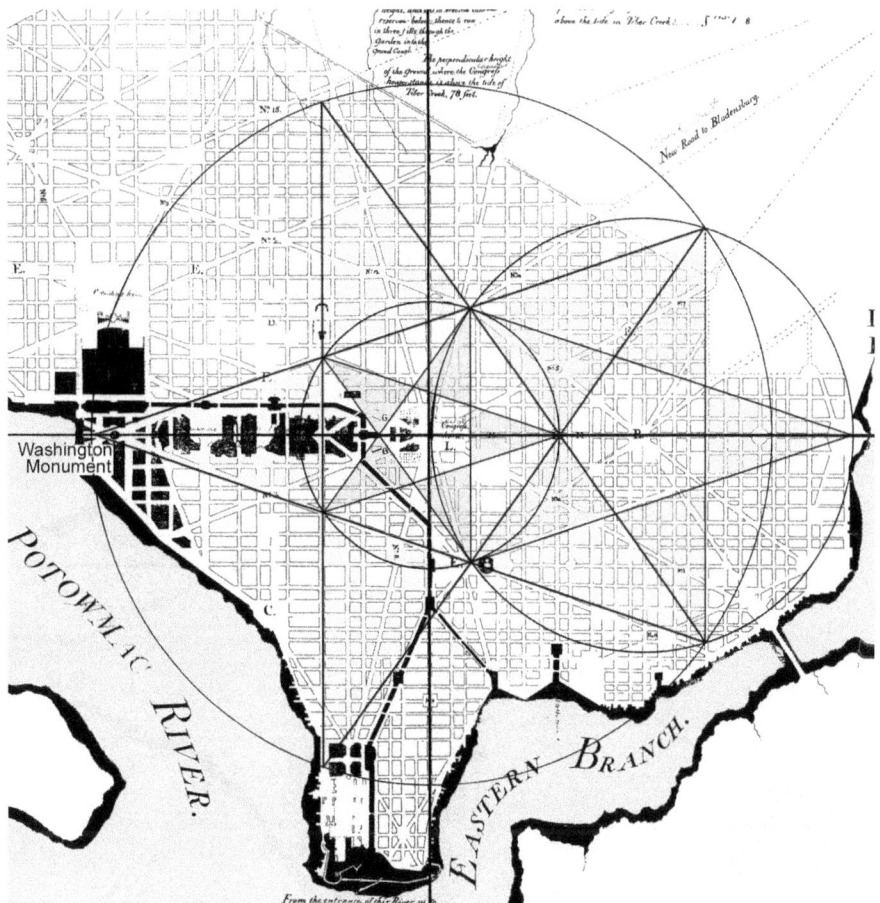

Figure 13.

From an initial or 'root' starting point in the area intended for a monument to George Washington, each star progresses to the next in the ratio of the Golden Section. In other words, one star generates another, so that it is in the same ratio to the other as the other is to the next in the series. The series may thus be imagined as extending infinitely, but any circle can be 'turned around' or inverted at any point to return to the initial root starting point. Each star is generated from or returns to a shared source in a sequence that although theoretically multiplying infinitely can turn around at any point and return to source. On the L'Enfant Plan, this inversion is demonstrated by the third primary circle, which contains the largest five-pointed star.

The Secret Geometry of Washington, D.C.

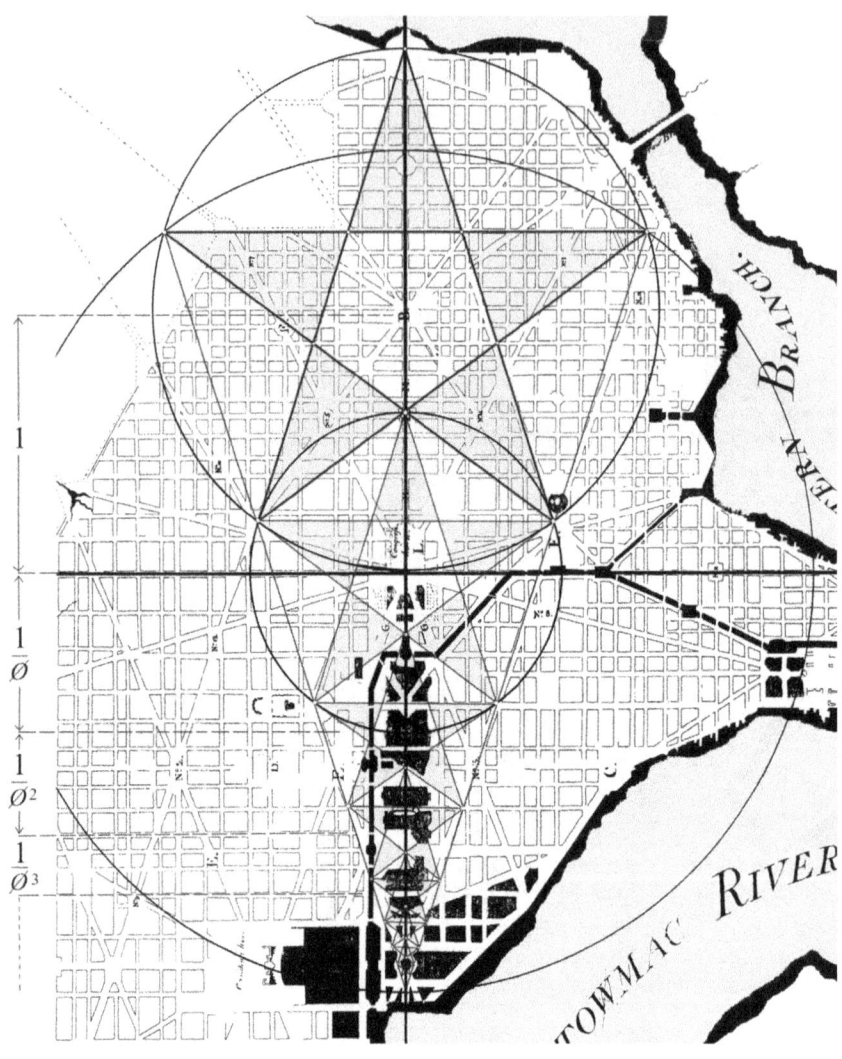

Figure 14.

At this point in the developmental sequence of the city's design, the prime locations and their functions are referred back to their founding source. This is represented on the ground by the large circle that passes through the area defined by the White House and the Washington Monument. See Figure 13. As we shall see, L'Enfant intended the first circle to represent the Capitol, the second circle the people, and the third circle the President or the Executive. The geometrical symbolism suggests that L'Enfant saw both the people, the bearers of sovereignty

The L'Enfant Plan and Traditional Geometry

Figure 15.

in the American Republic, and their representatives in the Legislature being referred back to their original bond or unity through the leadership of their President. L'Enfant's design was a stroke of genius that gave a symbolic answer to those critics of the Constitution who could not understand how sovereignty could reside among the many: *E Pluribus Unum*. (Note that as the third circle passes through the center of the White House and frames the location chosen for the Washington Monument – the initial or 'root' starting point of the pentagonal sequence – I refer to this whole area as the 'Presidential axis'.)

Figures 15 and 16 show different versions of the Golden Section pentagonal geometry that is present within the L'Enfant Plan. Figure 15 shows the essential, abstract geometry of the plan. It is a universal pattern of growth found throughout nature. The ratio can be achieved geometrically, using both sticks and cord on the ground, or a straight edge and a compass on paper. The Egyptians achieved almost unparalleled geometric precision using such simple tools. Anyone can acquire,

Figure 16.

work with and understand these kinds of traditional geometrical figures in this way.

THE GOLDEN SECTION TEMPLATE

Figure 17 is the critical diagram that shows how the center, the axes, the three circles (plus the two construction circles) and their pentagonal divisions generate the diagonal pattern of the city's squares and avenues. Once the widths of buildings are taken into account, the avenues of Washington always conform to the pattern that is generated by the underlying Golden Section circles, axes and center. This pattern was adhered to in the work of the McMillan Commission in the early 1900s; particularly in the extensions to the Mall which were provided by the Jefferson and Lincoln Memorials. The genius of L'Enfant, yet the difficultly of understanding his work, was due to the fact that he founded the City of Washington upon this geometrical template without ever providing a clear explanation of what he was doing.

The L'Enfant Plan and Traditional Geometry

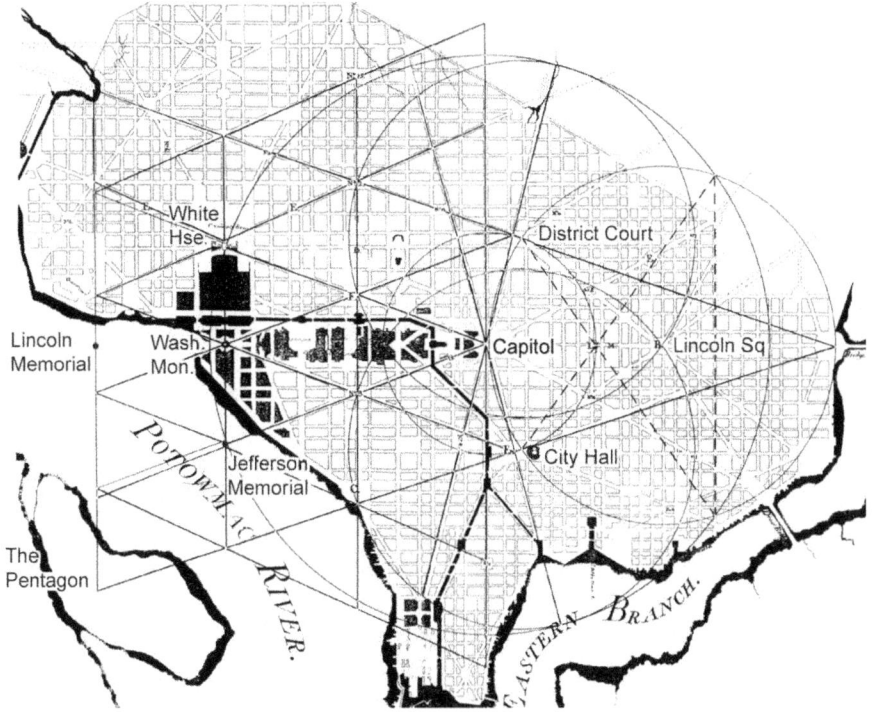

Figure 17.

The Golden Section and pentagonal sequencing present in the L'Enfant Plan of 1791 are fundamental to sacred geometry. This ratio lay behind many man-made structures of antiquity, such as the Parthenon of Athens and the Temple of Luxor in Egypt. The especial importance of this particular ratio of expansion or growth is that it is found throughout nature. The Greeks called this principle the *gnomon*: this is where new growth occurs in the same ratio to the original as the original structure or organism is to the whole finished structure or organism. The Golden Section is present throughout all the proportions of the body and is immediately evident in the growth of natural spiral forms. If the new growth of a spiral shell, for example, is given as 3 to an original of 5, then the total 8 is to the 5 as the 5 is to the 3. The subsequent expansions of 8 to 13, 13 to 21, 21 to 34, 34 to 55, and so on – as described in the series attributed to Fibonacci – come ever closer to the 'perfect' but unquantifiable ratio of the Golden Section, *phi*, written as Φ. If one was to try and mathematically quantify *phi*, it would be the ratio of 1 to 1.6180339 ... or 0.6180339 ... to 1. But it must be remembered that *phi* is a ratio, not a number. *Phi* has an important relationship to another 'irrational' proportion or number, *pi*. This relationship was explored by the Egyptians in the dimensions of the Great Pyramid; but that is another story.

Figure 16 is a version of the Golden Section template that shows pentacles emerging from a multiplicity of primary sources, each in a constant state of referral to the others. Flat, two-dimensional Figure 16, however, cannot show the wider potential that exists here for multidimensional development. The Golden Section provides a diverse, infinitely generative, self-reflexive and creative matrix. Its pentacles underlie the forms of life, and provide the key to all harmonically integrated natural systems. Leonardo da Vinci placed his figure of 'perfected man' within it. Renaissance Humanists called the pentacle the 'Figure of Life'. They pointed out that, as the measure into the multiplication of forms, the Golden Section ratio is superior to simple mirroring or doubling into two-, four-, six- and eight-fold forms. In biology, the pentagonal geometry visible in any microscopic section through the spiral strands of the genetic code establishes a complex, evolving sequence of DNA, rather than a simple repetitive one. In other words, it is the Golden Section that ensures the mysterious and marvellous diversity of creation.

The third, or final, pentacle in the sequence for Washington has been 'inverted'. As shown in Figure 14, the pentagonal sequence appears to emerge from a source around the area occupied by the Washington Monument, is developed up until the second primary circle – the 1 mile radius pentacle around the mile column – and then is inverted with the third primary circle, the 1.618 mile radius pentacle around the Capitol. One expands to two to three then returns to one. The geometric inversion re-emphasises the centrality of the Capitol; yet the template as a whole allows for a multiplicity of centers and relationships.

RISING OR FALLING STARS?

One rather narrow interpretation of this geometry maintains that when a sequence of emerging pentacles share the same relationship to their source, or when the pentacles all point upward from their source, it reveals a symbolic aspiration to spirit that acknowledges the primacy of spirit over matter. If a pentacle were to be inverted or reversed however, that is, point downwards, it would represent the predominance of matter over spirit. This interpretation, which has a Christian origin, although it is found in other contexts, ascribes a negative influence, even an evil one, to an inverted pentacle. However, in the case of Washington's geometry, the reversal of the third and final pentacle, pointing down to the Washington Monument, might be seen as countering and balancing the first two; thus no 'good' or 'bad' interpretation should necessarily be drawn.

As the inversion was achieved by the third and final pentacle, centered like the first on the Capitol, and contained within a circle on whose circumference lies the President's House, L'Enfant seems to be suggesting in his Golden Section symbolism that the nation's search for unity would be accomplished via the office of the President: *E Pluribus Unum*, 'From Many, One'. In the single figure of the President, the many people and the States of the nation are to be united as one. This extremely ancient and widespread concept of central power, or divine kingship, could well have been favoured by L'Enfant, with his childhood-ingrained aristocratic and monarchical values and his close client-patron relationship with George Washington.

If the symbolic equilibrium intended by the pentacles was ever to be disturbed, however, then the significance of this interpretation is that it suggests how the harmonious balance of the parts might easily be impaired. If the second pentacle were to become predominant, for example – that is, if the forces of the people were ever to outweigh those of government and law – then chaos could ensue across the country. If, on the other hand, the inverted pentacle were to become predominant – that is, if the forces of the Legislature or spirit were at some point outweighed by either those of the Executive or by narrow economic interests – then government would be separated from the people, and measures would need to be taken to restore the ideal republican balance between the design's different parts.

Whatever reading of this symbolism is made, the geometry makes it clear that L'Enfant designed the location of the avenues and the primary buildings of the Federal City to maintain a highly delicate balance of powerful, and sometimes opposing, forces. The architectural allegory he designed, in proportion, measure and number, saw the rising star of the American nation – shining through its people and its States, increased by the activities of commerce, governed by its constitutional principles and laws, and returned to unity through the office of its President – as a complex dynamic in which the equilibrium of all parts needed to be maintained. The House of Congress, the President's House, the Supreme Court, the places of the people, the monuments, the squares and courts of the Federal City, were each originally positioned on

Washington's Golden Section template in a relationship of measured order that was uniquely appropriate to the new republican federation.

THE FREEMASONS

Some writers maintain that an 'occult geometric system' guarded by a secret group of initiates emerged centuries ago as a result of observation of the properties of the circle and the square, and that the system then spread across the entire world. This is an important hypothesis, as it may throw light on the possible sources of L'Enfant ideas. Authors such as Tons Brunés have argued that this system was transmitted through secret organizations such as Freemasonry, and that a universal architectural template or 'canon' provided by them was used in the creation of temples, churches and other sacred spaces. It is for this reason that Freemasons are devoted to the architects who they believe first established the system, such as Hiram of Tyre, architect of the earliest Temple of Jerusalem, and Imhotep, designer of pyramids in Egypt's Old Kingdom. Yet Brunés, who is himself a Freemason, makes the assumption that because two knowledge systems are similar they must inevitably have originated from a shared source and could not have arisen independently. He is convinced there was one secret society, fraternity or priesthood, which held and transmitted these principles throughout the ages. Yet I don't believe that this was necessarily true.

As I describe in the closing chapters of this book, I could not find a single shred of positive proof that L'Enfant followed any existing architectural template in his geometrical design for the City of Washington. There is definitely no evidence that he derived his plan from a specific system of 'occult' knowledge such as Freemasonry. It is important to make this point clear from the start. I found plenty of concepts that influenced L'Enfant, especially ideas that circulated among the educated classes of his day, which of course included the Masons, but no evidence to prove that the architectural ideas in his design derived from an 'occult geometric system' that was passed onto him by Freemasons. It is far more likely that an inspired, idealistic, well-trained architect, working intuitively with the natural forms of a new landscape, may well have arrived at similar results to those who intentionally employed canonical proportions in their designs. For example, it cannot be proven that every time a 3-4-5 triangle appears at a 5,000 year old European stone circle or a 2,000 year old Hopewell mound complex that the architects were working with a

The L'Enfant Plan and Traditional Geometry

common set of theorems derived solely from Pythagoras! The appearance of 3-4-5 triangles, the Golden Section, the Platonic Solids and other geometric forms occurs in the work of mathematicians and architects working in quite separate cultural contexts, employing different methods and techniques of observation, astronomy and measure to arrive at the same result. It seems clear that since this geometry is universal, part of a living tradition, it was intuitively sensed by those working in form, measure and number. This may go some of the way to explain why L'Enfant did not or could not describe his geometry.

When I made a transparency of the geometry underlying the L'Enfant Plan and placed it over the ground plans of temples, cathedrals and cities as diverse as Stonehenge, Luxor and Angkor Wat, as shown in Figures 18, 19 and 20, some remarkable correlations appeared.

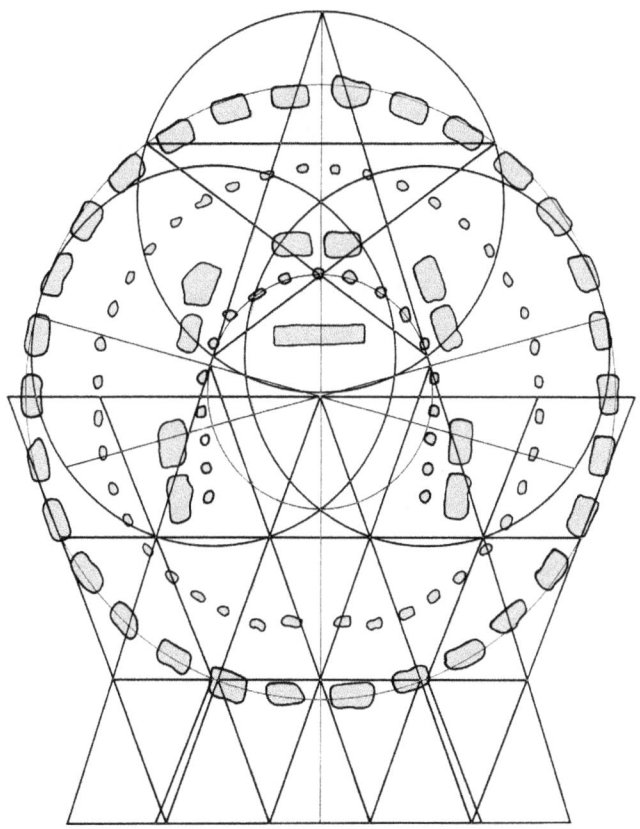

Figure 18. The geometry of the L'Enfant Plan superimposed upon the plan of a restoration of Stonehenge, England, 3100–1800 BCE.

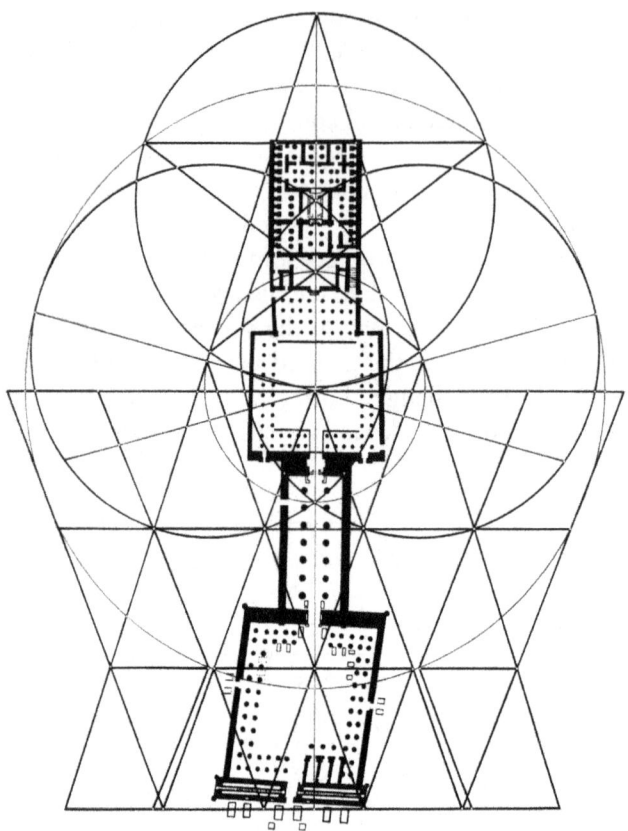

Figure 19. The L'Enfant Plan superimposed upon the Temple of Luxor, Egypt, begun c. 1400 BCE. The center of the pentacle, 'B' on the L'Enfant Plan, is placed upon the naos, the sanctuary where the statue of (the Netr) Amun stood.

However, these do not provide the evidence for a single source of occult knowledge. Instead, they confirm the presence of a universal pattern that links the proportions and measures of human and natural life. The architect or artist attuned to that knowledge, gained from observation, experience and the application of imagination, may intuitively and pre-conceptually infer the many diverse expressions of the pattern.

THE FLOWER OF LIFE

If any universal system or canon of sacred geometry does exist, one that can be transmitted over time and space, then it may be the deceptively

The L'Enfant Plan and Traditional Geometry

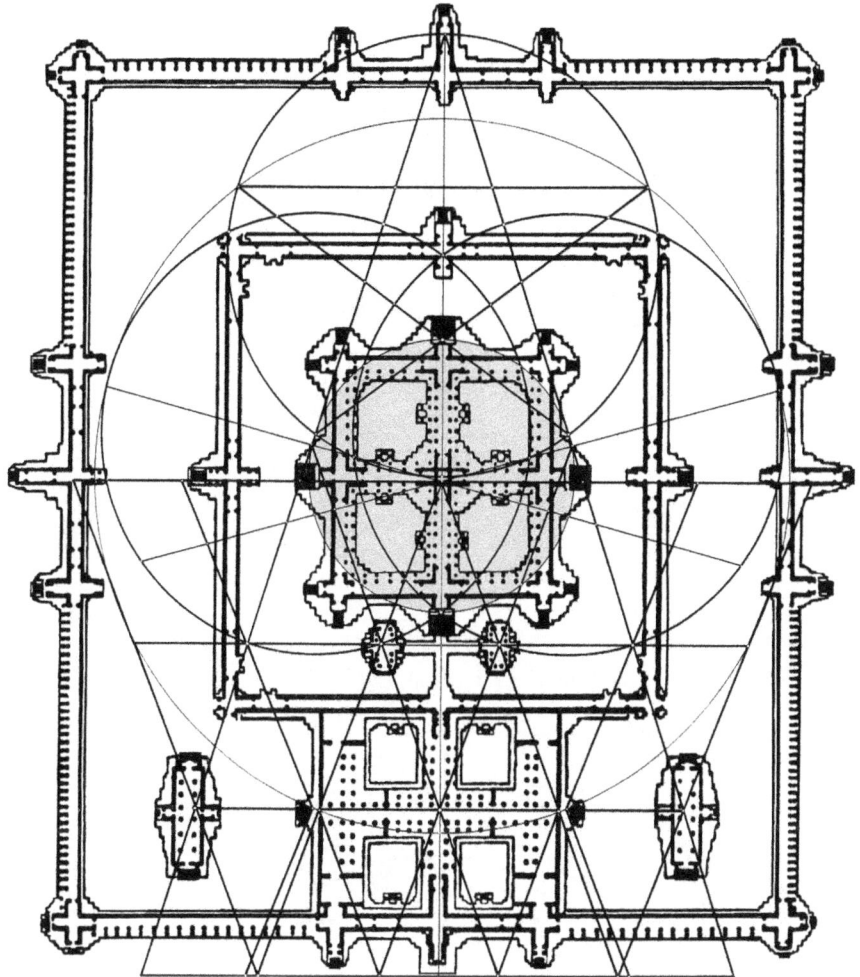

Figure 20. The L'Enfant plan superimposed upon the Khymer temple of Angkor Wat within the ceremonial city of Angkor Thom, Cambodia, 1100–1400 CE. The shaded central circle is the innermost circle of the L'Enfant Plan. The ratio of phi and its progressions are present not only in the layout of this vast inner temple but also in the total context of Angkor Thom, where square miles of formal landscape approximate the scale of the City of Washington.

simple set of overlapping circles shown in Figure 21. This pattern is known as the 'Flower of Life' or, as shown in Figure 22, 'Metatron's Cube'. (Metatron is the archangel who traditionally governs form.) The earliest known form of this figure is inscribed on the walls of a nineteenth dynasty (c. 1300 BCE) Egyptian temple at Abydos. If two circles

Figure 21. The 'Flower of Life'.

Figure 22. 'Metatron's Cube'.

The L'Enfant Plan and Traditional Geometry

Figure 23. The Dodecahedron.

of the same radius are drawn so that the circumference of one is on the center of the other (creating the *vesica piscis*), further circles around the first circle will divide it into six equal parts. As shown in Figure 21, the sequence can be extended indefinitely in every direction. When visualised in three dimensions, twelve spheres surround a central thirteenth sphere. It is possible to derive many geometrical figures from this matrix of overlapping circles, including the Platonic Solids. A Platonic Solid is one of the five regular solids: cube, tetrahedron, icosahedron, octahedron and dodecahedron – each can be inscribed within a sphere the length of whose edges and the measure of whose internal angles are the same. A dodecahedron is shown in Figure 23. The divisions of the circle shown by the Flower of Life diagram provide the basic measures of earth and heaven. Most traditional systems of geometry conceive of the division of circles and spheres in six-fold forms. Our use of 360 degrees to measure the horizon, 60 minutes to measure an hour, and 60 seconds to a minute, as well as our use of duodecimal (twelve-fold) measures, has widespread and ancient origins.

In the case of the City of Washington, however, its architect did not follow a six-fold scheme. Instead, L'Enfant deliberately drew the first circles of his design in the ratio of the Golden Section. In preference over of any other form, his design for the city focused upon pentagonal forms and Golden Section relationships. If L'Enfant did not inherit this idea directly from any pre-existing system, but arrived at it intuitively, why did he make this particular geometrical ratio the basis for the new American Capital City? Before pursuing this question in the following chapters of this book, it should be pointed out that because the pentacle and its five-sided forms are present among all the forms derived from the Flower of Life (the pentacle is present, for example, in Figure 23), the underlying design of the city does possess a relationship to all other primary geometrical forms.

2

The Creation of the Federal City

THE SEARCH FOR THE SITE

As soon as the War of Independence was over, the location of the site for the capital city of the new federation of American States became an extremely important and impassioned issue. As described in such works as Bob Arnebeck's *Through a Fiery Trial: Building Washington 1790–1800* and Kenneth Bowling's *The Creation of Washington, D.C.,* the site of the capital, the designs of the national flag, the currency and the Great Seal, were all seen as highly symbolic issues charged with immense importance. Many people attached great significance to the design of the new city, as well as to the character of the future federal buildings: the President's house, Congress and the courts. The city and its buildings were intended to be the equivalent of the cities, parliaments and royal palaces – Paris, London, Versailles or a Kremlin – of the Old World, but everyone at the time passionately believed that they must also suit the recently fought for political and spiritual character of the new American Republic.

I imagine that many of the early Americans would have felt the absence of a national center. For them, there was as yet no foundation place sanctified by years of usage and veneration; no place that expressed their values, or provided them with a setting for their national monuments and memorials to their heroes. And there was little the colonists could recognise as a center in the Native American tradition; significant native sites like Cahokia, or Mound City, in Illinois, were still unheard of, and besides, the indigenous tradition differed too greatly from their own. The center of the New World, wherever it was chosen to be, would have to be entirely new and laid out on a bare natural canvas. It fell on the newly elected President, George Washington, to select the appropriate site, and appoint someone with sufficient knowledge and vision to institute the creation of the capital of the new union.

The Secret Geometry of Washington, D.C.

As I read through the source material in the Library of Congress, I learnt that while the nascent States were initially concerned about excessive federal government, they also appreciated its importance. Federal power could not only protect them from the British but from any conflicts with each other. When the States realized the influence they could exert if the federal city lay within their own borders, the site of the capital for the new republic became a matter of great contention. With the advantage of hindsight, we can see that all the issues which were later so fiercely contested in the Civil War were already present in the Congressional debates over site selection. These debates focused on costs, the assumption of Revolutionary War debts, national and international security, slavery and commerce. But the main line of division over the location of the site was clearly drawn between the North and the South.

The question of selection dominated the First Federal Congress held in New York between 1789 and 1791. As committees appointed by Congress reviewed possible sites, including several along the Potomac, Virginia and Maryland offered money, New York and Philadelphia pressed their case on precedence, Delaware offered ten square miles of land, the South wanted Richmond to be selected, and Pennsylvania shamelessly promoted numerous sites along the Susquehanna River. By 1790, almost fifty locations for the capital had been proposed.

All agreed that a huge and unifying factor in the deliberations was George Washington himself. As a charismatic hero of the War of Independence and now President of the Federal Government, it was Washington who came to hold the deciding hand in the matter of selection. It was soon clear that he favored a site generally located midway between the North and the South, and in particular along the banks of the River Potomac.

George Washington's advocacy of the Potomac as the main route of communication between the east coast and the interior – despite the difficulties of navigation – was greatly influenced by the fact his family's vast estate, Mount Vernon, lay on the banks of this river. The records show that both his father and brother, along with other local property owners, had long held the vision of a great future for the Potomac and its associated settlements. This dream had motivated the growth of the colonial ports of Alexandria in Virginia and Georgetown in Maryland; by the mid 1780s, it had led to the creation of the 'Patowmack Canal' Company.

In 1785, Washington became president of the Patowmack Company. In a letter he wrote to Thomas Jefferson regarding the canal in the same year, he emphasized that 'Not a moment ought to be lost in recommencing this business'. Several historians, such as Bowling, think that in bringing together leaders of Virginia and Maryland at Mount Vernon later that year to ratify an agreement that established rights for the canal, Washington set the precedent for future meetings where much greater issues were decided. Indeed, Washington's wealth, success, political skill and charisma brought him to the presidency of the Constitutional Convention of 1789–91. Thereafter it would give him the deciding vote in the selection of the site for the federal capital.

By 1790, the rivalry between the States for selection had increased, and threatened to break apart the North and the South. But as a result of successful negotiations by Alexander Hamilton, James Madison and Thomas Jefferson, the South declared that it would agree to a Potomac site if the federal government assumed the Southern States' war debts. The North agreed not to block the location of the capital in the Potomac region and indeed, from their point of view, the site promised to be very good for trade; it was also a relief that it was no further south. The general location of the capital was then decided by Congress and made into law on July 16, 1790. This act established 'a district of territory, not exceeding ten miles square, to be located, as hereafter directed, on the river Potomac, at some place between the mouths of the Eastern Branch and Connochegue'. Congress went on to make sure that it would have exclusive jurisdiction in the new, independent, Federal District.

Although this decision was undoubtedly a compromise, apparently it proved an effective one. The selection of the exact site was being left to the President, and the members of Congress had known he favored the Potomac around Georgetown and his hometown, Alexandria. The choice appeased the South by placing the capital between two slave States. It accommodated the North by not being too far south and by the emphasis on the location's commercial potential.

THE POTOMAC AND THE NATIVE BACKGROUND

The Potomac River drains roughly fifteen thousand square miles of land before entering the Atlantic Ocean in the Chesapeake Bay. The bay itself and the tidal portion of the river offers plain sailing deep into the interior. Upstream, the main sources of the river, almost four hundred miles inland, are known as the North and South Branches. The Potomac is joined by the Shenandoah River, which in Algonquin means 'Daughter

The Secret Geometry of Washington, D.C.

Photo 1. The Potomac just above Great Falls.

of the Stars', at Harpers Ferry. The river then breaks through the last Appalachian mountain barrier before being joined by the Anacostia River at Washington and running to the sea. The head of navigation is determined by Little Falls just above Washington. Shortly above that, Great Falls presents an even greater – but very impressive – white water challenge to anyone wishing to run boats on the river.

After visiting the falls and seeing for myself that the river was extremely wild in places, shallow in others, and rocky everywhere, it was obvious that despite its great natural beauty the true commercial potential of the Potomac would not have been very great. To try and understand why George Washington had favoured it, my next step was to investigate the historical background.

I discovered that in the Algonquin, the universal language of the eastern seaboard tribes, 'Potomac' or more likely 'Patawomeck' can be translated in a variety of ways. According to the local Washington historian Frederick Gutheim, the meaning centers on a verbal noun for 'something brought' or the place 'where something is brought', allowing the translation of a 'meeting' or 'trading place'. Local tradition reports that the land due east of the Capitol, along with Greenleaf Point on the junction of the Potomac and the Eastern Branch, was used as meeting places for both tribal commerce and councils. Was George Washington therefore following a long established tradition in his enthusiasm for the new capital to become a great center of trade?

Petroglyphs, spear points, arrowheads and stone axes found in this area testify that people have fished and hunted along the river since about 9,000 BCE. The first inhabitants settled into villages and farmed the land from at least 700 CE. At this time, many villages lay along the estuary and its side branches. The river was to become an important meeting place between tribes of the coast and those of the interior, with the area around Great Falls being the natural point of connection between them. This was also the most convenient point for communication and trading between north and south – a fact not lost on the first European settlers, who included the family of George Washington. The Lowland tribes of the Potomac region traded shell currency, arrowheads and dyes with the interior tribes, who supplied them with copper and pelts.

I also found it interesting that the influence of the Six Nation Iroquois Confederacy in the north had evidently reached along the river to Great Falls and beyond. The Confederacy comprised the Mohawk, Oneida, Onondaga, Cayuga, Seneca and eventually the Tuscarora nations. (The latter, driven out of North Carolina, joined the confederacy in about 1722.) The Iroquois Confederacy had also strongly influenced the Delaware to the south and the Shawnee to the west. The upper reaches of the Potomac lay in Shawnee territory. So could this enlightened and indigenous confederacy – in which Benjamin Franklin had a great interest – have had some effect upon the factors that contributed to the selection of the site?

Another factor seemed to be that when the English colonist Captain John Smith first scouted Chesapeake Bay in 1608, he reported about thirty tribes along the shores. The Manahoacs and the Monacans, Smith observed, were the principal tribes between the York and Potomac Rivers. These tribes appeared to be continuously at war with the Powhatans, living to the south in what was to become Virginia. Smith noted that another tribe, the Nacotchants, lived beside the Anacostia River – between what is now Pennsylvania Avenue and Benning Road. South of the Nacotchants were the Potowomeks, who lived on what is now Potomac Creek. Indeed, there were many native settlements throughout the entire area: on Theodore Roosevelt Island, near Little Falls, and beside a large soapstone quarry located in the valley of Rock Creek. John Smith wrote that both the local individual tribes and the larger group to which they all belonged, the Piscataway, were friendly. Mostly dwelling on the east bank of the Potomac, these tribes were caught between the Powhatan Confederacy of the south and the Susquehannocs of the north. It seems that the Piscataway as a whole saw the white colonists as potential allies in their struggle against their hostile neighbors and had consequently encouraged them to settle in the area.

As I absorbed this information, I felt I was coming to understand something of the influence the Native Americans had once exerted in the area and also some of the factors that contributed towards its selection as the site for the national capital. It was especially moving to learn that key meeting places for the surrounding tribal groups had existed in the area, and that one in particular was thought to have lain on the summit of the hill due east of the Capitol. There was also a 'Treaty Oak' site in the area that I will describe in detail in the next chapter. The white settlers described the natives who lived on this junction of territories and natural trade routes, and especially the Potowomeks, as 'the best Marchants'. The most successful of early white traders had adopted the operating methods of the long established native trading system and adapted these to their own needs. Certainly the established native routes along the river seemed to be the key factor that made the Washington family favor the site. However, it also seemed clear that the Washingtons seriously overestimated the ability of its waters to carry increasingly larger and much heavier cargoes.

THE FIRST SETTLERS AND GEORGE WASHINGTON'S CANAL

The comprehensive records I studied in the Library of Congress showed that between 1663 and 1703 all the lands of the future city of Washington had been acquired by grant or purchase by about eighteen landowners. In 1664, for example, a John Langworth owned a piece of land in this area known as the 'Widow's Mite'. On a map made by Baron Christophle De Graffenried in 1711, an estate belonging to the property investor Ninian Beall is noted at Georgetown. This estate included land north of the Tiber, or Goose Creek, as it was then known.

In keeping with the interests and activities of the native people, the idea of developing the Potomac as the link between the Atlantic and the interior via the Ohio River was advocated by the first white settlers. Thomas Lee, agent for the five million northern Virginia acres owned by the Fairfax family, pursued this idea from as early as 1711. Lee purchased twenty thousand acres from Little Falls to above Great Falls

The Creation of the Federal City

at that time, with the intention of it becoming the site of Virginia's great commercial city. This was quite a vision to have imagined so long before even the idea of the City of Washington.

In 1747, Lee and others, including Lawrence Washington, formed the Ohio Company to promote this goal. Lawrence Washington had by now settled on a plantation in Virginia that he had called Mount Vernon (this was granted to his great-grandfather in 1687), and he promoted the town of Alexandria as the great Virginian commercial center. When Lawrence died in 1752, his younger half-brother, twenty-two year old George, inherited the Mount Vernon estate, and his family's hopes for the region.

Apparently George Washington loved the area and passionately believed in its commercial and industrial potential. Inspired by the hopes of his ancestors and the activities of the native people before them, Washington dreamt of the waterways of the Potomac carrying cargoes in every direction. He wrote, unrealistically as it turned out, that the 'navigation of this river is equal if not superior to any in the Union ... this will become the great avenue into the Western Country'. Washington pushed for the creation of the Patowmack Company since he believed a canal would enable the white settlers to overcome all the natural obstacles of the river. Through marriage, Washington owned considerable amounts of land in the adjacent interior, as well as twelve hundred acres in the future District of Columbia on the Virginia side. He was honest enough in his private letters to admit his self-interest in the project.

The canal was intended to take manufactured goods from Georgetown, the westernmost point that could be reached by ships travelling along the east coast, into the interior. From the Ohio, through the town of Cumberland further up the Potomac, raw material was to come back. The most easterly road from north to south crossed the Potomac at Georgetown. By 1789, Georgetown was a thriving port, and Washington believed that everything was present in this area for a great city to grow.

I went back to the river to have a look at the remains of the canal. It was evident that, due to Washington's determination, all the major obstacles to the creation of the canal were overcome. The impressive set of locks at Little Falls opened in 1795, but the even more impressive five locks over three-quarters of a mile that were needed to navigate the spectacular seventy-seven-foot drop of Great Falls did not open until 1802, more than two years after Washington's death. It was pointed out to me by the Park Service guides that some of the masons who worked on the Capitol and the White House had left their marks on the stones of the locks.

With the benefit of hindsight, it is obvious that the presumed commercial potential of the Potomac had put it on the map. It continued the age-old tradition, inherited from the Native Americans, of a lively trading place. Even though the Patowmack Company went bankrupt in 1828 this did not stop another canal company, the Chesapeake and Ohio, from breaking ground in the same year. It took twenty-two years, seventy-four locks, eleven aqueducts and seven dams for this canal along the north bank of the Potomac to reach Cumberland, by which time the Baltimore and Ohio Railroad had already made it redundant. By the early nineteenth-century, it was already clear that Washington as a future center of trade was unviable; but this conclusion had been unthinkable in the last decades of the eighteenth century.

THE SITE OF THE FEDERAL CITY

Once I had looked at the historical and geographical background and reviewed the reasons for the selection of the site, it was time for me to return to the reading room of the Library of Congress. I learnt that with the passing of the act by Congress for the creation of a federal city on the Potomac, it was time for President Washington and his Secretary of State Thomas Jefferson to really get down to business. Washington had already commissioned surveys of several possible local sites; by August 1790, Jefferson was drafting tentative plans.

Jefferson visited Georgetown in September 1790 with James Madison. Apparently they liked the general location and Jefferson proposed various ideas in his notes and sketches. With one eye on the tightness of the federal budget, Jefferson still favored a small city with wide streets, large squares and low houses arranged in a simple grid, to be situated just to the east of Georgetown. Washington himself visited the area in October and also looked at various sites. Excitement now ran high among the locals concerning exactly which location would be chosen. The proponents of each area pressed their case. A lot of barrels were opened in the inns and bets were placed. Yet few had any idea how large an area of land was eventually to be expropriated.

In the same way as the terms of the act of 1790 gave the President final responsibility for the choice of the site, it also gave him the authority to appoint the District Commissioners who were to oversee its overall development. Accordingly, in January 1791, Washington appointed three commissioners who were to define and purchase the land for the federal territory and the city that was to lie within it. These District Commissioners were Thomas Johnson, Daniel Carroll and David Stuart. All three were distinguished citizens, professional men, supporters of the Patowmack Canal, slave-owners – and friends of the President. Like Washington, Carroll and Stuart were Freemasons. The Commissioners were to be directed by Washington and Jefferson. Two days later, with a grand flourish, the President issued the proclamation that finally located the Federal Territory on the banks of the Potomac near Georgetown.

The site that had been chosen for the city was a triangular piece of ground at the confluence of the Potomac and its tributary, the Eastern Branch. This was soon renamed the Anacostia River after the Nacotchants who had lived there; although by 1791 the tribe had moved elsewhere. The federal district was to include Alexandria in Virginia and the undeveloped towns of Carrollsburg and Hamburg in Maryland. The land to be appropriated was mostly woodland and farms. It had many appealing qualities but some less than congenial ones. The site was hot and humid in summer and much of the area was swampy. The natives liked to fish in Goose Creek, which descended past Jenkins Hill through tidewater flats and marshlands into the Potomac. It was not long before Goose Creek was renamed Tiber Creek after the river of ancient Rome.

Several roads already existed in the area that took advantage of ridges of higher ground. The Bladensburg-Ferry Road, which approximates to Maryland Avenue today, and the Georgetown-Ferry Road that approximates to Pennsylvania Avenue, formed a diagonal cross through Jenkins Hill. Apart from the hills to the north, the densely wooded Jenkins Hill was the highest point in the center of the territory of the future city.

SURVEYING THE DISTRICT

Next, Washington appointed one of the nation's leading surveyors, Andrew Ellicott, to conduct an exact survey of the Federal District and mark its boundaries. Writing to Ellicott in February 1791, Jefferson requested him to begin the survey. Ellicott was told to carefully ascertain 'a true Meridian, and the latitude of the place', and to mark the rivers. The first survey of the site would determine a great deal about the city that was to stand there. But who was Ellicott, and what were his motives and background?

The Secret Geometry of Washington, D.C.

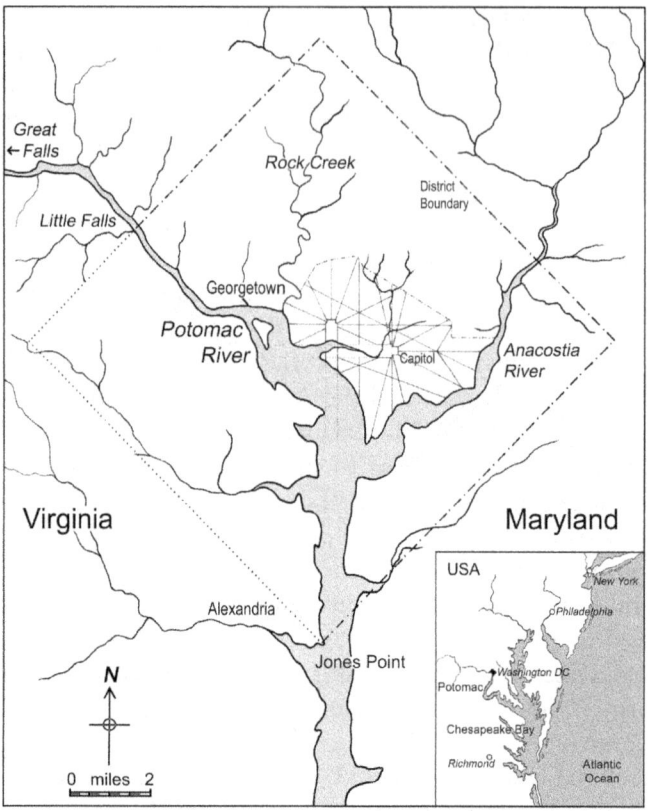

Figure 24. The ten-mile square 'diamond' of the Federal District in 1791. The western portion was returned to Virginia in 1846. The White House was located to look down the length of the Potomac. The densest concentration of native villages was originally on the eastern shore of the Anacostia.

I learnt from Silvio Bedini's work, in the *Records* of the Columbia Historical Society and in *Washington History,* that Andrew Ellicott, born in 1754, was an astronomer and surveyor of Pennsylvania Quaker stock. He had surveyed and mapped many state lines and U.S. frontiers. He later became a professor of mathematics at West Point. Although the low-lying land around the Potomac did not particularly impress him, Ellicott liked being outdoors, which was fortunate as the spring of 1791 was particularly wet and foggy. The astronomer, almanac writer and surveyor Benjamin Banneker assisted Ellicott. Despite being a black man in a slave culture, Banneker was self-taught. It is well known that Banneker was an adept mathematician, and provided Ellicott with all the necessary chronological and astronomical calculations. Banneker could calculate not only solar and lunar movements but also those of the planets and the stars. At that time sixty years of age, Banneker's health was apparently affected by the poor weather and he left the area in late April.

I found it particularly striking that Ellicott recommended that the ten-mile square district begin at the well-known landmark Jones Point on the Potomac near Alexandria and be oriented from there. This key point of orientation, used by navigators on the tidal waters of the deep inland bays, was promptly accepted. The result was that the corners of the ten-mile square originally chosen by Washington and approved by Congress slid around to point north, south, east and west. In this way, the ten-mile square on the map gives the impression of being a diamond.

NAMING THE DISTRICT

The *Records* of the Columbia Historical Society state that late in the afternoon on April 15, 1791, the boundary stone at the southernmost tip of the Federal Territory, Jones Point, was laid in a full Masonic ceremony. The unnamed master of Alexandria Lodge No. 22 officiated, assisted by Master Mason and District Commissioner David Stuart. Commissioner Daniel Carroll of Maryland Lodge No. 16 also attended. Ellicott (who was not a mason) was there to confirm the exact position of the stone. Survey lines were then run northwest and northeast. Forty stones were placed to mark off the miles around the district. Thirty-seven stones remain in place, many of them now in rather poor condition after the trials of the Civil War.

Congress approved Ellicott's survey, with the amendment that all the public buildings should be on the Maryland side of the river. The territory was then officially named the District of Columbia and the city within it was named the City of Washington. Ellicott completed the district map fieldwork in December 1792, and a map of the new district – on Jefferson's suggestion, to be hung as a diamond – was subsequently produced. (In 1846, however, with little interest in the western shore and limited funds to develop the city, Congress returned to Virginia the land it had given to the District of Columbia. The aristocratic town of Alexandria had never been happy about its alliance with what was becoming an extremely scruffy federal construction site and was only too glad to be returned to Virginia. But, as a result, the design of the diamond was seriously flawed.)

While it was clear to me why the city was given its name, I needed to find out more about the origin of the name for the district. I called up more books from the shelves of the Library of Congress and made the discovery that the name for the new District of Columbia derived from a popular feminine personification of the new nation. This was an important revelation, as with my background in ancient history and anthropology, I knew not only that names carry an important message about the essential qualities of a place, but also that in European mythology it was often a goddess who was the eponymous or naming deity of a country. Europe for example is said to be named after the goddess Europa. Was Columbia a similar eponymous goddess?

I learnt that the figure of Columbia had origins in classical and European tradition, in American craft traditions and in early American representations of native women. She had become popular during the Revolution, when many towns on the North American continent were named after her. Images of Columbia were omnipresent on eighteenth- and nineteenth-century coins, paintings, wood-carvings, sculpture and were present in newspapers. These showed her with the liberty cap, the liberty pole or staff, broken chains, the scales of justice, the American flag and eagle and most often the legend 'Liberty'. Columbia was sometimes accompanied by the classical goddess Minerva, or by other figures of 'Justice' or 'Concord'. The name itself is curious, and seemed to have derived from a feminized mixture of Columbus – the navigator credited with the discovery of the continent – and the Gaelic word *columba*, which means 'dove'. The great Irish and Scottish saint known as Columba was credited, like Columbus, with an important voyage. But in the European tradition, allegorical figures of sovereignty, justice, peace, liberty and so on tend to be female.

Columbia's image as a goddess was developed by poets such as the African American Phillis Wheatley. In a poem addressed to George Washington in 1775, Wheatley combined neoclassical motifs and values with the idea of the nation emerging as the Goddess Columbia, virtuous and free, out of the wild, native landscape. Wheatley told Washington:

> 'Proceed, great chief, with virtue on thy side,
> Thy ev'ry action let the goddess guide.
> A crown, a mansion, and a throne that shine,
> With gold unfading, WASHINGTON! be thine'.

This imagery of Columbia was later developed in engravings and paintings that depicted the goddess as 'Justice'; and eventually even as 'Manifest Destiny'. Apart from such images as the Lady of Freedom and the Statue of Liberty (described in the next chapter), Columbia still appears today, with her shining lamp, at the beginning of every film by the movie company of the same name.

Photo 2. If lines are drawn between the points of the 'diamond' of the Federal District of Columbia, they cross at the O.A.S. or Pan-American Union building on 17th and Constitution, not far from the Washington Monument. At the rear of the building, at the exact center of the district, sits a statue of Xochipilli, 'prince of flowers', a pre-Columbian, Toltec/Aztec deity.

Some of the poetry in the mixture of motivations behind the creation of the city was now becoming clear to me. Local tribes had always seen the area as a meeting place. The site was beautiful. The romantic river provoked classical and neoclassical allusions. The conception of the district as a diamond was imaginative. The marking of its outline in full Masonic ceremony was dramatic. And the naming of it after a popular goddess – whom poets could evoke – was highly symbolic. I wondered if there were any other properties of the site that lent themselves to the imagery of idealism and symbolism found at other national centers. Were there any images, myths and legends, especially from the native tribes or possibly from the early settlers, which explored the qualities and fundamental nature of the region?

3

The Power of Place in the Place of Power

THE WIDOW'S MITE

Apart from the thin scattering of archaeological evidence and the few accounts by early explorers or settlers, we have little data to help us imagine the Federal District before European colonisation. The Native peoples didn't write anything down. Nevertheless, one afternoon when I was working in the reading room of the Columbia Historical Society, I found an account of a significant local legend. It opened a small but vital window into the ideas that the early colonists had held about the indigenous Americans. The legend also told me a great deal about the colonists' early perception of the place selected for their national capital. The legend is known as *The Widow's Mite*.

> The Anacostia Indian Tribe once lived in a vast forest in the region where the City of Washington now stands. Their chief, Mannacasset, set up his wigwam near a mighty oak that stood upon a high hill. From there, he governed the surrounding land.
>
> One day, among the captives taken by the tribe in war, was a young mother and her daughter. The chief wanted the woman to be his wife. She repeatedly turned down his requests. So Mannacasset decreed that although custom prevented him from taking her by force, she would be killed if she wandered beyond the shade of the great oak tree.
>
> As the years passed, the mother drew pleasure from the raising of her child, Gwawa, which means 'hope'. Gwawa found a playmate in a half-Indian, half-white boy called Tschagarag. When the chief died, perhaps in battle with the whites, the treaty for peace and for the purchase of the land from the Indians

was signed under the spreading branches of the oak tree. Washington himself, 'the Father of our Country', signed the treaty. The woman was released from her imprisonment. The tree is the Treaty Oak.

Although offered several homes, the woman insisted on remaining in the shelter of the tree. She was granted the land around the tree; which from that day forth became known as the Widow's Mite. She was offered large sums of money for the hill upon which the great oak stood – the site of the U.S. Capitol or the White House – but the widow clung to the land.

Upon her death, she willed the property to her daughter, who had now married Tschagarag. She said to her daughter: 'Regard the oak which overspreads our cottage as an ancient relic; cherish it through life as the talisman of a resigned sufferer. And should you be blessed with offspring, instil them with the reverence for the tree as will transmit from generation to generation. These fulfilled, accept my thanks and consider the little I give you ... as the Widow's Mite to her posterity'.

When I examined the early maps of this area I found that the land known as the Widow's Mite lay between 18th Street, 22nd Street and Pennsylvania Avenue, with Rock Creek lying to the north. Records show it originally lay on a six hundred acre estate that was first deeded to a white settler, a man named John Langworth, in 1664. At that time white settlement of the area was still opposed by native peoples; the record reported that his children were killed in a native uprising shortly afterwards.

The hill in the northern part of this area (Connecticut Avenue and Florida,) provided the setting for the story. A great white oak, known as the Treaty Tree or the Treaty Oak, and in the 1940s judged to be between four and six hundred years old, stood on a property known as Oak Lawns. The original building by settlers on the site was put up in 1820 amid 'a forest of white oaks'. In 1922 the site, then about nine acres, was acquired by the Masonic Grand Lodge of the district and christened 'Temple Heights'. Several Masonic temples and headquarters of various Masonic organizations were planned for this location. The Masons' plans show that the Treaty Oak was to have been preserved in the forecourt. Due to the Depression, however, the temple was never built, but the Freemasons tried for several years to leave their mark on this key site in the city, given its highly unusual foundation legend.

Figure 25. 'Temple Heights Mansion to Fall – This old building at Connecticut and Florida avenues N.W. will be dismantled by wrecking crews beginning this week. Also to go is the "Treaty Oak" at left center'. Washington Post, April 4, 1948.

After the Masons abandoned their plans another great scheme was proposed for the Widow's Mite. This was the innovative and very expensive 'Crystal City' designed by no less an architect than Frank Lloyd Wright. This design would also have preserved the Treaty Oak, but the Second World War stopped Wright's project. After the war, the tree did not fare well. The adjacent mansion fell into disrepair and one side of the tree was severely burnt in a fire. Despite appeals by antiquarians, local protests and the introduction of bills in Congress to preserve the site, the mansion was torn down and the tree felled in 1948. In 1953 the developer offered its wood for sale to any who were interested on the understanding that this was the tree of legend. Today the Hilton Hotel stands on or close to the site. There is no sign nearby that refers to the story of the widow and the oak.

Washington writer and historian John Claggart Proctor was among those who appealed for the preservation of the tree. It was through Proctor's column in the Washington Sunday Star that the legend of the Widow's Mite first became well known, although Proctor later became skeptical about the legend's authenticity. In 1934, he printed a letter from a Miss M. E. Gillespie whose family had owned the property of Oak Lawns, in which she said the stories about the Treaty Oak 'were invented by my great uncle' for children. Other stories later appeared debunking the legend. The criticism focused on the inconsistent dating. How could George Washington have been there at such an early time? But I knew from my academic background in anthropology that this insistence on precise factuality was at the expense of the meaning of the story – a quality that stories for children can express and preserve.

'NATURE TO CULTURE' IN THE AMERICAN LANDSCAPE

What does the legend mean? Whether it relates to real events or to fiction, it seized the imagination of the residents of Washington in the early twentieth-century. Can its imagery provide an understanding of the quality of the area selected for the nation's capital? I think the legend does this in a very illuminating manner.

Although the times given for the 'purchase' from the native people and for Washington and the building of the Capitol are inconsistent, there is a striking consistency in the story of the Widow's Mite. Two quite separate times appear to be conflated, yet the structure of the story remains the same in each. There are two different scenarios here that nonetheless possess similar features. First, there is a leader who is a chief, and secondly there is a leader who is a President. There is the center of power as a 'wigwam' and then there is the center of power as the Capitol. There is the woman's refusal of her marriage to the chief and then there is her refusal to those offering to buy the land – in other words, we move from the wish to possess her own body to the wish to possess her land. Finally, there is her right to control her own body and later her right to control her own property.

Although the details of this story may have become garbled, glossed over and modernised, its essential structural quality seems to have been preserved in the relationships and parallels between its different parts. In each case, the key relationships or the structural consistencies between the two scenarios revolve around the single feature of the tree.

The tree is the constant that does not change. The tree is the clue that something mythic, something profound, is going on.

The tree is used in the legend in a manner that connects it to the world center, the world axis or the *axis mundi*. It represents the center, the marker or *gnomon*, around which the world turns. In Nordic mythology, for example, the world tree, *Yggdrasil*, unites the lower, the middle and the upper worlds – it stands at the center of existence. In the tradition of the Iroquois Confederacy, a similar world tree marked a place of power and peace, the place where the councils gather. A tree is an auspicious and appropriate symbol for any site of symbolic importance. In this legend, the tree's centrality helps to illustrate an important shift in how the American people viewed their recently settled land.

In the first scenario – likely to derive from seventeenth-century or earlier conceptions of the land – the tree is a symbol of power. It is described as the place from which the chief establishes sovereignty over the surrounding land. He governs from the tree. Yet when the woman in the legend enters the sphere of the tree, she not only becomes inviolable; she also assumes this power. And when the chief finally gives her the center, what was her former prison actually serves to establish her sovereign rights to the land. Her freedom and life become bound up with that of the tree. There is a sense therefore in which she becomes aligned with the tree and the sovereignty it represents. She now symbolizes the land of America, conceived as a Native American woman. This image of the continent emerged in the art and the imagination of the time as an Indian princess, a goddess or a queen, dwelling in a wild and wooded landscape.

In the second scenario, we find ourselves in the city of Washington in the late eighteenth and early nineteenth centuries. Here, the symbol of freedom, power and sovereignty has shifted from the tree to something more sophisticated: the Capitol or the President's House. The woman has also made the transition from a wild, untamed Native American – probably dressed in nothing but feathers and wielding a tomahawk – to a woman with all the cultural attributes of a white land-owner. She is now a 'widow' with clearly defined legal rights to the land.

In essence, the legend describes a nation redefining itself in relation to wild nature as it makes the transition from woodland to urban living. It traces the changes from tribal living to the sophistication of an industrialized nation. The legend underlines the movement from nature to culture, from wild to domestic, from natural to legal. In human terms, there is also the shift from the status of a captive – but free under the branches of the tree – to the status of a free woman able to do what she likes within the bounds of what is now her property. These transitions can be formulated in terms of a fundamental polarity of 'Nature to Culture'.

NATURE	→	CULTURE
Tree	→	Monument
Chief	→	President
Tipi/Wigwam	→	President's House/Capitol
Shade of tree	→	Property boundary
Forest	→	City
No mating	→	No sale
Rights to body	→	Rights to property
Captive	→	Free
Confined	→	Independent
Slave	→	Land Owner
Wild/Savage	→	Tame/Civilized
Woman, Unmarried	→	'Widow', Married
Mother	→	Daughter

At the same time as the story tracks the progression from mother to daughter, chief to President, captive to free, monuments in the new urban landscape replace the tree. The new American nation comes out of the wilderness into secure townships and becomes more complex and sophisticated in its cultural, commercial, political, legal and civil development. Anthropology describes this as the well-documented transition from Nature to Culture; and, in keeping with the popular ideas of the time as well as those of antiquity, this transition of the new nation from one state to another is symbolically and allegorically perceived in terms of the body of a woman. In this case, the woman is not only described in the story of the Native American 'Widow', but my assumption is that she is also perceived as an aspect of the popular Goddess Columbia.

I understood from analysis of these transitions that the legend of the Widow's Mite described the very real concerns of the people of the region. It tells us about the experience and the imagination of the American colonists from as early as the seventeenth century onwards. It deals with the threats, real and perceived, that they encountered as they worked to find a foothold in their new country. It contains information about the view people had of the place eventually chosen for their national capital. It does not really matter if the chief, the woman and the relationship between them ever really existed. What does matter is the fact that the people coming into the area thought that they had. It is human nature to seek antecedents for our actions – the older the better – as through this practice, new activities, however innovative, can be legitimated and established.

THE SPIRIT OF PLACE

In one of the several versions of the story recorded by John Claggart Proctor, the captive is a white woman, Magadalena Noyes. As a free, white widow she represents on the one hand the stubborn refusal of the settlers to give in to the natives. She answers to no one. On the other hand, this white woman offers an allegory of the spatial limits which the early white settlers felt were imposed on them by what then were the all-surrounding Native Americans and the wild, heavily wooded and unfamiliar landscape. Though it was only small, a 'mite' surrounded by the vast forest and easily threatened, at least the settlers had legal rights to their property as the indigenous tribes gave, or sold it to them.

In my view, the story of the Widow's Mite is a fictional attempt to place the rights of the colonising Americans back in time. It was especially important to do this in the place where the capital city of the white settlers was being founded. If there was no concrete evidence for Greenleaf Point or Jenkins Hill being places for native councils then it would have been important for the people of the area to create the tradition that they were such places. It was also necessary to provide legitimation for the displacement of the native peoples by creating stories of friendships, treaties and intermarriage. It was also necessary to move from the primitive 'wigwams', log cabins and woods of 'nature' into the sophisticated buildings and monuments of 'culture'. Above all, it was necessary to have a Treaty Tree, a symbol of rightful ownership confirming the right of sovereignty over the land and its people.

I find it intriguing that the perceived power of this place, even if its founding legend may have been greatly enhanced by Miss Gillespie's great uncle, was sufficient to draw plans for three huge buildings to the site of the Treaty Oak in the twentieth-century, one of which – admittedly not the most fabulous – was eventually built.

The legend of the Widow's Mite is strongly imbued with mythological quality. Myths that are specific to a particular area, although they may be factually incorrect, always provide us with important insights into its presiding *genius loci*, or the 'spirit of place'. This is the geomantic signature or the essential quality that pervades a locality, is usually present in its name, and that will influence and be increased by the imagination and actions of whoever dwells or goes there. To my mind, the legend of the Widow's Mite speaks volumes about the qualities attributed to the land that was about to become the site of the new national capital.

STATUE OF FREEDOM

The more I reflected upon the legend of the Widow's Mite and the more I immersed myself in American culture, the more remarkable and complex appeared the ideals of liberty and freedom that surrounded the central figure. As a woman (and possibly even a 'Magdalene'), she is independent and autonomous in every choice – including her sexual choices. The woman refuses to be defined by her relationship to a man. In most versions of the legend she remains unnamed, and there is even a sense that she is uncomfortable with the label of 'widow'. The sole thing that does confine the woman is her imprisonment by Mannacasset to a specific location. But, as I suggested above, the woman is not so much confined by the place – the place of power as it happens – as it is she who comes to circumscribe and define it. She becomes the place. She becomes the tree, the symbol, not only of the spirit of place of the capital city, but also of the independent spirit, liberty and freedom of the new America. Within the boundaries of her body and her land, she WILL be free; and from here, she will spread out her branches and grow.

Ideals of independence and liberty were and still are hugely important to the American mind. This became very clear to me within weeks of my arrival in America in 1987. I could hear it in the city council meetings I attended and among the citizens I met. It became rapidly obvious that the nation still remembered its original foundation as an act of resistance to imperial rule and as a strongly felt commitment to republican and democratic virtues. The concept of personal freedom was enshrined in the Constitution, the Bill of Rights, the Oath of Allegiance and in every symbol of the nation: from the anthem to the flag, the bell, the eagle, the liberty cap and the liberty staff. Republican and democratic ideals of independence, individual sovereignty and personal freedom are also present in the highly charged and singularly American motifs of the freed slave, the law man, the pioneer and the cowboy. They also inform the only too evident American dislike of high taxation, centralised government and over-regulation of commercial development. Certainly the figure of liberty, in the image of a woman, was introduced at a very early stage in American history and has continued to be extremely important to American identity as the nation has developed.

The first American symbols of liberty appeared, as early as the sixteenth century, in representations of a woman who became known as Columbia. This figure may have evolved from ancient European traditions of sovereign goddesses of the land and been represented in images of native Americans 'princesses', but she was gradually influenced by neoclassical figures of wisdom, liberty and justice. Columbia appeared as a representation of the democratic ideals of the nation in many popular contexts throughout the eighteenth century. The coin, *Immunis Columbia*, 'free, without constraint', for example, produced in 1785, featured the Goddess of Liberty with cap, staff, national flag and the scales of justice. Sometimes accompanied by the Goddess Minerva, Columbia appeared in magazines, books, statues, paintings and poems. As an expression of popular American values, the female figure of Columbia conveniently avoided any monarchic and imperial exaltation of its individual, and male, Presidents and leaders.

An anonymous essay of 1795 described the national capital and especially the Capitol building as 'a temple erected to liberty'. The author described Liberty in the manner of a classical goddess and wanted an 'altar of Liberty' to be placed in the center of the eastern forecourt of the Capitol, 'around which the United States will be represented under the figures of young women'. The city architect, L'Enfant – evidently in full agreement with this plan – wanted another sculptural group on the west side of the Capitol, featuring a huge woman beside a forty-foot cascade of water. This was to be called 'Liberty hailing Nature out of its slumber'.

Photo 3. *The United States Capitol from the West. The Statue of Freedom crowns the central dome.*

Although these early plans were later changed or remained unrealised, images of American Liberty as a monumental woman were eventually achieved both in the Statue of Liberty in New York and in the Statue of Freedom that stands upon the dome of the Capitol building in Washington, D.C.. The Statue of Liberty needs no further comment from me; it comes instantly to mind as the iconic representation of American ideals.

In 1992 the Statue of Freedom or 'Lady Liberty' was removed from the dome of the Capitol for restoration and stood within a wire cage in the Capitol forecourt. I was conducting my research in Washington at the time, and so was able to examine from only a few feet away a bronze sculpture of a proud and noble woman, nearly twenty feet tall, carrying a sheathed sword and a shield. I noticed that the statue combined neoclassical motifs with Native American elements. Her extraordinary taloned and billed eagle headdress sprouts ostrich plumes; there are Union motifs in the five-pointed stars on a band around her brow; there is bear fur trim on her Grecian influenced robe, and stars and stripes on her shield. 'US' for the United States is inscribed on a medallion on the statue's chest. She holds a sword in one hand and either an olive branch of peace or a laurel wreath of victory in the other. The statue, dedicated on December 2, 1863, stands upon a globe inscribed with the national motto, *E Pluribus Unum*. The designer of the statue, Thomas Crawford, drew upon many cultural traditions for his inspiration.

As well as symbolizing independence, liberty, peace and victory, the Statue of Freedom also embodies the theme of justice; in this respect she bears all the attributes of Columbia. Classical figures of justice conventionally bear a sword. The eagle headdress acknowledges the Native American tradition, while ostrich feathers are a familiar symbol of the principle of divine justice in the culture of ancient Egypt. Fully restored just after I moved away from the city in 1993, when she was remounted upon the dome of the Capitol, 'Lady Liberty' or the 'Lady of Freedom' is not only a powerful symbol of an ideal central to American identity and consciousness; she also encodes layers of meaning that are yet to be fully understood by the average American.

CITY OF LIBERTY

As I thought further about the legend of the Widow's Mite, I became increasingly convinced that it contained themes which illuminated the

The Secret Geometry of Washington, D.C.

Photo 4. The Statue or 'Lady of Freedom' that crowns the US Capitol.

national spirit that had prevailed at the time of the foundation of the Federal City. These themes can be summarized as follows:

1. Firstly, the spirit of American liberty, individuality, independence and sovereignty, symbolized in iconography as a woman or goddess (and, it must be said, controlled in European history by men), is conceptualised in the minds of those around the site for the new American capital city. It is seen as the relationship of a free, native woman confined to a place by a native man. The man, the chief, represents the surrounding, hostile, indigenous tribes and the raw, inhospitable and untrained landscape. (See those items that appear in the left-hand column of the table above.) In the art of the time, native women were repeatedly depicted as naked, voluptuous, exotic, independent and dangerous figures – all the qualities associated by the settlers with the new land.

2. Secondly, as the transition to fully coherent forms of American identity and independence takes place, the migrants themselves become the 'native' Americans, the land is conquered and tamed, and the woman is no longer seen as symbolically confined. Now she and the land are free (or at least for sale). The spirit of sovereignty now appears depicted as enrobed and increasingly Caucasian and neoclassical figures of women in architectural spaces dedicated to liberty.
3. Finally, the ideals of liberty, freedom, justice and sovereignty are synthesized in the form of a monumental statue of a woman – now fully integrating both native and classical symbolism – upon the building that houses the seat of government (even though, ironically, this government was still denying women, slaves and Native Americans their freedom and was, and still is, dominated by men). The Federal District itself is named after the most popular manifestation of this figure, the goddess Columbia. (See those items in the right-hand column of the table above.)

This analysis suggests how the legend contains the seeds of the ambivalent American attitude to empire. How has a nation founded on independent, republican, democratic values and anti-imperial ideologies reconciled itself to a strong, centralized federal government, to almost unprecedented continental expansion and to subsequent world empire building? Living for over twelve years in the southwest deserts of Arizona, New Mexico and Utah made it only too clear to me how this historical and cultural contradiction between domination and freedom has continued in repeated tensions between American attitudes to the environment as a resource to be exploited and a wilderness to be protected.

This contradiction also emerges in the ongoing debate concerning who is included within the circle of the nation and who is excluded from it. The debate is exemplified in American history by the dichotomies between the North and the South, between the free and the slaves, between the colonists and native peoples, between citizens and immigrants. Perhaps, above all, the contradiction continues in the early twenty-first century, in the pronounced tension between a perceived need for strong national security and the conflict and national soul-searching over appropriate forms of international intervention by a democratic and freedom-conscious country.

I had concluded that the legend of the Widow's Mite was essentially a contemporary story that had been retrospectively projected onto a mythologized past. It drew upon the key themes of American history as they were alive in the minds of those living in the vicinity of Washington during and after the time it was established as the federal capital. The legend provides suggestive insights into the subtle relationship between the American people – their innermost thoughts, feelings, aspirations, symbols and beliefs – and their chosen place of power.

This chapter has been conceived as an exercise in 'geomythics', which seeks to analyse and map the thoughts and feelings of people in relation to place. In their totality, such feelings form the *genius loci* or the 'spirit of place', and are extremely relevant to the creation of any city. The legend of the Widow's Mite offers us a window on the ideals and perspectives of the people involved in the birth of the American Federal City – not just the leaders, but the people who lived and farmed in the area and worked in the city and on its construction. And reinterpreting the legend for our own time may open a window into the consciousness of the American people of today. For it may now be possible to see that 'coming out from the shade of the tree' carries more ambivalent meanings for this generation, which is beginning to take responsibility for its ancestors' mistreatment of Native American peoples and is also attempting to reverse the terrible environmental degradation of the Potomac and Anacostia river basins.

4

Major Pierre Charles L'Enfant

'BETTER QUALIFIED THAN ANY ONE'

While the Commissioners oversaw the development of the Federal District, and Ellicott and Banneker surveyed and mapped the area, it was a Frenchman, Major Pierre Charles L'Enfant, who was asked by President Washington, through Secretary of State Thomas Jefferson, to design the new federal city. L'Enfant was also asked to design the important public buildings including the President's House, the House of Congress and the Supreme Court. It was clear that L'Enfant had inspired exceptional trust in the two most powerful men in the country (although he was shortly to lose this trust from Jefferson).

By March 1791, L'Enfant had completed his preliminary drawings; Washington now authorized him to lay out the plan for the city. On June 22 L'Enfant took a report and a 'progress map' to the President at Mount Vernon. Apart from a few small changes this was approved, and by late August L'Enfant was busy preparing a detailed map of the new city for engraving. Washington wrote a letter to his friend, fellow Masonic Lodge member and District Commissioner David Stuart, on November 20, where he explained his choice of L'Enfant by stating that 'for projecting public works, and carrying them into effect, he was better qualified than any one who had come within my knowledge in this Country, or indeed in any other'.

But who precisely was L'Enfant? Why did Washington consider him to be the most qualified for the job? And how was he able to produce a plan for a major city in the space of a few months?

L'Enfant was born in Paris on August, 2nd 1754. As a boy he lived for a while at Versailles. Of course, both Paris and the royal palace were the scene of some remarkable architectural achievements during this period. In 1771 L'Enfant had enrolled as a student at the Académie

Royale de Peinture et de Sculpture in Paris, where his father was an instructor. His father was a painter in commission to king Louis XV, with special expertise in landscape, battle scenes and fortifications. L'Enfant was thus born into an environment of professional artistry and noble patronage. Just as significantly, he spent his formative years amidst the finest urban architecture of the day. Living in Europe just prior to the French Revolution, L'Enfant – like European visitors Thomas Jefferson and Benjamin Franklin – was also exposed to a climate of radical political ideas.

In August 1776, L'Enfant, by now a Lieutenant of Infantry in the French Colonial Troops, volunteered to serve in the American War of Independence. He was deeply inspired by the American cause and not just because the war was against the British. L'Enfant worked as an engineer, drawing plans and illustrating military texts. During the winter of 1777, he was at Valley Forge where he drew sketches of several officers, including George Washington. In 1778, he was made a Captain of Engineers in the U.S. Army and began to move in circles that included the Marquis de la Fayette and General Steuben. He dined with the generals on many occasions. In 1779, he fought and received a severe gunshot wound in the leg at the Siege of Savannah. He was captured by the British and imprisoned for eighteen months. After the war, in May 1783, Congress appointed L'Enfant a Brevet Major in the Corps of Engineers. By then, he was in personal correspondence with George Washington, had become a close friend of Alexander Hamilton, and was proud of his new American identity. He began signing his name 'Peter'.

According to his biographer, Hans Paul Caemmerer, L'Enfant was by now in great demand as an architect in New York City. There, during the succeeding years, he converted the old City Hall on Wall Street into Federal Hall. He employed singularly American motifs, placing thirteen stars in the metopes of the pediment – one for each of the States – and above them, an eagle clutching thirteen arrows in its talons. In 1789 George Washington was inaugurated in this building, then considered to be the 'most beautiful in the country'.

In this period, L'Enfant drew many portraits, and built or re-modelled many private residences, including the mansion of Alexander Hamilton. He was commissioned to design banqueting halls, furniture, cabinets, a pageant, a fortress, coins and several medals. He always demanded the highest quality of material and excellence in craftsmanship, which was often beyond his clients' budgets. 'Due in part to L'Enfant's influence', Caemmerer wrote, 'this country has never seen better wares than those made 1784 to 1820'. In 1783, L'Enfant was commissioned by Washington to design a gold insignia medal, 'the Eagle', for the Society of the Cincinnati. The society was made up of officers who had fought in the American Revolution. It was styled on neoclassical values and as a military lodge of the Masonic order, although the Masons did not officially charter it. Its founder and president, George Washington, drew upon Roman republican ideals and his Masonic background for its rituals and regalia. It is also said that L'Enfant designed the medal that later became the Purple Heart.

From 1786 to 1788, L'Enfant worked on St. Paul's Chapel in New York. Here he designed the 'Glory' over its altar. L'Enfant used mystical Old Testament symbolism in this work: symbolism to which he must have been exposed at the Académie Royale in France. On the monument to General Montgomery in the same chapel, he placed a sun rising behind a pyramid with thirteen rays illuminating the American portion of a globe. These motifs were also in use among Freemasons at that time, but there is not a single piece of evidence to show that L'Enfant was initiated into the order. Above the Montgomery pyramid, an American eagle flies from east to west bearing a curtain of stars. Because of his inventiveness and his preference for such typically American ciphers and symbols, some believe L'Enfant worked on the design of the Great Seal of the United States; but other sources clearly state who was involved and L'Enfant was not named among them. The Great Seal, however, with all its classical allusions and Masonic symbolism, bears close comparison to the Eagle of the Society of the Cincinnati. By 1790 Major L'Enfant had become a highly acclaimed, prominent and popular member of American society. He was also a candidate for the Congressional committee that was to locate the federal district beside the Delaware River.

L'Enfant's idiosyncratic temperament emerges in the few brief descriptions of him that survive. Although no accurate portrait of him is known to exist, it is from these accounts, from his own letters and from what we know of his time in Washington that the following characterization can be made. He was tall, finely proportioned, 'nose prominent'; he was noticeable in a crowd and was of military bearing. His disposition was 'courtly', aloof, enthusiastic, zealous, ambitious, high-spirited, quick-tempered – Washington later used the word 'untoward' – determined, impulsive, meticulous, generous and extravagant. He was concerned for his honor and reputation, could be vainglorious, and was of course, highly artistic in his temperament and inclination.

His seconds and workmen were intensely loyal to L'Enfant, even though or perhaps because he demanded the highest standard of work

The Secret Geometry of Washington, D.C.

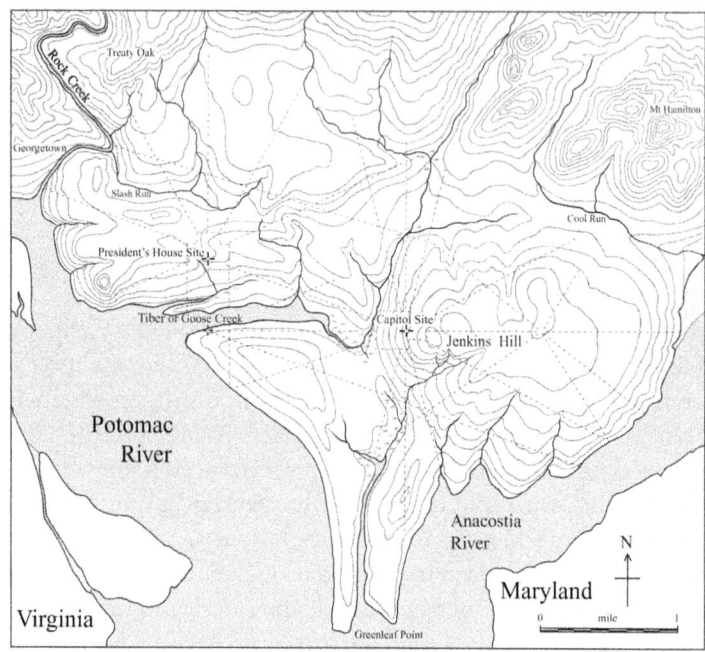

Figure 26A. Plan of the basic topographical features in the region when L'Enfant began his survey. Steep gullies cut into the circular hill above the Eastern Branch. The locations of the principal avenues and squares are shown in hatched lines.

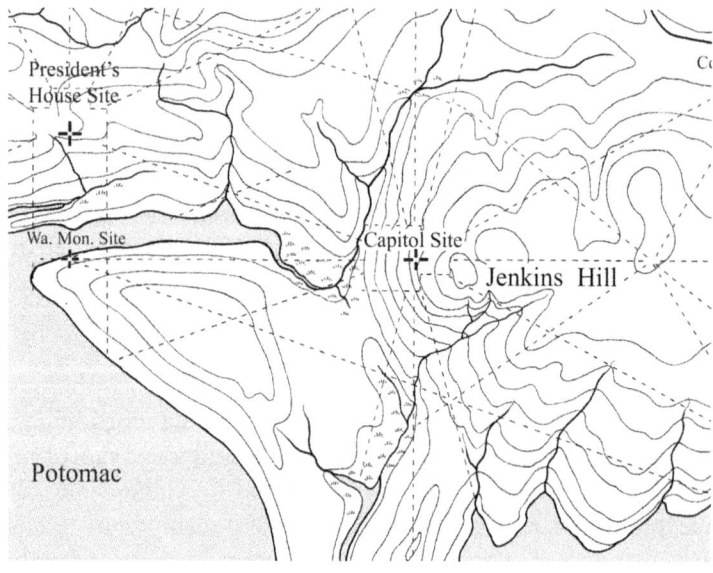

Figure 26B. Central detail of area map.

from them. He would tear down substandard work and have it done again. He insisted on his workers having two ounces of cocoa butter in their rations every day and he abhorred the use of low paid, unskilled and, noticeably for the time, slave labour. His bill at the tavern in Georgetown where he was accommodated was far greater than Andrew Ellicott's. On August 9, 1791, the surveyor Ellicott wrote to his wife Sally that L'Enfant was 'a most worthy French Gentleman and though not one of the most handsome of men he is from his good breeding and native politeness a first rate favorite among the ladies'. Although one liaison produced a child, there is no official record of a permanent female partner in L'Enfant's life. He seems to have preferred spending his time and sharing residences with men, something entirely unremarkable for the day. The author Bob Arnebeck is slowly compiling evidence of L'Enfant's close relationships with men; although what that would have meant in the homosocial culture of the eighteenth century may be quite different from what it means today.

L'ENFANT ACCEPTS THE COMMISSION

On September 11, 1789, in a remarkable letter sent to President Washington, L'Enfant made it plain that he saw the extraordinary opportunities presented in the task of designing the new capital. 'No nation', he wrote somewhat obliquely, for of course he knew he meant the President, 'had ever before the opportunity offered them of deliberately deciding on the spot where their Capital City should be fixed'. L'Enfant requested the position of architect in charge and straightforwardly admitted this would be an 'occasion for acquiring reputation'. Ever practical, he stressed the new city's need for fortifications and coastal defenses. But above all, he had already grasped the scale of what was required and had the beginnings of the vision that would lead to his Grand Plan. 'The plan should be drawn on such a scale', he wrote, 'as to leave room for that aggrandizement & embellishment which the increase of the wealth of the Nation will permit it to pursue at any period however remote'. It is obvious, with the benefit of historical hindsight, that no contemporary matched L'Enfant in the grandness and wisdom of this vision; at that time perhaps only the President shared with him an accurate assessment of the future size and importance of the capital.

L'Enfant continued his private work in New York City as the debate about the location of the federal city rolled on to its conclusion. He claimed later, with some justification, that he had undertaken commissioned work to the value of a million dollars on property there. Early in 1791 his close friend, Treasurer Alexander Hamilton, was consulting L'Enfant over a design for a U.S. coin; but in March the President asked L'Enfant to 'proceed to Georgetown' to begin a survey of the land for the city. He dropped all his other work and left New York immediately.

Despite the mud, rain, cold and thick fog, Major L'Enfant was enamored by the land he encountered on the banks of the Potomac. In a fervent and highly significant letter written in early April, he wrote to Jefferson, 'It is my wish and shall be my endeavor to delineate in a new and original way the plan the contrivance of which the President has left to me without any restriction soever'.

L'ENFANT'S GRAND PLAN

From scrutiny of the papers at the Library of Congress it is clear that by the time of L'Enfant's appointment – like the District Commissioners and the surveyors, not by Congress, but by President Washington – Thomas Jefferson had already conceived his own and very different plan for the new city. This was for a small federal city to be situated close to Georgetown and in which the President's House would be barely half a mile from the Capitol. Jefferson envisaged that the city could develop as required along the lines of an expandable grid very similar to the rectangular pattern of Philadelphia. This was a pragmatic but unimaginative solution that accommodated the political and financial realities of the day. L'Enfant, however, had other ideas and conforming to limited budgets was not among them.

When the President arrived on site late in March 1791, L'Enfant had to persuade him to ignore Jefferson and to consider the city's potential for development further east. He argued that the choice of hills beside Georgetown would limit the scope of the plan. He explained that it was the Anacostia, the Eastern Branch of the Potomac, which would offer the best deep-water harbour necessary for the commerce which Washington wanted to promote. L'Enfant wanted bridges built over the Eastern Branch and Rock Creek and a road between them to encourage the growth of the city. This road was to become Pennsylvania Avenue. It appears that Washington had no trouble seeing the larger plan and, after doing what was necessary to persuade local landowners to sell land for the city on reasonable terms, he instructed L'Enfant to proceed.

Major Pierre Charles L'Enfant

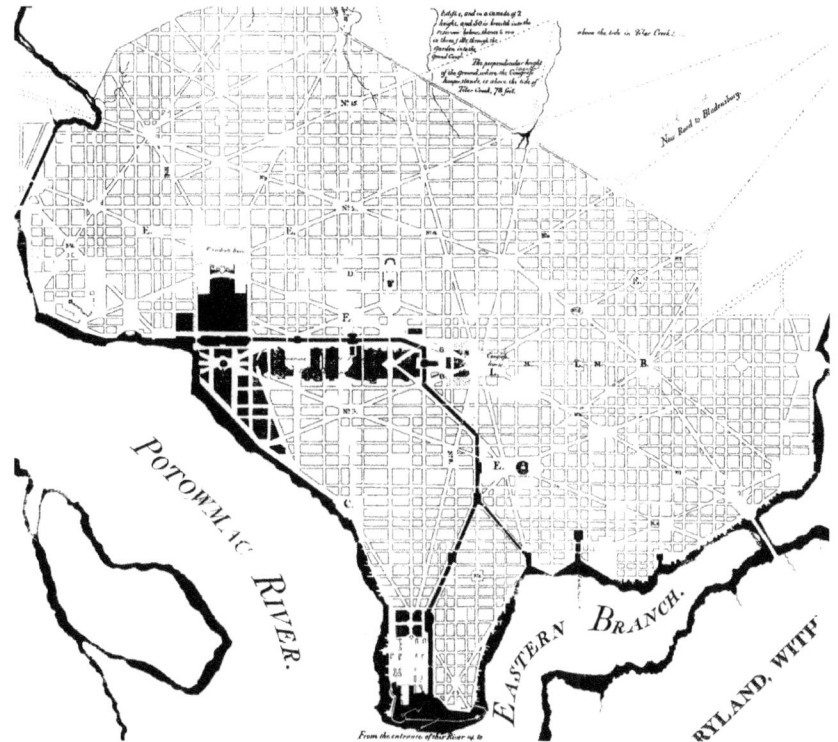

Figure 27.A. The L'Enfant Plan of 1791. This is probably the plan L'Enfant submitted to the President in August. 1991 facsimile, Library of Congress.

At this point, in early April, Jefferson supplied L'Enfant with plans of Paris, Orleans, Bordeaux, Lyons, Montpellier, Amsterdam, Frankfurt am Main, Karlsruhe, Strasbourg, Turin and Milan. Yet it seems L'Enfant may have been playing the diplomat by viewing these plans, for he returned them to Jefferson very quickly. L'Enfant was already familiar with planned American cities such as Annapolis and Williamsburg and probably with the European cities above. At this point he began to insist that his plan would not be a copy of any existing scheme. Instead, it would be original and unique. 'I would reprobate the idea of imitating', L'Enfant wrote to Jefferson not soon after the request was made; adding that 'the contemplation of what exists ... even the parallel of these with defective ones, may serve to suggest a variety of new ideas'. Jefferson was, at the time, apparently happy to let the planning of the city go 'in such good hands', but he could not resist adding some suggestions of his own. He proposed that 'very liberal reservations' should be made for public buildings and these could 'be about the Tyber'. In keeping

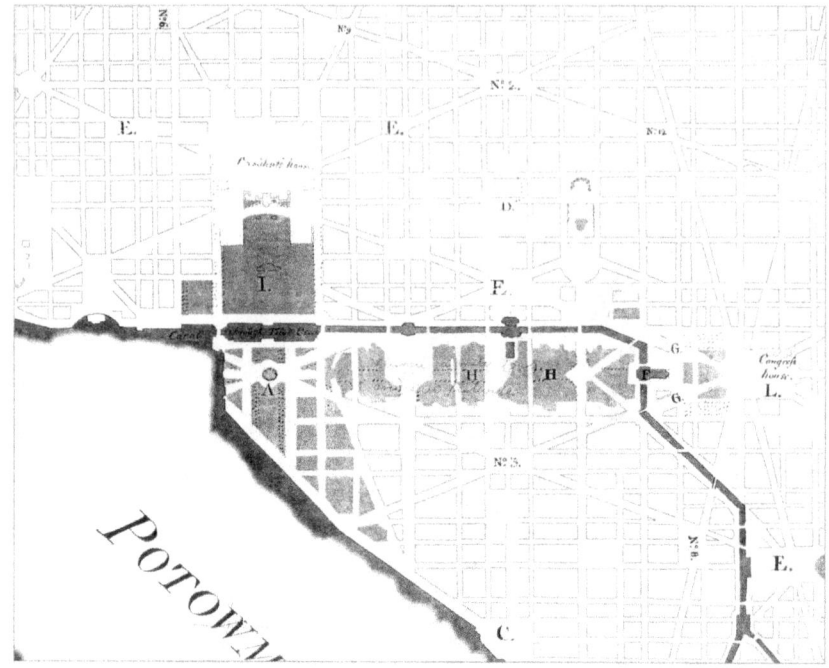

Figure 27B. Detail of the central portion of the L'Enfant Plan. H is the Mall. D was to be the location of the 'National Church', while just to the right of D was the intended location for the Supreme Court.

with the neoclassical style of the day, he preferred 'one of the models of antiquity' for the Capitol and a 'modern' design for the President's House. The Secretary of State would eventually get his way, especially in matters of symbolism relating to the design.

His records and personal letters reveal that, having received his instructions, L'Enfant got down to work. He was apparently delighted with the harmonious disposition of the land and the evidence shows that he soon became intimate with it. It is obvious that he came to know every hill, slope, gully, spring, creek, harbor and road, as his natural exuberance and enthusiasm fired the vision for the new city that would one day transform them. At this time, he was still only thirty-six years of age and at the height of his creative powers. In the words of the ambassador and historian, J. J. Jusserand, 'Rarely was a brain more busy than that of L'Enfant during the first half of the year 1791'!

In June, L'Enfant submitted 'an Incompleat drawing' and a report to the President. The drawing no longer survives. But dated June 22, the revealing report which accompanied it contains an important description of L'Enfant's intentions and methods. In the circumlocutions that were characteristic of his English, L'Enfant wrote:

> Having first determined some principal points to which I wished making the rest subordinate I next made the distribution regular with Streets at right angle north–south & East–West but afterwards I opened others on various directions as avenues to & from Every principal place ... principally to connect each part of the City ... making the real distance less from place to place ... giving to them a reciprocity of sight and making them thus seemingly connected promot a rapide stellement over the whole so that the most remot may become an addition to the principal ...

For the city's central site, the congressional building, L'Enfant said that he could not find a location with more advantage than 'that on the west of Jenkins height which stands as a pedestal waiting for a monument'. He wrote elsewhere that on this hill a 'grand building would rear with a majestick aspect over the Country all round ...'.

For the 'Presidential palace' L'Enfant agreed that a ridge above the Tiber that had captured Washington's attention during his visit was the perfect location. But he chose a spot further east and slightly higher on the ridge. As shown in Figure 24, this was to command views down the length of the Potomac as it opened into its tidal estuary. Below this view was to be a canal and park 'in the center of which, and at the point of intersection of the sight from each of the Houses, would be ... an equestrian statue'. This was L'Enfant's initial version of the Washington Monument. The two houses, water, land, monuments and formal landscape would thus be joined on two bold axes, and, when all was complete, this 'would produce a most grand effect'.

One week later, the President, Andrew Ellicott and L'Enfant rode over the site. Once again it was damp and foggy, but Washington expressed his satisfaction with L'Enfant's plan and it was shown to the local landholders. They were told that this was not a final plan. Washington said, but behind L'Enfant's back, that the diagonal avenues 'would not be so numerous'. The executive offices not yet shown on the plan, he explained, would flank the President's House, which would be further to the west.

In his ensuing correspondence with Washington and Jefferson, L'Enfant, nothing daunted, went on to explain his ideas. He campaigned vigorously for the realization of the points of his plan in every detail. Contrary to the report of June 22 that seemed to give priority to the north–south and east west orientation of the streets, he now said that he disliked this gridiron order favored by Jefferson. Streets arranged in this pattern 'become at last tiresome and insipide', he wrote, and emphasized that his very different plan, with its great avenues, conformed to existing topography and lines of sight, such as that from the President's House down the Potomac River.

THE 'LEADING AVENUES'

Despite the similarity of L'Enfant's focal points and radial avenues to those favoured in Baroque palaces, grand houses and in Paris and other European cities, no confirmation is given in any of his writing that he drew upon existing cities, or indeed on any traditional aesthetic or geometric formulae, for his inspiration. On the contrary, L'Enfant always claimed that his plan was 'original' and 'wholy new'. Not once did L'Enfant justify himself in terms of tradition. He always insisted upon the originality of his plan.

Although he would have noted the beauty and power of diagonal avenues as a youth when he lived at Versailles, L'Enfant explained the avenues in the City of Washington in functional terms as 'principally to connect each part of the city ... making the real distance less from place to place'. This was not the language of a monarchist concerned with enhancing executive power. Instead his repeated concern was that the city of the new republic would be able to grow in a natural way, and attract throngs of people, shops and businesses to the spaces created by its broad squares and avenues. L'Enfant believed that in designing the city as a unified whole, with each part interconnected by long avenues, it would be able to flourish as a whole. It would thus be financed by the high price of lots throughout the entire city. While the President was busy promoting the building of the Potomac canal as the channel of commerce with the interior of the continent, L'Enfant was proposing to turn the Tiber into a canal, thereby facilitating greater commercial activity within the city. Furthermore, the earth used to fill the creek would help level the ground to the south, making a 'Grand Avenue', later to be known as the Mall. When bordered with gardens, sculpture and edifices, L'Enfant envisaged his Grand Avenue becoming the center of the artistic and intellectual life of the city, and as integrating local commerce with entertainment and education.

The extensive distance between Congress House and the President's House (Jefferson made sure that its original designation of 'palace' was quickly dropped) was appropriate, L'Enfant thought, as a 'sort of decorum' was required between these two branches of government. A glance at his plan shows that both buildings are set on rises to command views over the surrounding landscape. But the third branch of government, the Judiciary, was to be sited without any linking avenues to surrounding landmarks, in order to underline its independent nature. 'To denote the freedom of the judiciary from political influence', L'Enfant wrote, 'the avenues from Judiciary Square would not run to them'. That is, no radial avenues would run from the Supreme Court to the President's House or to Congress House. It was clear that right from the beginning of the design process, such details were seen by L'Enfant as highly important symbolic but also political considerations.

The extant L'Enfant Plan of 1791 consists of a system of diagonal avenues radiating from focal points or converging upon irregular open spaces, squares and circles. L'Enfant explained in the legend on his plan that great attention was 'paid to the passing of those leading Avenues over the most favorable ground for prospect and convenience'. The Capitol and the President's House – in addition to some other sites, as will be shown – form the principal focal points for these radial avenues and also for the dominant east–west and north–south axes. The north–south axis through the President's House was also aligned on the Potomac. These principal points, L'Enfant wrote, 'were first determined on the most advantageous ground', thus marrying topography with geometric order.

Fifteen squares were reserved for the States of the Union, to be decorated as each state saw fit. Further squares were set aside for public buildings such as the Supreme Court, the District Court and City Hall. Finally, in reports sent to Washington in August, written in his typically exuberant style, L'Enfant explained that the

> North and South lines, intersected by others running due East and West, make the distribution of the City into Streets, Squares &c ... those lines have been so combined as to meet at certain given points with those divergent Avenues, so as to form on the spaces 'first determined', the different Squares or Areas, which are all proportional in Magnitude to the number of Avenues leading to them.

In other words, since the initial report of June 22, L'Enfant had changed his priorities. He made the principal points and the avenues come first, and only then came the gridiron pattern for the streets.

As the City of Washington was intended to be politically powerful, to integrate all the activities of the people and to be financially prosperous, L'Enfant planned a large commercial district to be sited east of

Photo 5. View west from the Capitol. Pennsylvania Avenue is to the right, Maryland Avenue to the left, the Mall in the center. This view must be close to what L'Enfant intended.

the Capitol. On the shore of the Anacostia River, he proposed a location for the 'General Exchange'. Where the National Museum of American Art and the National Portrait Gallery are now located L'Enfant also suggested a church 'intended for national purposes ... assigned to the special use of no particular Sect or denomination, but equally open to all'. Reservations were also made for future public buildings and for undefined monuments. As his letters make only too clear, L'Enfant was marshalling all the elements necessary for a great city equal to any European equivalent of the day and capable of fulfilling the unique requirements of the capital of the new republic.

THE CITY SPACES

The stages of L'Enfant's planning can be summarized as follows. First, he examined the topography and determined the best location for the two principal sites: the Capitol and the President's House. Then he determined other important centers and laid out broad avenues between them. The avenues had to be at least a hundred and sixty feet in width to create the desired aesthetic and commanding effect. Pennsylvania Avenue was described by L'Enfant in August 1791 as 'a direct & large avenue from the bridge on the potowmack to that on the Eastern branch ... proportioned to the Greatnes which a City the Capitale of a powerfull Empire ought to manifest'. The main avenue between the Capitol and the President's House was to be the 'foundation' of the city. Finally, there came the cross streets and the numerous architectural details which would make the city vibrant and viable.

The architect J. L. Sibley Jennings Jr. thinks that L'Enfant did not envisage his avenues as long, even, open roads. He suggests that L'Enfant saw them instead as tree-filled 'greenways' of short stretches, converging on squares, filled with moving people, arcaded stores, differently treated facades, monuments and fountains, and interspersed – in the European manner – by archways or even houses spanning the street. The avenues on the L'Enfant Plan, together with the many irregular squares, create a great variety of differently treated 'architectonic' spaces. When built, the city's extraordinary variety of shapes, textures, perspectives, modulated planes, deep shadows, light-filled squares, sculptures and monumental points in space, was intended to provide many different experiences and even surprises for those who lived in the city or visited it.

Given the variety of settings created by his plan, it appeared that L'Enfant deeply understood the need of ordinary people for opportunities for commerce, recreation, entertainment and housing at different social levels. He understood the need for the inhabitants to become intimately involved with the formal architectural space of their city. Its people would be the energy that was going to drive the city, and its architectonic spaces would not come alive unless people could work, dwell and feel comfortable among them. I think this counters the charge often made against L'Enfant that his radiant avenues and emphasis on broad vistas were better suited for the capital of an empire rather than a republic. L'Enfant adapted the grand architecture of monarchic Europe to the political, social and commercial reality of the new American republic. Contrary to the prevailing elitism of the Age of Enlightenment, the political and spatial awareness of L'Enfant allowed him to conceive of a city in service to a democracy.

A CITY FOR SALE

At some point either on or just before August 26, 1791, L'Enfant travelled to Philadelphia to lay the outline of his design for the federal city before the President. Written in the margins of the plan shown to the President were the observations and references quoted above. Authorities such as Richard Stephenson of its Geography and Map Division consider that the plan preserved in the Library of Congress is 'almost certainly' this working drawing, although L'Enfant's 'original' or 'large plan', as he described it, has not survived.

After the Secretary of State had examined the plan – for alterations to L'Enfant's wording appear in Jefferson's handwriting upon it – it was entirely approved. Acting on the President's instructions, L'Enfant now began preparing it for engraving. In order to finance the city's construction, Washington and Jefferson felt it was imperative that the sale of lots took place as soon as possible and to this end it was a necessity to produce and exhibit the plan of the new city.

Contemporary texts reveal that this pressure led L'Enfant into a series of conflicts. Above all, he was an artist. He seems to have seen President Washington as his patron in the 'Grand Tradition' of the European school of architecture. In fact L'Enfant didn't even have a contract, for his work was being based upon an old comrade's courtly code of gentlemanly agreements. Moreover, L'Enfant's vision was of his ideal city rising from the earth of the District of Columbia all at once on a 'Grand Scale'. He, the Nation's Engineer and Architect, was to build it with the munificence that would pour in through his presidential patron. Then other patrons, in the form of the States – following the lead of their President – would construct and embellish their designated portions. L'Enfant seems to have anticipated that as the city grew, and especially when the infrastructure of roads, canals, bridges and public utilities was complete, then the investors, developers, traders and the common people would move in, purchase their lots at a high price and bring the city to life.

But alas, the new American Republic was operating in an entirely different manner from that which L'Enfant imagined. While the States did not want to fund a distant and potentially overbearing federal capital, and the federal government itself had no cash, the many speculators, land-owners, investors, commissioners and bureaucrats all wanted their say as well as their piece of the pie. L'Enfant, for all his visionary thinking, could never quite overcome his aristocratic upbringing and understand the need for compromise and expediency which this situation imposed. In his mind he was still attributing powers to President Washington that his father would have witnessed in the person of the French king. And he loathed the speculators who were gathering in the area, who would of course have included many local businessmen and Masons. His disdain of these speculators would soon lead to his downfall. But at this point we should turn and examine L'Enfant's plan for the city in more detail.

5
The Geometric Order of the Federal City

A *TABULA RASA*

When I first studied L'Enfant's plan during the autumn of 1992, I was eager to see what pattern I would find within its detail. But I also had to avoid rushing to conclusions. I knew that I had first to get inside the mind of the architect and find out how he had worked in order to see the deeper pattern in his work, rather than attempt to confine what L'Enfant had done within any pre-existing theory of my own. Fortunately I had no axe to grind. I had no preconceived attachment to the possibility of a federal conspiracy, no affiliation with any interest group, not even any pro- or anti-Masonic theory to prove. I was a resident of the US, but had not been born there; like L'Enfant, I was by birth and temperament a European. Perhaps my position as an outsider and independent scholar could give me some extra objectivity and insight into the way this other European and friend to America had been thinking almost exactly 200 years before? The following sections will describe the steps, deduced from the plan of 1791, which I believe L'Enfant followed to lay out the city.

It was clear that after the selection of the sites for the Capitol and the President's House, L'Enfant had defined the other key sites and the avenues between them. These primary sites and avenues were determined, as he said, after the careful consideration of the existing topographical features. He was not constrained by anything else. Now that George Washington had personally seen to the purchase of all the necessary land, the ground was a *tabula rasa*, a 'clean slate', and L'Enfant could literally create *ex nihilo*, 'from out of nothing', without any impediment. He was about to design what most architects could only dream of. He had the extremely rare opportunity to create the capital city of a powerful emerging nation from the ground up. How would he use this opportunity?

The Secret Geometry of Washington, D.C.

A short answer to this question is that L'Enfant allowed his imagination to rove over the relatively untrammelled landscape, to see where and how the most harmonious relationships between the forms of nature and the forms required by the capital city would be achieved. In the words attributed to the architect Frank Lloyd Wright, he did not 'build on' the land; he 'built with it'. He filled in some deeply eroded gullies – especially on the flanks of Jenkins Hill, the Capitol site – he drained marshes, and he planned to canal the Tiber; but above all, he was sensitive to the contours of the landscape and alive to the potentials of the location. L'Enfant was not a pragmatic city planner, flattening and throwing a fixed plan, a gridiron, onto the ground regardless of its character. Instead he acted intuitively, as a true geomancer, or as 'a diviner of the earth'; using all his senses to assess every topographical and subtle influence to arrive at the most favorable aspects for the city.

Yet at the same time, it seems L'Enfant was not content to simply allow his imagination and the natural features of the place determine the design. It was evident that he wanted to create a striking and carefully developed urban pattern that was in harmony with the landscape, but he also had something to say beyond this. After all, the new city was to be the capital of a vast, powerful and rapidly emerging nation that had just taken on and defeated the greatest colonial power on earth; and the ideas behind the nation's birth came from real, revolutionary and highly aspiring principles. So L'Enfant selected a design that sprang from observation of the natural world combined with his desire to build a symbolic approximation of the ideal order of his new nation on earth.

'AN HISTORIC COLUMN'

As I studied the plan, I became certain that after the Capitol and the President's House, the next principal point selected by L'Enfant lay a mile east of the Capitol. This is (and I think this is significant) the square that was marked with a large 'B' on the plan. This point is in the center of the elevation whose western brow is Jenkins Hill. Its topographical significance can be seen from Figure 26. The main entrance of the Capitol looks east to Square B along what is now a tree-lined, residential street. This modest vista, however, was not what L'Enfant originally had in mind.

L'Enfant intended Square B to be reached by a great avenue, East Capitol Street, along which a prosperous commercial district was to

The Geometric Order of the Federal City

grow. At the center of the square was to be placed a 'historic Column ... a Mile or itinerary column', L'Enfant wrote on his plan, 'from whose station, all distances of places through the continent, are to be calculated'. East Capitol Street and the square at B were to be the commercial center of the new city. They were to provide its economic heart. But the symbolic column was never realized, nor was the commercial district. The area became a residential one and the square became Lincoln Park. I first visited it one cool and breezy October day, and found that the Emancipation Monument, a bronze sculpture unveiled in 1876 and depicting Lincoln freeing a slave, now sits at the center of the square.

The growth of the eastern part of the Federal City was extremely important to L'Enfant; in fact it was essential to his entire plan for the development of the city. As explained above, while desiring a grand and imposing capital, L'Enfant also shared Washington's vision of the city becoming a metropolis of commerce. L'Enfant's repeated concern, as his work progressed, was that the commercial district in the east would be neglected in favor of the federal buildings in the western part of the city. This is precisely what happened over the following years and in the succeeding centuries. L'Enfant wanted his city to be realized as a whole. It would only be achieved as businesses, banks, shops, cafés and people moved in to occupy and vitalize its many different districts. To this end every part of the city had to be developed together to make it attractive to purchasers. But the District Commissioners wanted to direct all available funds to the development of the main public buildings in the west. Despite this, L'Enfant instructed his work crews to carry on construction over the whole area of his plan. The result, his critics complained, was a city full of streets without houses. It appeared to be a city, as Charles Dickens dismissively said, of nothing more than 'magnificent intentions'.

His conflict with the Commissioners was eventually to bring about L'Enfant's downfall and undermine his plan for the city. In retrospect, it is clear that both parties were partly right and partly wrong. The commercial city dreamt of by both the President and L'Enfant was never developed, mainly because the Potomac was intrinsically unsuitable for trade. Today, the distinctiveness of Washington, D.C. arises precisely from its identity as a Federal City, not a commercial center. But eventually the city did become large enough to fill all of L'Enfant's sweeping panoramas. He was merely ahead of his time.

I shall return to this point later; but for now I should emphasise that it was Square B and its Mile Column that had enabled me to understand L'Enfant's intentions for the first steps of his grand plan. With this firmly fixed in my mind, I was able to return to and review the beginning of the plan – the Capitol.

THE CENTER

From my study of traditional architecture, I knew that the first act in the building of any important settlement, city or sanctuary was the location of the center. The center was always located first and only then came the definition of the boundary, the finding of the directions, and the marking of their measures. Cities and towns as various as Rome, Jerusalem, Cuzco, Medina and the Imperial City of China, the temples of Egypt and the classical world, as well as the pueblos of the Southwest United States, were all founded through this measured sequence of apparently simple acts.

In traditional architecture, the center is seen as the place of origin, of beginnings. It is the place of creative power from which emerges the generative order of life. The center is also the symbolic focus of unity, and is therefore the preferred seat of authority and government in many cities. The center is the place from which the right order of things is established and from which order is maintained throughout the land.

The center is also the key point upon the horizontal surface of the earth that possesses a vertical dimension. It always has a vertical axis that connects the center to the above and to the below. The center is the point of connection between the terrestrial realm, the heavenly realm and the underworld. In different traditions this vertical axis is symbolically represented by a tree, a mound, a pyramid, a mountain, a fissure, shaft or cave, a spring, a stone, a ladder, a column or some other kind of pillar set in the ground and reaching to the sky. The axis may be marked by a hearth, a depression in the ground, or a hole in the roof. It may be marked by a monument, a temple, or a palace. The vertical axis is the *axis mundi*, the 'world axis'. The marker at its very center is described in Greek tradition as the *omphalos*, the 'navel of the world'.

I think the reason why these qualities are imputed to the center originates in our experience of the human body. From the experience of standing on the surface of the Earth, we become aware of our bodies defining a vertical axis in space. The earth is beneath our feet, the sky above our heads. This defines our primary axis, and one that is distinctively human. Ahead and behind us on the horizontal plane is our next significant axis, while to our right and to our left is a third primary axis. Whatever we are – heart, mind, body, soul, spirit, senses, nerves and so on – is experienced as being at the center.

As humanity evolved over immense periods of time, our ideas of space became ordered and categorised by this common physical experience of the body upon the earth. As our brains and memory developed, we acquired a language of space and time that was structured by our interaction with our surroundings. These spatial experiences and observations included a developing awareness of our movement over the Earth's surface, the passage of the seasons, migrations, movement of the heavenly bodies, the direction of the Earth's polar axis and so on. The relationship of our bodies to these things formed the primary perceptual categories, the fundamental structural language, the values and conceptual orientations of our minds.

'THE TEMPLE OF MAN'

According to the philosopher and Egyptologist Schwaller de Lubicz, whose book *The Temple of Man* has the same title as this section, it was inevitable that, for humans, the body itself would become the primary image and the measure of the order of life. Whether conceived in the Christian 'image of the divine', as the Pythagorean's 'perfect' expression in human form of the creative impulse, or as Leonardo da Vinci's 'Vitruvian Man', the body has come to provide us with the model for the order of life. The structural form provided by the body influences us enormously not just in our occasional thoughts but in the very nature of our minds.

The past, spatial and temporal experience of the human body came to structure the form of what Schwaller de Lubicz called the 'Temple'. This can be understood as any intended architectural manifestation in the world of the divine or sacred order. In all religious traditions, some aspect of the Temple will always be modelled upon the body, and its forms and values will derive from the human perception of the divine order of life. In other words, the Temple is structured both by our experience of the body and by our idea of the primary, divine order. We imprint the earth with our idea of the generative order of things, just as we are aware that that order imprints itself upon us. The most fundamental expression of this idea, deriving from our experience of the body, is the center and the three axes. The simplest and most universal form of the Temple involves the definition of the center and the three axial divisions of space.

The Secret Geometry of Washington, D.C.

Once a center and the three primary axes are established, the volumes that an individual temple may actually assume in architectural space can become very complicated, as many other spatial and temporal forms will influence its design. Some temples are dedicated to the sun, the moon, the stars; some to other expressions of the creative divine order. The volumes of the temple can manifest according to fundamental mathematical or geometric patterns: the square, the circle, the triangle, the sphere, the cube and so on. These forms express the many observable divisions and dimensions of the order of our spatial experience. But I think it is true to say that in the building of any temple – whether this is a cathedral, a mosque, a stone circle, a medicine wheel, or a central foundation – the primary desire of the builders is to explore the most generative, the most creative, the most primal and therefore the simplest order. The axiom that is implicitly followed is that the more inclusive the perceived order, the more primal it will be, and the simpler – and at the same time, the more powerful – it must be.

The primal order of the Temple is an expression of the human idea of fundamental unity and origins. The Temple represents our concept of source, the place we have originated from. Given that our modern experience is generally that of being no longer one with the source, the Temple may now represent something and somewhere in the past that we see ourselves as having become separated from; something we may have lost and which must be restored or returned to. The word 'temple' not only includes the meaning of space, *templum*, the spatial order, but it also alludes to our situation in time, *tempus*, the temporal order. The Temple may therefore evoke something and somewhere back in time: a special place that is connected to the original source. As a gateway suggests movement and a journey through space and time, gateways are nearly always fundamental to the fabric of the Temple. Some Egyptian temples, for example, are designed predominantly as a succession of gateways, known as *pylons*, which progressively take the visitor deeper and deeper on a journey through space and time that leads back to the primordial point of unity and origins, located in the temple *naos* or sanctuary.

As the experience of the human body always involves a linear progression through birth, life and death, so the builders of a Temple sometimes represented its gateway as the opening to the womb. The builders of the megalithic passage mounds, for example, appear to have conceived the place of origins as a cave-temple with a uterine passageway to the generative power of the divine archetypal feminine – the 'Great Goddess'. Yet life is also a passage toward death, and the megalithic

The Geometric Order of the Federal City

builders also appear to have conceived of their chambered mounds as tombs. Mircea Eliade observed that the archetypal symbols of the womb and the tomb are synonymous; they share with the symbols of the tree, the cave and the *omphalos* a numinous power that suggests something beyond the one-way journey of this life. Thus the temple can suggest an 'eternal return', wrote Eliade, an 'ever-recurring cycle', a renewal of original power, rebirth, resurrection and re-incarnation.

A gateway, or a procession through successively more exclusive spaces within a Temple, allows the visitor to arrive at a focused single point. This may be described as a sanctuary, a shrine, or a 'holy of holies'. This ultimate chamber of the temple, usually accessible only to a few, is the attempt to express in form the gateway from our present experience in time and space into another. It may feature a final gateway, one that only a spirit or a deity can pass through. This part of the Temple mirrors human attempts to reconcile the realm of the immeasurable, the unquantifiable, the transcendent, with the dimensions of this world. To the Jews, for example, the Ark of the Covenant – once enshrined in the Holy of Holies of the Temple of Solomon, but now lost – was understood as the point where God had touched this world. This relationship found symbolic expression in the geometrical proportions of the Ark and of the Temple in Jerusalem – both of which are thought to have been those of the cube (see Figure 22). The statue of the particular *Netr*, or divine principle, to whom an Egyptian temple was dedicated, which stood in its *naos*, was likewise understood to be the symbol of the divine presence on earth.

The space of the Temple itself is always sacred, a sanctuary set apart from human life. As the place of spiritual power its boundaries are not to be transgressed by the profane. It may have terrifying guardians and closed doors. It may exhibit the most amazing, varied and bewildering displays of human ingenuity. Its proportions, acoustics and decorations may express every facet of the human idea of the Divine Mind. Sometimes the Temple may be dedicated to a particular form of a life entity: an animal, a god, a goddess, a *Netr*, a tree, a spirit of place – an embodiment of the *genius loci*, the local spirit or *daemon*. At other times the Temple may uphold something supremely philosophical and abstract. But, according to Eliade, all these diverse archetypal threads run parallel to each other. While each temple would have developed a system of meaning that accords with its culture and location, the dimensions of every temple are all connected by the unifying image of the center. The Temple always helps those who visit it to feel connected; to feel the unifying or archetypal patterns within everything; to become aware of the measured dimensions of the single, primary source and hence of a unifying order behind the seeming chaos of ordinary existence.

THE HOUSE AT THE CENTER

> I have ... every hope that the grand work we have done today will be handed down ... to a late posterity, as the like work of that ever memorable temple to our order erected by our ancient Grand Master Solomon.
> Maryland Grand Master Joseph Clark, September 18, 1793, at the laying of the cornerstone of the Capitol.

> It would be unbecoming the representatives of this Nation to assemble for the first time in this solemn Temple without looking up to the Supreme Ruler of the Universe and imploring His blessing.
> President Adams, November 22, 1800, opening the Second Session of the Sixth Congress in the new Capitol building.

It was unequivocally clear that L'Enfant intended to make the House of Congress the center of both the Federal District and of the United States. The Capitol, as it is now known – otherwise and (mostly) affectionately called 'the Hill' – was described by everyone at the time of its foundation as a temple.

When President Washington laid the cornerstone of the Capitol building in 1793, the Masonic lodges of the area provided the grandest dedication ceremony possible. As shown in the many paintings of the event, everyone who was anyone was present. The importance of this ceremony to Freemasons can be judged by the portion of the oration quoted above. The building was vividly described as being akin to the Temple of Solomon in Jerusalem. To the Masons, present in all their finery, the cornerstone – whose location is now unknown – represented a renewed covenant with the divine in the land of America. The cornerstone carried echoes of the founding of the temple of Jerusalem as well as the Ark of the Covenant. At the time, George Washington was Master of Virginia Lodge No. 39 in Alexandria. And on the evidence of President Adams' opening remarks, also quoted above, when Congress first sat in the building a few years later it was viewed in a very similar way. The divine or the 'Supreme Ruler of the Universe' was invoked by Adams 'in this solemn Temple'.

Such acts, words and ideas were entirely in accordance with the traditions that have always surrounded the foundation of a world

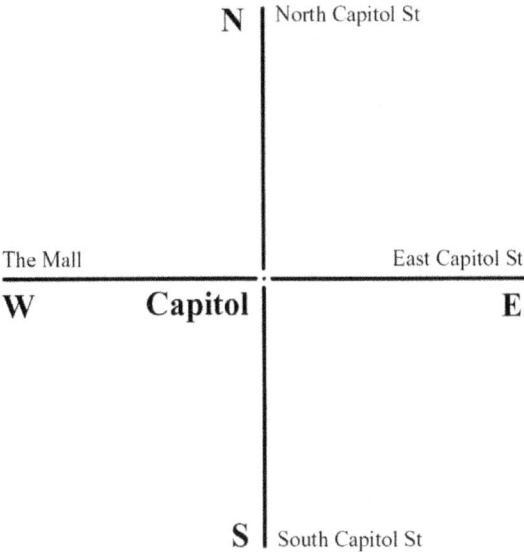

Figure 28. The Center and Axes. Aligned to the cardinal directions, the axial center of the new world was to be the site chosen for the House of Congress. All agreed with L'Enfant's estimation of the hill, the highest ground in the center of the city, as being 'a pedestal waiting for a superstructure'.

center and the creation of a Temple. It was customary that the site selected for the center was the highest point in the area and, in keeping with this tradition, L'Enfant located Congress House on Jenkins Hill. He even described the location as his 'pedestal waiting for a superstructure'. The hill established the center and the vertical axis in space. It symbolically connected the House of Congress to the above, to the transcendent dimension. Only under the rotunda of the central dome of the Capitol can someone lie in state in the USA. This was to be the place where the qualities of the divine order – or the 'Supreme Ruler' according to President Adams – were to be attuned to and mirrored on the terrestrial sphere. L'Enfant's intentions were entirely clear on this matter.

Then, to emphasise the centrality of Congress, and still in keeping with temple-building tradition, L'Enfant ran the two horizontal axes of the city: north, south, east and west, straight through its site.

THE 'TRUE MERIDIAN'

In one bold and extraordinary masterstroke, L'Enfant put the new prime or zero meridian of longitude through the site for the Capitol building on

The Secret Geometry of Washington, D.C.

Jenkins Hill. In the notes accompanying his 1791 plan, L'Enfant wrote:

> Mr. Ellicott drew a true Meridienal line by celestial observation which passes through the Area intended for the Congress house; this line he crossed by another due East and West ... These lines were accurately measured and made the bases on which the whole plan was executed.

Andrew Ellicott, assisted by Benjamin Banneker, surveyed the exact orientation of the north–south polar axis from the intended center of the Capitol site on Jenkins Hill and defined its line of longitude as a new 0° prime meridian, from which all other positions on the earth were to be measured. This new, zero-degree global meridian was then marked by a survey of North Capitol and South Capitol Streets. This inspired and extraordinary act not only affirmed independence from Britain – who had already defined the prime meridian as running through Greenwich, London – but it also defined the center of the New World. The Congress House was to be the center of an order, defined by lines of 'celestial observation': north–south, east–west, that were, furthermore, 'the bases on which the whole plan was executed'. From its 'meridienal' base lines centered on the Capitol, the order of the New World was to be governed and measured, and from here it was to grow.

This was impressive temple building activity, directly described by the architect. But there was one thing that didn't quite add up. As was made clear at the beginning of this chapter, L'Enfant intended to place at a distance of one mile from the Capitol, at Square B, a 'historic Column ... a Mile or itinerary column, from whose station, all distances of places through the continent, are to be calculated'. At first, I could not understand why the defining measures of the New World order were to run from the Mile Column and not from the Capitol. Surely, in keeping with temple-building tradition, the measures of the first spatial creative acts should emerge from the chosen center, the Capitol itself?

I went away and thought about this for a while. I returned to the high, white marble steps at the entrance to the Capitol and walked from there along East Capitol Street. As I walked the mile to Lincoln Square with late autumn leaves swirling about my feet, it occurred to me that the name of the Mile Column itself was the clue. By establishing a marker at one mile from the center along a primary axis – hence the 'Mile' Column – L'Enfant was defining the number 1 and the mile as the first acts of measure. It seemed that L'Enfant realised the measures that emerged from the center and quantified space should not run through the unquantifiable center but instead should pass through a marker set at a propitious distance from it. The Capitol is the center, the place of unity; but as the primary source, it is understood as itself being outside or 'beyond' measure or direction. The work of measure was therefore the task of the Mile Column.

I was to learn that the number 1, the mile – the initial step to Square B in the east – defined all the subsequent measures, orders and numbers of the spatial dynamics of the city. But to understand how this symbolism was developed by L'Enfant in his plan, I first had to do a lot more walking in the city.

THE BOUNDARY OR CIRCUMFERENCE

After choosing the location of the center, I knew that the next steps taken by traditional architecture to establish the most advantageous spatial order involved finding and delineating the directions, as well as marking the measures and the boundaries of the area that enclosed the center. According to the geometer Robert Lawlor, the boundary differentiated the 'ground of the primal creative unity within' from the ordinary ground without. In antiquity, this boundary would have enclosed an area known to the Greeks as the *temenos* (and to the Celts as the *nemeton,* which literally means 'the sacred grove').

It was from Robert – with whom I hiked around a canyon in Arizona in the following year and who is the translator of Schwaller de Lubicz's opus, *The Temple of Man* – that I learnt the Greek word *temenos* is related to the Latin words for temple and template, as well as to space, *templum* and to time, *tempus.* The temple not only defines space and time, it also provides the template for defining that which is within and that which is without: that which is the 'ultimate cause' and that which is its effect. This was the kind of ordering of symbolic power and authority that nation states were eager to put into their city plans.

In traditional systems of city design, the *temenos* laid out on the ground may take the form of a circle, a square, a rectangle or some other prime geometrical form. Plato's ideal city of Magnesia was circular, Medina of the Prophet is square, and the Imperial city of China employed rectangles. In the case of Washington D.C., the *temenos* was surely the one hundred square miles of the Federal District. This ten-mile square, defined by Article 1 of the U.S. Constitution, located by Washington, turned into a 'diamond' by Jefferson and anchored on Jones Point by the surveys of Ellicott and Banneker, forms the boundary and defines the inner space of what is, in effect, the national Temple. As shown in

Figure 24, the corners of the square point north, south, east and west; in this way, they set the District of Columbia quite apart from the orthogonal grid that defines the rest of the United States.

Once the shape of the federal 'diamond' was decided upon, I felt it must have had a profound conceptual impact upon many people at the time. How did they see it and what did it mean to them? When I learnt that Masons were involved with the marking of the boundaries of the district – and knowing that in Masonic tradition the square was held as an important figure – I decided to go and ask them what this had meant for them.

I met the Grand Archivist of the very well appointed Lodge of the Scottish Order in Washington D.C.. He was also a thirty-third degree Freemason. He gave me as much access as I wanted to the books in their library, and when he learnt what I was researching, he also gave me generous amounts of his time. From the start, he made what he felt was an important distinction between the majority of Masons, who were mostly concerned with charitable and community work, and those others – far fewer in number – who had a definite mystical inclination. The views of the latter, he said, were diverse. They were the responsibility of each individual and no reliable version of a 'Masonic' tradition of knowledge should be drawn from any one of them. Having made what sounded like a disclaimer, he went on to agree that the Freemasons of the area would have considered the square boundary of the district to be of great significance in the creation of the federal city.

The Grand Archivist showed me various designs for Masonic lodges, adding that the ideas behind them had been developed in the eighteenth century as a result of increasing information about ancient architectural tradition. Earlier stonemason guilds and the Knights Templar had already speculated on the nature of Solomon's Temple; but it was the enormous flood of information made available in the 'Age of Enlightenment' that had stimulated the foundation of the Fraternity of Freemasonry in 1717. This, together with other social factors like the rise of a wealthy middle class, had led to a huge increase in the number of Masons and to the building of many new lodges. The archivist credited Masonry for upholding moral and mystical values during a period of increasing secularism and rationalism. He regretted that this inevitably brought it into conflict with the Church, who insisted on being the sole authority in such matters. As the wealth and influence of the fraternity increased this had led to hostility from other quarters, including, he said somewhat defensively, the anti-Masonry conspiracy theories that still abound today.

The Geometric Order of the Federal City

The archivist told me that through the marking of geometrical forms on the floor of the Masonic temple, the profane terrestrial realm was restored to the harmony of the ideal forms of the heavenly realm. It was his view – and one which he believed he shared with many other Masons – that the ideal forms, numbers and measures which order the irregularity, if not to say the chaos, of earth were only to be found in the heavens.

I asked him about the square. He gave me access to texts that described the 'square of virtue' as the form that denoted or created the first settled, 'concrete' or solid order in space. Composed of four right-angles, the texts said that the square enclosed an area upon the earth where a Mason could stand firmly upon the moral virtues that ultimately came from God. Using the essential tools of Masonry, the square and the compass – that originally came from Egypt – the 'right' angles could be created for the proper regulation of human activities upon Earth. Some of the sources went on to say that the compass and the circle represented the spiritual realm, while the square represented the material, the human realm. I also read such things as that the upward-pointing 'lunar' triangle, although sublimely generative, is deemed too 'active' for terrestrial affairs unless complemented by its downward-pointing partner to form a six, the 'solar' hexagon.

This was all helpful in my attempt to understand what Masons thought about the square; however I couldn't be certain, as Masonic interpretations of the square differed from text to text. Yet further reading in their tradition tended to confirm the archivist's view that the ideal or 'perfect' measures of the heavens were the template for the correct order of human affairs on earth. Everyone seemed to agree on this. Pythagoras, Plato and the early neo-Platonists had clearly influenced the Masons, and all these philosophers held that harmony, law and correct governance emerged from such primary forms as the circle, the triangle and the square. They said that the origins of these archetypal forms lay outside of the earthly realm, in the heavenly realm; but when these forms were imprinted upon earth by the hands and minds of those attuned to this celestial order, then the temple, the holy city, could be built on earth. If the eighteenth-century Masons had access to this sort of information – and the date of some of the texts in the library suggests they did – then Masonic sensibilities must have been very affected by the day the square boundary of the city was marked out.

Masonic tradition seemed to hold some of the clues that would allow me to open a window into understanding the ideas that prevailed at the time the city was built. But I had to tread very carefully as I walked over this territory. For one thing, I certainly wasn't being told

The Secret Geometry of Washington, D.C.

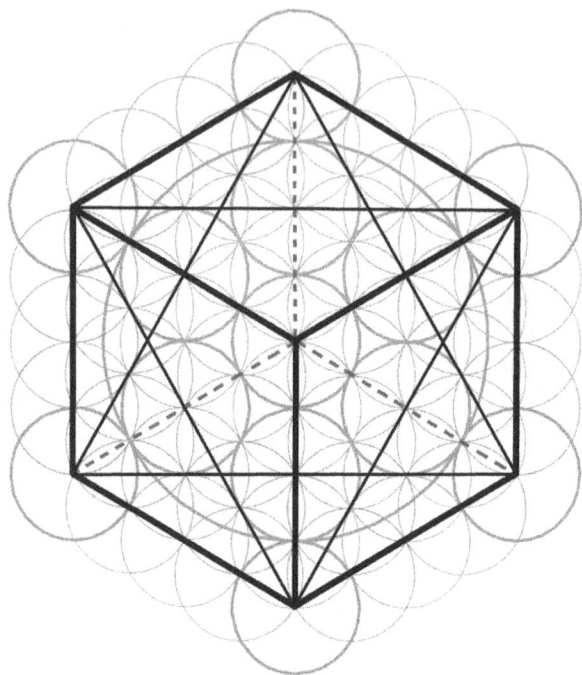

Figure 29. The six-pointed star present within the cubic ashlar.

everything; for another, some of what I was being told may not have been strictly true. And whatever I learnt, it would still be hard to know what the key protagonists of the time of Washington's foundation – especially L'Enfant – had really believed.

THE CARDINAL DIRECTIONS

In traditional systems of cosmology and architecture, the drawing of the boundary is accompanied by a division of the prime geometrical figure it encloses. The center, the 'sacred ground' or *temenos*, has to be divided into specific measures and directions. This first division of space is, as a rule, along the three major axes. While the vertical axis is aligned to the above and the below, the other two axes are aligned horizontally to the four cardinal directions – north, south, east and west. The prime geometrical figure that forms the central unity is thus divided by three axes into six directions. The square of the Federal District could therefore be divided into quadrants, vectors, planes and directions arranged and measured in a variety of ways.

The Geometric Order of the Federal City

On the horizontal surface of the earth, the cardinal directions are determined by the earth's polar axis – north–south – and by the direction of its apparent rotation – east–west – through space. Observation of the star Polaris can provide an indicator of true north; while observation of the sun can confirm east–west. On a level horizon, a line drawn between the point of the rising and the point of the setting sun on any day will establish the east–west axis. All traditional architecture considered it vital to recognise and align the horizontal axes of their foundations to these geo-celestial coordinates. My research into Egyptian, Greek, Indian and Middle Eastern architecture indicated that the four directions were usually marked by avenues and gateways, or by some other significant features on the points where they intersected the boundaries of the central city, temple or palace. The cardinal axes and their four gateways, north, south, east, west aligned the heavenly to the terrestrial sphere and allowed the movement of beneficent forces between the center and every quarter of the realm.

In April 1791, surveyors and Freemasons marked the cardinal directions on the ten-mile square *temenos* of the city – the Federal District – with large boundary stones, and went on to divide the space between them with further stones at one-mile intervals: this was a total of forty stones in all.

I returned to the Masonic library, where I was reminded that if there was a tradition shared by all the members of the Fraternity of Freemasonry it was the creation of the 'ashlar' – a block of stone cut into a cube. The act of squaring the surfaces of the ashlar to form the basic building stone was considered to be the primary task of the Mason, however speculative, or 'non-operative', he might be. This act was seen as the main source of order in the world. Ancient Egyptian masons went to extraordinary lengths to lay out the perfect 'cubic ashlar' in stone with only a compass, a plumb line and a square. The ashlar was considered the manifestation of the prime, geometrical, heavenly figure in the stone of earth. The ashlar, the cube, is one of five figures that can be inscribed within a sphere whose lines are of equal length and whose internal angles are the same. These five figures – the cube, the tetrahedron, the octahedron, the icosahedron and the dodecahedron (Figure 23) – are known as the Platonic Solids. When visualised set inside each other, the five 'solids' were considered by the Neo-Platonic tradition – which in its Renaissance flowering had a great influence upon Freemasonry – to emanate the 'music of the spheres'.

The ashlar can be conceived as having an outer boundary whose six faces directly correspond to the three inner axes. The six sides, or planes, of the cubic ashlar look to the four cardinal directions – north, south, east and west – and also to the heavens above and the earth below. Altogether, the cubic ashlar has twelve edges, representing the twelve tribes, the twelve apostles, the twelve houses of the Zodiac, and so on. According to the soldier, prolific author and nineteenth-century Freemason Albert Pike (the source of much of this information), the six sides of the ashlar, only three of which are visible and three are invisible at any one time, represent the earthly and the spiritual powers of creation. Pike says the two sets of three are also represented in the two triangles of the six-pointed star, the 'Seal of Solomon'. As shown in Figure 29, this figure appears when a cube is viewed diagonally and the three hidden sides are imagined, or the cube is made transparent. All the Platonic Solids are also present in the cube or the ashlar. I think it is safe to say that for many Masons, it is this type of geometry that approaches most closely the mysterious order of the exemplary terrestrial foundation, the Temple of Solomon.

Pike also pointed out that the ashlar contains the figure made by 'doubling' the tetrahedron. Known as the star tetrahedron, the 'cubic star', or 'Merkabah', this figure can be imagined by drawing a fourth point from each of the three corners of the two triangles of the six-pointed star. As shown in Figure 30, this creates two three-dimensional pyramids or tetrahedrons that combine to make the cubic star. The lines of symmetry of the star tetrahedron bisect the three primary axes and point to the eight intersecting directions at the corners of the ashlar to form another manifestation of the prime order of the archetypal temple. Elaborations of such three-, four-, six- and eight-fold geometry reached a peak of expression in Islamic architecture.

If this was the sort of thing Masons were thinking about as they inaugurated the boundary stones on the four corners of the federal district, was it occupying L'Enfant? He was, after all, laying out his cardinal axes in the design of the city at the same time. L'Enfant was not a Mason; but since Masonic ideas were enjoying a huge revival during the eighteenth century, he certainly would have read books describing the temples of the ancient world, not only while training in France but also during his years in America. L'Enfant clearly went to great pains to emphasise the three-fold axial treatment of space in his design for Washington, and, of course, he would have been directly exposed to this principle during his youth in Europe.

In its great cathedrals, as in all the churches of Europe, the spatial order that emerges from the central point is always defined by the three primary axes. I can think of no exception to this rule. The vertical

The Geometric Order of the Federal City

Figure 30. The star tetrahedron.

axis was considered the most auspicious. The central tower or spire of the cathedral formed the connection between heaven and earth. It pointed to God. The principal cardinal axis invariably lay east–west. Defined by the nave, the crossing, the choir and the apse, the altar gave emphasis to the east. The third axis was defined by the transepts on the north and south sides of the great central crossing.

This three-fold, axial treatment of space is found in architecture throughout the world and the axial extension to the east is often the one given preferential treatment on the horizontal plane. In Chinese architecture, for example, the east–west axis was considered the most propitious for human affairs. Whenever the nation was metaphorically compared to a body – which was often – the direction to the east was considered the principal 'artery'. In Middle Eastern architecture, the east–west axis was again considered the most auspicious and was usually defined by the bazaar. The bazaar was a straight and often covered road that ran for a measured distance to the east of the center – either the mosque or the palace – and along which the vital commerce of the nation flowed.

EAST CAPITOL STREET

As I studied the L'Enfant Plan and read his notes, it became obvious that L'Enfant was giving East Capitol Street the most auspicious relationship to the center of the city. East Capitol Street was the avenue leading from the main doorway of the Capitol to the east. L'Enfant wrote in the references on his plan:

> ... around the Square [to the east] of the Capitol [and] along the Avenue from the two bridges to the Federal house, the pavement on each side will pass under an arched way, under whose cover Shops will be most conveniently and agreeably situated. This street is 160 feet in breadth, and a mile long.

This was L'Enfant's intention for the eastward extension of the main axis to the square at B, with its 'historic' or 'mile column'. L'Enfant intended this one-mile avenue to connect the commercial district of the new city – apparently so favorably situated on the junction of natural trade routes – to the Capitol at the center. East Capitol Street was designed to carry the life-blood of the nation to its heart.

L'Enfant described his design for the city in terms of the body. 'The avenues', he wrote to George Washington in June, would

> insure a rapide Inter course with all the parts of the City to which they will Serve as does the main vains in the animal body to diffuse life through smaller vessels in quickening the active motion of the heart.

This was to provide me with a particularly intriguing insight. It seems likely that L'Enfant – like all those influenced by the ideals of the Age of Enlightenment – conceived the city, all social commerce, the economy and even the Constitution of the country, as a self-regulating organism that would grow and flourish through the participation of the individuals involved within it. The country would only thrive if the people were allowed their independence and the freedom to pursue their own goals. Sovereignty, after all, as brilliantly expressed by the opening lines of the 1787 Constitution, was invested in the people. Government, it was thought, had the role of defining and harmonising the many parts of the whole, but should intervene as little and as lightly as possible, and most especially should not tax the people too highly. Protected, directed, led, but sovereign and unencumbered, the American people were seen as the driving force of the economy and the wealth of the new nation. The one-mile avenue along the main axis to the east – the place of sunrise, inception and vitality – was intended by L'Enfant to serve as a symbolic expression of this purpose.

In keeping with President Washington's wishes, dominant interests and Age of Enlightenment ideals, L'Enfant's intention was to architecturally express and enhance the idea of the flow of the forces of commerce along East Capitol Street. L'Enfant conceived the one mile eastern avenue between the Capitol and Square B as the main artery of the nation. All commercial activity would thus symbolically fall under the eye of government as it financed and invigorated the city. At the same time as it was intended to keep the center connected with the whole – with the people across the nation – East Capitol Street was also intended to keep the people connected with the center. The Capitol was to look directly into the thriving heart of the city.

I think this concept can be favorably compared to both the European cathedral and the traditional Middle Eastern bazaar. In the case of the former, East Capitol Street corresponded to the pre-eminent line that passes from the axial crossing through the choir to the high altar. In the case of the latter, it is important to remember the Middle Eastern bazaar is not merely a commercial concept. In its treatment of space, the bazaar allows direct and immediate movement by people between all the centers, temples, palaces and peripheries of the state. It is thus a profoundly integrative and allegorical concept. Plato, for example, writes in his *Laws* (778) that the temples of his ideal city of Magnesia must be erected 'all round the market-place and in a circle round the whole city, on the highest ground'. For Plato, the free flow of people within the *agora*, the street market and meeting place, was central to the ideal order of a state modelled on heaven. The activities of the people must fall, Plato stated, within the sphere governed by divine law.

In ancient Rome a similar concept applied to the Forum. This was the meeting place of the people, close to the temples, where business and every other human affair was conducted. In the center of the Forum stood the 'Golden Milestone', from which all distances were measured and to which all the roads of the empire were symbolically oriented. Although nowhere does L'Enfant state that he was making a direct analogy between Washington and Rome, many people were naturally drawing that comparison at the time; his Mile Column was to stand, like the Golden Milestone in the Forum, at the center of the great commercial district and provide the marker from which the distances on the country's highways to the capital were to be measured. The Roman republican model of government, rather than the Greek idea of democracy, was much in favour in America in the late eighteenth century. And Roman analogies were certainly plentiful in the Federal District: Goose Creek became the Tiber; Congress housed a Senate; and Congress itself became known as the 'Capitol' after the Capitoline Hill in Rome. The Roman Capitoline Hill had stood directly above the Forum and was surmounted by the temple of the leader of the gods, Jupiter. The activities of the people in the Forum thus fell under the eye of the gods, thereby integrating the life of the whole with the life of the center.

The distance one mile east from the Capitol, along the highest ground, also placed the center of the commercial district – Square B – directly in the area where the Nacotchant tribe were said to have held their meetings and conducted trade. L'Enfant may thus have had a strong local precedent for placing his commercial district there. And I should note in passing that for Native American peoples, trading, social and spiritual activities – like those described in Plato's *Republic* – were wholly integrated practices.

Finally, I knew that the distance of one mile was itself highly significant. The mile originates from ancient systems of measure based upon exact 'geodetic' or terrestrial measures. John Michell has pointed out, for example, that when the earth's equatorial circumference of 24,902.95 miles is divided by 360 – the degrees of a circle – the resultant measure of 365,243 feet is directly equivalent to the 365.243 days of the year. It was evidently this kind of mathematical equivalence that motivated L'Enfant to choose a distance of one mile; yet this is also stating the obvious – for one mile was also the obvious distance to choose. But the emphasis in L'Enfant's plan upon the mile measure had conveniently brought my attention to the importance of number. The mile column was the clue that made me begin to pay attention to L'Enfant's subtle use of all the symbolic aspects of measure: its ratios, its distances, and its numbers.

A 'GRAND AVENUE'

L'Enfant complemented the area to the east of the Capitol with an equally significant but very different architectural treatment to the west. Running west from the Capitol, he envisaged a 'Grand Avenue, 400 feet in breadth, and about a mile in length, bordered with gardens'. This is shown in Figure 27B on page 58. The Grand Avenue was to be a lively place for the perambulation and the gathering of people. In the analogy of the city to a cathedral, this area was to be the nave. Or perhaps in the better analogy of the Middle Eastern bazaar, this was to be a place where people relaxed, met, talked and were entertained. Although providing some formality, the places for ceremony and for memorials were to lie

The Geometric Order of the Federal City

for the most part elsewhere than the Grand Avenue. L'Enfant described this avenue to George Washington in June 1791 as, 'a place of general resort ... all along side of which may be placed play houses, rooms of assembly, academies and all such sort of places as may be attractive to the learned and afford diversion to the idle'. It was also to have 'spacious houses and gardens, such as may accommodate foreign Ministers, &c'.

Although it went through several different phases in its history, this Grand Avenue was eventually realized in the Washington Mall. But the Mall today is not at all what L'Enfant had envisaged. With its straight lines of trees, rectangular lawns and pools, with a central width of over 600 feet and over two miles in length, bordered by Federal buildings and containing numerous museums and galleries such as the National Gallery of Art and the Smithsonian, the Mall establishes an enormous formal space at the center of the city. It is not a place to linger or socialise. After office and museum hours it is more or less devoid of the sort of activities that L'Enfant had had in mind for this site. The location, although it affords a spectacular statement of state power, is chilly and impersonal and does not really enable informal gatherings of people. The only assemblies of people here that are not orchestrated by the government are those of political protestors. The Mall is framed by the Capitol to the east, the White House to the north, the Lincoln Memorial to the west and the Jefferson Memorial to the south. These four white, columned and neoclassical buildings appear to look inwards upon the giant obelisk of the Washington Monument in their midst.

It was always L'Enfant's intention to design a monument to President George Washington in the city that was to bear his name. This monument or memorial was to be placed at the western end of the 'Grand Avenue' on the intersection with the north–south axis of the 'President's House'. L'Enfant suggested a fairly low monument that would probably have included colonnades and sculpture – possibly fountains – set within gardens. He never intended a formal obelisk at the center of an enormous cross. His city was centered on the Capitol and was designed to look outwards, not within. This point will be so important to my analysis of the history of the city plan that it is discussed at length in the closing chapters, while the Washington Monument is the focus of Chapter 9.

SUMMARY OF THE ORDER OF EVENTS

In keeping with traditional architecture and in an impressive display of imaginative boldness, Major L'Enfant had by the end of March 1791 completed the first acts in the design of the order of the new city. He had established the center of the city at the Capitol, had outlined its form, and had set it upon an elevation that accentuated its vertical axis, connecting the above and the below. The circumference of the Federal District of Columbia was marked with a square that dramatically set it apart from the nation around it. At the same time, with a glance at the heavens, L'Enfant – with the aid of Ellicott and Banneker – had established the order of the New World with a new, zero, global meridian. From the center, they had defined the four cardinal directions with the four axial streets – East, West, South and North Capitol Streets. The quadrants, names and numbers of the city streets originate from the Capitol to this day. L'Enfant placed especial emphasis upon the east–west axis; and on this axis, one mile to the east, he had located an exact point of measure, Square B. This axis and square with its 'Golden Milestone' – conceived after the original milestone in Rome – was intended to provide a forum, a commercial district for the people. The Mile Column was to define all subsequent measures throughout the land, as well as those of its capital city.

In these actions, L'Enfant repeated the ancient and traditional acts used to create the Temple – understood as the replication of the idea of the divine order of space and time – upon the earth. In this instance, by placing Congress House at the center, L'Enfant symbolically placed law, the Legislature – not the Church, the Presidency or the monarchy – at the center of the order of the city and the continent it was to govern. It was the Legislature, the house of the elected representatives of the people and the States, that was to occupy the central position in the new, distinctly American, federal and democratic world order.

L'Enfant also made an explicit statement when he placed commerce, the market, and the social and cultural activities of the people on the main axis to the east of Congress, and then again emphasised the west, the north and the south, with their grand avenues, courts and halls, as places of the people. It was the republican ideal of liberty and sovereign power residing within the people, who elected their representatives, judges and even their leaders, which had radically transformed the nature of political power in the new world and distinguished America's Constitution from all others existing at that time in the world. But what symbolic intent lay behind L'Enfant's subsequent acts, which included the location of the Executive and the Judiciary?

6
The Golden Section

AN 'ALTAR OF LIBERTY'

I had to ponder the basic elements that L'Enfant had drawn upon his plan, as center, directions, axes and measures for a long time. As I walked two whippets on the blue Appalachian ridges and beside the broad, but shallow, rivers of the area, I was not viewing the city in its sprawling twentieth-century form, but as the design L'Enfant had set out two hundred years before. Finally, I decided that I should continue my analysis by using the two circles, one larger than the other, that could be drawn around the Capitol and Square B.

In Figures 31 and 32, the first and smaller circle shows the distance that the avenues radiating from the Capitol have to run before meeting their first squares. The radius of this circle is approximately 1087 yards. The second circle, centered on Square B, has, as L'Enfant stated, a radius of exactly one mile or 1760 yards. The circumference of this circle now passes through the east side of the Capitol building, point C1.

Let me immediately explain that today C1 is a not particularly prominent point to the east of the center of the Capitol, point C. However, as L'Enfant envisaged a much larger building or group of buildings on the site, the circumference of the one-mile circle was originally intended to have passed through a very significant point in what was intended to become, in effect, the 'Capitol complex'.

It is highly likely that L'Enfant intended this point (C1) to lie within a central court, with the houses of the representatives on either side. At the center of the court was to be an 'altar of liberty'. Around the sides of the court were to be statues of women symbolically representing each of the States. It is probable that the first architect appointed to build the Capitol in 1793, Etienne or Stephen Hallet, endorsed this idea, as Hallet worked as L'Enfant's draftsman late in 1791. This theory is borne out by Hallet's complex arrangement of buildings for the Capitol, shown in Figure 33, almost as extensive as that in place today

The Secret Geometry of Washington, D.C.

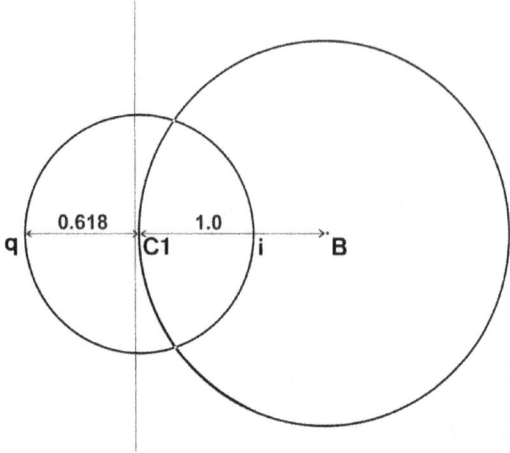

Figure 31. Circle center C1 (east side of Capitol) is in proportion to circle center B (Lincoln Square) as 1 to 1.618 or 0.618 to 1. This is the proportion known as the Golden Section. The centers of the two circles are one mile apart.

but significantly wider. It is also demonstrated by the engravings of the Ellicott Plan, meant to be copies of a L'Enfant plan drafted by Hallet, that show an enormous complex of courts and buildings. (See Figure 50.)

One of the reasons why I selected the two circles was because the circumference of each circle intersects the circumference of the other, through what L'Enfant obviously intended to be two extremely important squares. He marked these squares 'D' and 'E' on the plan. Yet there is far more significance to the circles than this. For as explained in Chapter 1, the relationship between the two circles demonstrates the geometrical ratio of *phi*, the Golden Section.

The adjective 'golden' in the Golden Section, the Golden Ratio, the Golden Mean, the Golden Proportion and so on, indicates that the ancients considered this ratio to be both invaluable and ideal. They described it as the 'perfect' ratio, where the lesser is to the greater as the greater is to the whole: that is, A is to B as B is to A plus B, or $A:B::B:A+B$. The Golden Section defines the proportions of the human body and the face, which we judge to be beautiful to the degree that its parts accord to the ratio. The orbits of the planet named after the Roman Goddess of beauty and love, Venus, were considered to be in the ratio of the Golden Section to those of the Earth. According to Robert Lawlor, *phi* is the asymmetrical division of unity that leads to the diversity of creation and back to unity again: one to two to three to one.

The Golden Section

Figure 32. The Golden Section imposed upon the L'Enfant Plan. The square at B was described by L'Enfant as containing 'An historic Column, also intended for a Mile or itinerary Column, from whose station [a mile from the Capitol], all distances of places through the Continent are to be calculated'. Unlike other important squares the radiant avenues of B converge upon a single point. It seems clear that L'Enfant called this square 'B' because it was the second principal point in the geometry that underlies the city. Around the square east of the Capitol, and through points L and M, L'Enfant wanted 'an arched way, under whose cover Shops will be most conveniently and agreeably situated'. D and E were to be important squares: D was intended to be the District Courts; E was probably to be the site for City Hall. E was described by L'Enfant as one of five squares with 'grand fountains intended with a constant spout of water'.

As *phi* is, strictly speaking, a proportion or a ratio, it is unsatisfactory to express it numerically as 0.618˙ is to 1 as 1 is to 1.618˙. It is better to say that the line q, B in Figure 31 is divided by the Capitol at C1 in the proportion of the Golden Section than it is to say that the radius of the second circle of the L'Enfant Plan is 1.618 times larger than the radius of the first circle. The line C1, B is, of course, divided at *i* in the same way. However, as the radius of his second circle was clearly intended by L'Enfant to be one mile, the radius of his first, primary circle was therefore intended to be 0.618 of a mile, or 1087 yards.

The Secret Geometry of Washington, D.C.

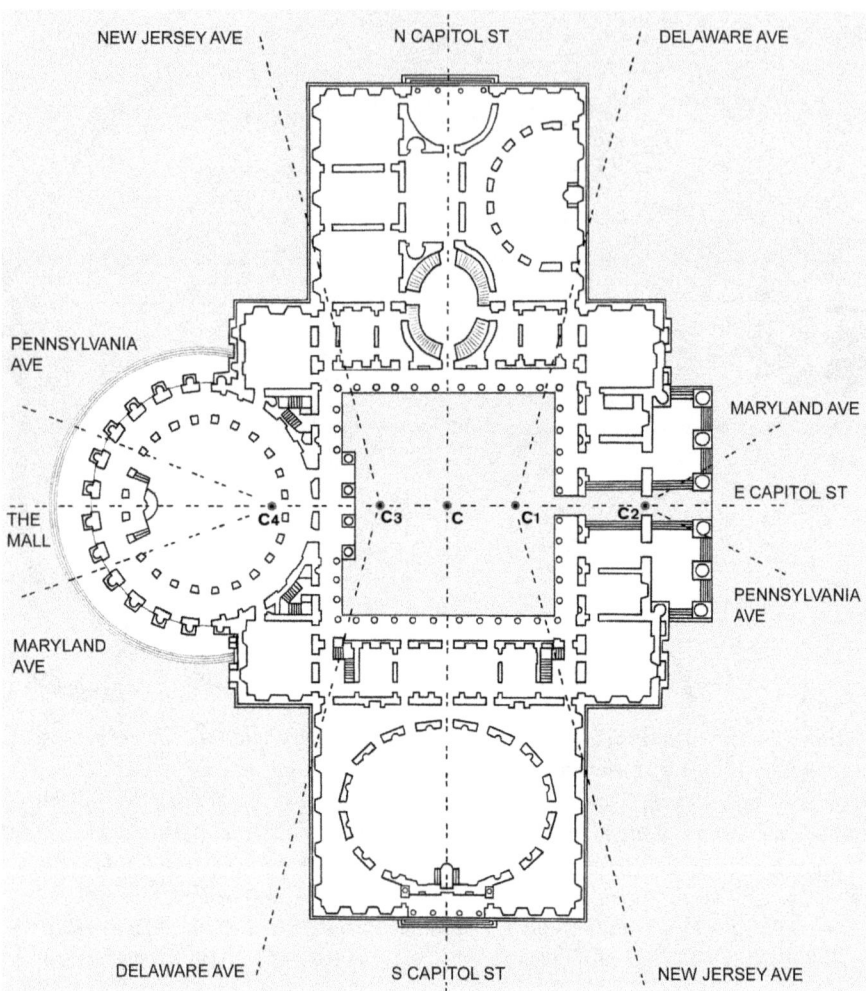

Figure 33. A simplified drawing of Etienne or Stephen Hallet's plan for the Capitol, c. 1791. This design incorporates the ideas of L'Enfant and shows the different points of focus (C through C4) for the principal axes and diagonal avenues. The many points of focus allow the avenues to achieve commanding vistas from the entrances of buildings while maintaining their proper relationship to the overall design of the city. Hallet was dismissed as architect of the Capitol as his plan for a central court was contrary to the ideas of Congress.

The Golden Section is a fascinating idea: one that is well worth dwelling on for a moment longer. Plato made *phi*, the Golden Section ratio, the mathematical key to the physics of the cosmos. The Egyptians considered it the symbol of the power that gave forth to the endless series of numbers, measures and proportions – the whole procession of creation. Many of their finest temples, tombs and monuments, such as the Temple of Luxor, the Oseirion at Abydos, and the Great Pyramid, are known to incorporate this ratio into their design.

As well as being present in all the proportions of the human body, *phi* is also the governing ratio of the five-sided figure, the pentagon; and the five-pointed star, the pentacle. As shown in Figure 39 on page 99, the ratio is present between all the lengths of the pentacle. *Phi*, and its associated pentacle, was considered by the ancients to establish the perfect harmony between the terrestrial, the material and the heavenly spheres. The pentacle was understood as the symbol of life. The Pythagoreans saw the pentacle as the primary symbol of the Golden Section. They described it as the 'gateway' to hidden knowledge and to the other worlds. In Egyptian tradition, *phi* and the pentacle were held as the number of humanity; in life, but able to reach beyond it. The Egyptian mysteries and the teachings of the Pythagoreans have had a great influence upon Freemasonry. Yet, while ideas associated with the Golden Section flourished among eighteenth-century Masons, it was quite unnecessary for L'Enfant to become a Freemason to discover them. The same ideas were present in much Baroque architecture and art; indeed, they pervaded the neoclassical thinking of his day.

THE VESICA PISCIS

Each of the two 'construction' circles centered on points D and E has a radius equal to the second circle with its center at B; that is, a distance of exactly one mile. This is shown in Figure 35. I knew from my work with sacred geometry – especially the analysis of Christian cathedrals – that each circle would create a *vesica piscis,* and further *phi* ratios, in relation to the second circle.

A vesica is formed by the intersection of two arcs or circles. When the center of each circle is on the circumference of the other, the resulting oval shape is known as the *vesica piscis. Piscis* is Latin for fish and this fish-shaped vesica became a Christian symbol. As shown in Figure 34, one of the properties of the *vesica piscis* is that if the line between the centers of the two circles is given the value of 1, then the figure generates the three fundamental root relationships of 2, 3 and 5. These square roots generate many of the geometrical principles underlying form, including the mathematics of three-dimensional figures such as cubes. The square

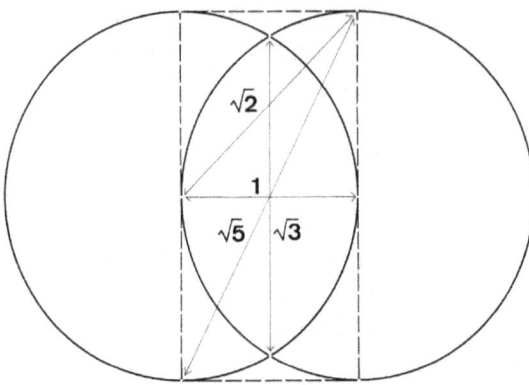

Figure 34. The Vesica Piscis. This easily created and simple figure of two overlapping circles is the starting point of sacred geometry. If the distance between the circles is given a value of 1, then the figure generates the fundamental square roots of 2, 3 and 5. If further circles are drawn with the same relationship around the first two, as in Figure 21, then the basis is established for generating many geometrical figures, including the Platonic Solids.

roots are especially important to those working in areas and volumes; such as masons working with ashlars, blocks of stone.

The simple figure of the *vesica piscis* is considered supremely generative of all form. It is understood as the intersection of opposites: of spirit and matter, heaven and earth, male and female. It represents an opening or gateway between these polarities, through which creation can take place. When not just two but multiple circles of the same radius are drawn around each other's circumference, this leads to the construction of the equilateral triangle, the square, the pentagon, hexagon, octagon, decagon and so on, as well as to all the Platonic Solids and the ratio of *phi*. The medieval masons illustrated these generative properties of the *vesica piscis* by framing Christ or his mother, or both together, within a vesica above many cathedral doors.

The two construction circles – with centers D and E as shown in Figures 9 and 35 – provided the next step in unravelling the geometry underlying the design of the city of Washington. The vesica formed by the overlap of the construction circles links the two primary circles in the ratio of *phi*. The line q, B is bisected at C1 in the ratio of the Golden Section. If another circle, as shown in Figure 35, centered on C1, is drawn around the circumference of the two construction circles, then it is in the same ratio to those circles as those circles are to the first circle. If the radius of the second circle B, C1 is one mile, and the

The Golden Section

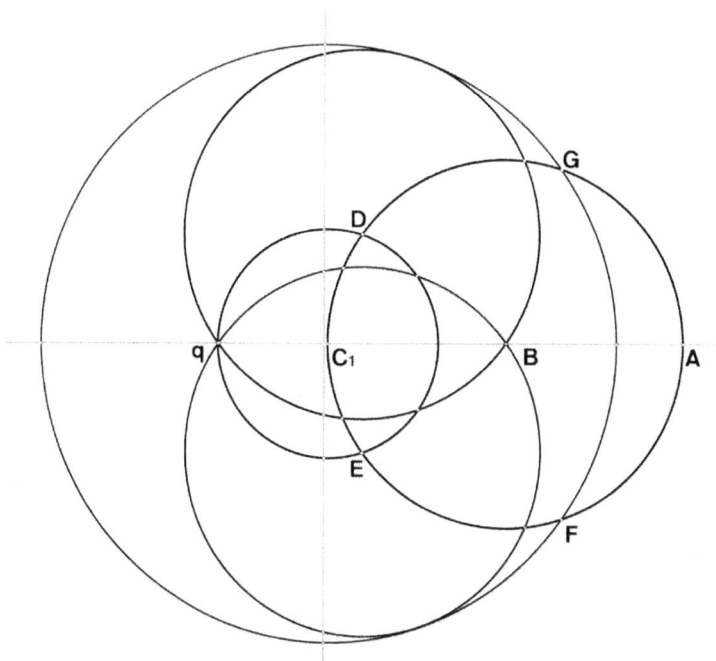

Figure 35. The circles center D and E are equal in size to the second circle, center B, and form a vesica piscis in relation to it. A further circle is drawn around them, center C1. The radius of the first circle is 0.618 of a mile. The common radius of the circles, centers D, E and B, is one mile. The radius of the third circle is 1.618 of a mile, demonstrating that the circles are in a Golden Section relationship to each other. The points A, G, D, E and F divide circle center B into five equal parts. The second and third circles can also be divided into five equal parts. Figures 9 and 13 show these circles and their internal pentacles superimposed upon the plan of the city.

radius of the first circle C_1, q is 0.618 miles or 1087 yards, then the radius of the third, the largest circle, is 1.618 miles or 2848 yards. These are all Golden section ratios. I had arrived at a crucial stage in my discovery of the significant relationships and distances in the plan that L'Enfant had for Washington, D.C..

THE PENTACLE AND THE NUMBER 5

As is shown in Figure 35, the first and second circles divide each other into five equal parts by their intersection at the important squares D and E. Points F and G of the division of the second circle are also marked by

The Secret Geometry of Washington, D.C.

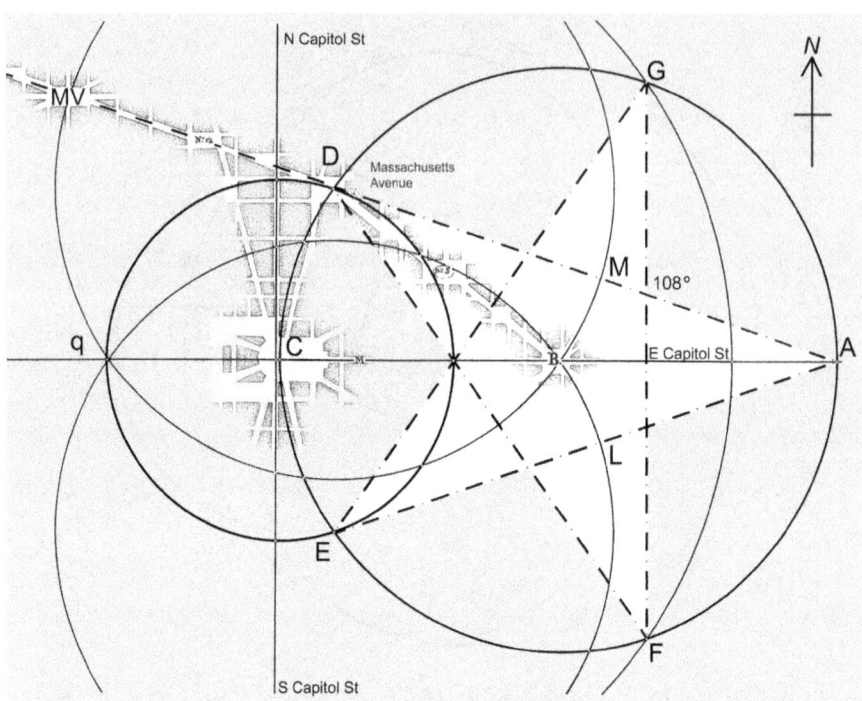

Figure 36. The five-fold division of the one-mile radius circle is fundamental to the pattern of all subsequent features in the city. Line A, D is the orientation of L'Enfant's Massachusetts Avenue (108 or 288 degrees). D, B is the avenue within the circle. MV is Mount Vernon Square. MV is the same distance from D as D is from B, that is, one mile. Intervening squares lie at half-mile distances.

the intersection of the third primary circle, and its fifth point is at A, on the far east of the primary axis. When the five points A, D, E, F, G are connected they form a five-pointed star or a pentacle. As described above, the pentacle and the number five were considered in ancient tradition to represent life; especially its manifestation in humanity. The pentacle was understood to represent the link between the human and the heavenly realm. The five of the pentacle stood one step up from the earthly number four, but was still one below the heavenly number six.

As shown in Figures 11 and 36, line A, D of the pentacle was aligned to the intended orientation of Massachusetts Avenue. The pentacle also defined the alignment of the avenue between squares D and B. The orientation L'Enfant planned for Massachusetts Avenue was eighteen degrees from the main axis A, B, C; like that of its corresponding partner, South Carolina Avenue A, E, its global orientation was therefore

The Golden Section

meant to be 108 degrees from north. As I will show, this hidden or underlying pentacle provides the basis for the orientation of nearly all the significant avenues in Washington. The pentacle was very deliberately aligned to point toward the east and for avenues to open and radiate westwards from it. It is completely integral to the plan of the city, and provides the key that unlocks the pattern of the avenues. Because of its fundamental Golden Section ratio, the pentacle had also enabled me to understand the geometry on which the city was designed and built. This was another turning point in my research.

It seems clear that L'Enfant intended point A of the pentacle, the most easterly point of the new city, to symbolically 'open' the city's geometry, which was then intended to radiate from the east into the vast and still uncharted territories to the west. The introduction of an eastern-oriented pentacle also allowed L'Enfant to make a symbolic statement, albeit covert, about spiritual, cultural and political origins in the east. In traditional geomancy – as in most spiritual traditions, including Masonry – the east is the place to which altars are oriented. The east is the place of inception; the source of new energy and beginnings. In some branches of Freemasonry, the five-pointed star or pentacle was called the 'Eastern Star', and was set in the eastern part of the Lodge. The east is of course where the stars rise on the horizon each night and the sun rises each day. The orientation of the city avenues at 108 or 288 degrees to North may have pointed to several significant astronomical events on the eastern horizon. Some of these – such as the rising of first magnitude stars – are suggested by the author David Ovason in his book, *The Secret Zodiacs of Washington, D.C.*. As an astronomer, Benjamin Banneker would have been well aware of the positions of the major stars – indeed, he went on to produce almanacs – and Ovason suggests that the royal star Regulus would have figured in his charts. L'Enfant may well have intended the lines of the pentacle, oriented east along the main axis of the city, to symbolically usher in stellar and auspicious qualities appropriate to the birth of the new nation. I could easily imagine L'Enfant, in his ebullient Parisian style, wanting to place classical figures of nymphs and Muses – perhaps of star goddesses – in the statuary of the square at A or perhaps beside the bridge over the river. If only he had had the budget!

While it is unclear exactly what purpose L'Enfant intended for the square at A – it may have been planned to have a commercial exchange – its location beside a bridge over the Anacostia obviously meant it was seen as a highly important point of entry to the city. The bridge is still there today and the square is now the Robert F. Kennedy Stadium.

RADIANT AVENUES

In the same way that the second circle is divided into five parts, so the first circle drawn around the Capitol can be divided into five parts. As is described in Chapter 1, and shown in Figures 4 and 5, the squares at D and E, the square at 'L' on the east–west axis, and two other points (one in the plaza before the intended location for the Supreme Court), divide the primary circle into five equal parts.

The two 'construction circles' with their centers at D and E can also be divided into five parts. See Figures 37 and 38. This division of the primary circles contributes to the definition of the orientation of New Jersey and Delaware Avenues. These avenues radiate either side of north–south, from the Capitol. The symbolic significance of these avenues cannot be missed; L'Enfant intended them to emphasize the centrality of the Capitol. Their orientation is marked by the points O and J, the center of the Capitol, point C, and the points J1 and O. But as New Jersey and Delaware Avenues are actually offset to points C1 and C3 of the Capitol, I had to explain this. The avenues appeared to deviate from, and thus perhaps undermine, what I was beginning to see as L'Enfant's underlying geometrical design.

As should be clear from the L'Enfant Plan shown in Figure 38, the offset of Delaware and New Jersey Avenues from a single point of focus is particularly noticeable on the eastern side of the Capitol. This departure from what I was now hypothesising as the underlying geometry of the city occurs several times in the L'Enfant Plan. I returned to the steps of the Capitol, stood at the main entrance and looked at the avenues. To my embarrassment, as I felt I should have noticed this sooner, I saw that the pairs of avenues radiate outward from the entrance in order to accommodate the point of view of the observer. All the avenues radiate from the entrances and not from the centers of the buildings in the city. Maryland and Pennsylvania Avenues, for example, are oriented to the entrances in the center of the east and west sides of the Capitol. If they had radiated out from its actual center they would have not looked or felt right to the viewer who was either approaching on the ground or emerging from the building. They would have looked too far apart – as though they had 'missed' the alignment to the center. In the same manner, the avenues radiating out from either side of North and South Capitol Street appear to converge upon the center from almost any approach, but because of the length and the width of the Capitol they in fact converge elsewhere. Figure 33 gives a good idea of the manner in which an architect adjusted pairs of avenues to converge upon different

The Golden Section

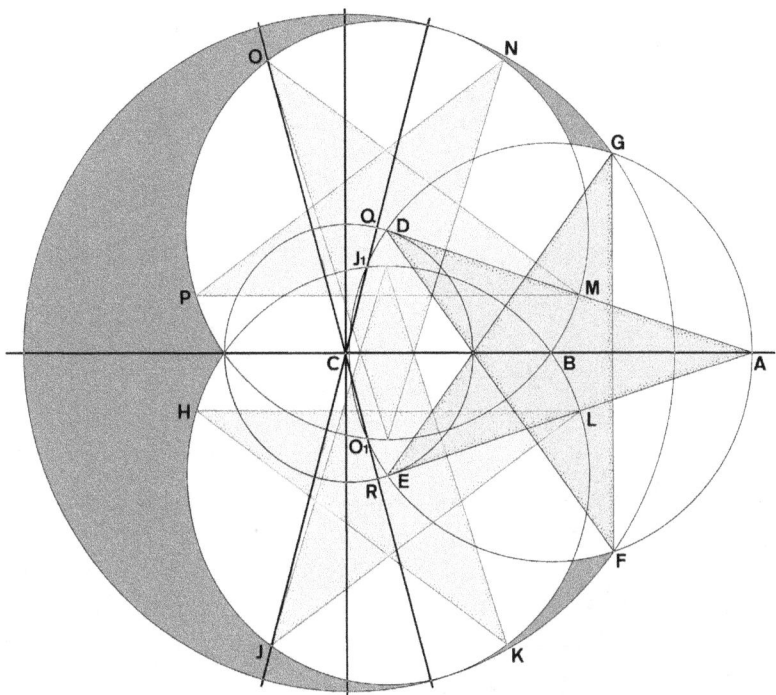

Figure 37. The three circles of one mile radius. Line J, C, J1, Q creates the orientation for Delaware Avenue. Line O, C, O1, R creates New Jersey Avenue. Points Q and R – points of departure for subsequent geometry – lie within squares D and E. Like the squares of the White House and the Capitol, D and E have more than one center. L'Enfant intended important buildings – City Hall and the District Courts – to be placed within them.

centers. L'Enfant was a genius at understanding how a two-dimensional plan must be adjusted in order to look and feel right to the passer-by who was moving in real time through space.

This adjustment creates a variety of interesting architectural views and spaces along the avenues; but it was also carried out for the purpose of accommodating buildings of size, such as the Capitol and the White House, into the underlying pattern for the diagonal avenues. The avenues are adjusted away from the underlying geometry, to point to the entranceway or to a corner of a building, so as to appear to radiate correctly to people moving through the perspective of horizontal space. The avenues give the appearance of being oriented to their center through an orientation to multiple centers. Yet – as the diagrams show – the underlying geometry always defines the orientation

The Secret Geometry of Washington, D.C.

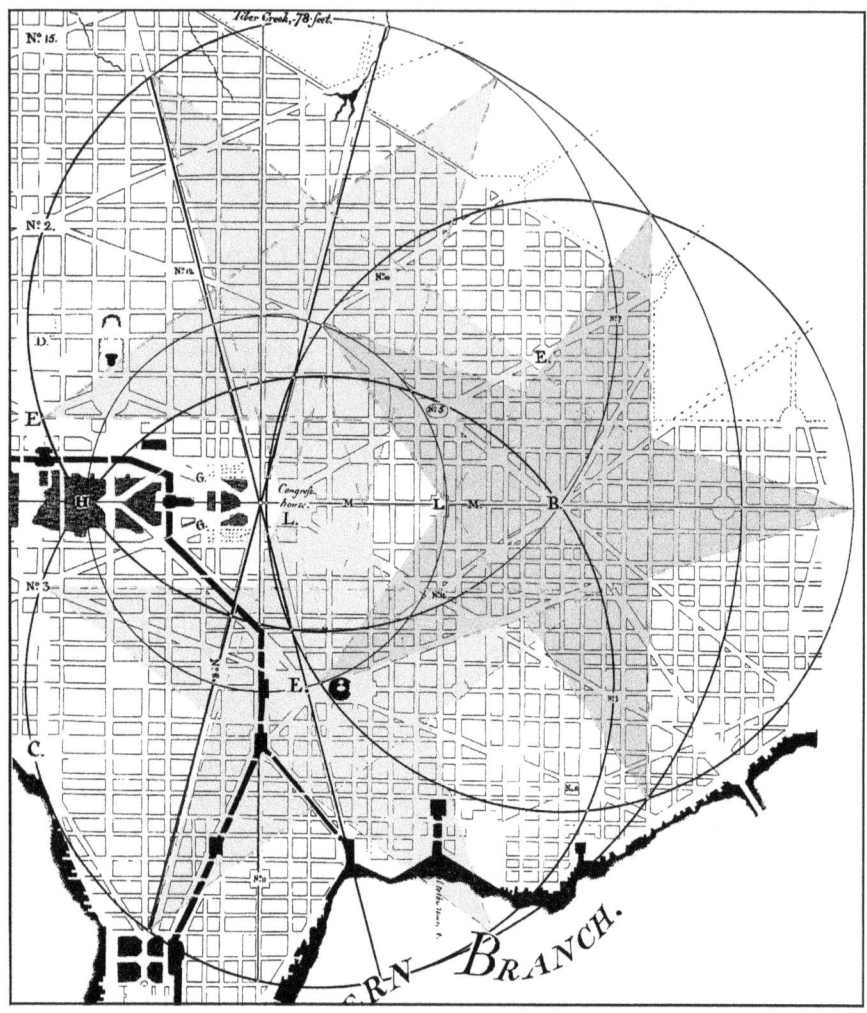

Figure 38. The three circles of one mile radius superimposed upon the L'Enfant Plan.

that the radiant avenues will return to once the spatial requirements of the buildings' size have been met.

I should mention here that, unlike in the Capitol where the avenues cannot run through the center of the building but must radiate from multiple points of focus such as the entranceways for their proper effect, the central feature of Square B, the Mile Column, did provide L'Enfant with a single point of focus. Figure 47 shows how L'Enfant wished the Mile Column to serve as a single point of focus at the center of the 'Eastern Star'. Once the pure geometry of the pentacle is

The Golden Section

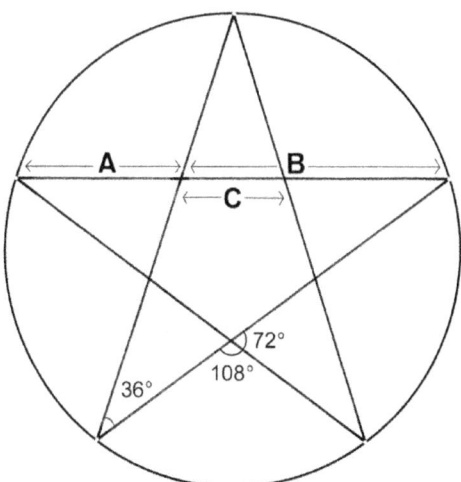

Figure 39. The internal lines of a pentacle are divided into sections A, B, C, according to the proportion of phi, the Golden Section. This ratio also defines the measures of the human body. The angles of the pentacle: 108, 72, 54, 144 and 36 degrees, are multiples of 18. The ancient Egyptians used the ratios found in the pentacle in trigonometry, surveying and the Great Pyramid. It was also a symbol of Thoth, the god with an ibis head, who was the first surveyor of the land after it emerged from the annual inundation.

seen, there can be no doubt of its role in defining the avenues in the eastern part of the city.

THE FIVE-POINTED STAR

Why did L'Enfant choose five-fold, Golden Section geometry based upon the pentacle for the development of his leading avenues? As Jefferson had already shown, a simple grid would have been much easier both to survey and construct. In medieval Europe, the Masons and the Knights Templar had usually employed a four-fold, square; a six-fold, hexagonal; or an eight-fold, octagonal, geometrical system for the construction of their churches and temples. These systems appear to have been influenced by Islam and the Middle East. But L'Enfant does not follow any of these ideas.

I went back to the Masonic library and read more about the symbolism traditionally assigned to the Golden Section and the pentacle in geometry. Most writers thought the pentacle – because of its alliance with the Golden Section – underlay the body and organic life. As the

The Secret Geometry of Washington, D.C.

pentacle frames the outstretched limbs of a human figure, defines human proportions and counts the five fingers, toes, senses and so on, it has always been associated with humanity. To the Egyptians the pentacle was the measure of creation and associated with the divine measurer or the first architect, Thoth. To the Pythagoreans the pentacle was a symbol of health and humanistic science. To Christian mystics the pentacle represented the man or the human aspect of Jesus Christ. To the Freemasons, where it is known as the 'pentalpha' (five A's), the 'Signet of Solomon', the 'Eastern' or the 'Blazing Star', the pentacle is a symbol of divine providence, light, life or eternity. The pentacle is always associated with human balance, harmony and integration with life. Some Freemasons insist that the pentacle has actually very little to do with Masonry. They say the pentacle was never a symbol they were very much interested in. This statement is confirmed by study of the symbolism in their regalia and in their lodges.

In contrast, L'Enfant was evidently very interested in the pentacle indeed. It divides his primary circles; it defines the location of his principal squares; and it governs the orientation he intended for the primary avenues radiating from or terminating at these squares. The principal arms of the second pentacle, that were intended to define Massachusetts and South Carolina Avenue, lie at 108-degrees from north. As the governing angle of the pentacle is 108-degrees, I wondered if L'Enfant thought of this measure as having a correspondence with the radius of the first circle around the Capitol. The 108-degree angle does appear to define the intended orientation of the major avenues of the city. Maryland and Pennsylvania Avenues still retain this orientation today. According to the investigator into the traditions of ancient science John Michell, 108 or 1080 is the lunar and earthly number, concerned with the order of human affairs. 'Throughout the world', Michell writes, ' in every traditional code of architectural proportion, computation of time and wherever number is involved, 1080 is always prominent: and its reference universally is to the "yin" side of nature, in contrast to the solar or "yang" significance of the number 666'. Did L'Enfant think that this numerology and symbolism was appropriate for the legislative branch of government? Michell notes that when the solar number 666 is added to the lunar and earthly number 1080, it yields 1746. This is close to the mile radius, 1760 yards, of the second primary circle. According to *gematria*, the ancient Hebrew science of number – where it is legitimate to round out large numbers – 1746 is the number of fusion and harmony.

Did any of this show that L'Enfant was using pentagonal geometry and its *phi* ratio in his design to deliberately create an allegory for the new form of democratic government? Was L'Enfant intentionally selecting pentagonal geometry because of its ancient significance?

THE AVENUES

Figure 40 is the key, as it shows the development of the central avenues in the L'Enfant Plan for the city. It should be clear by now, once the need to accommodate the width of buildings is understood, how the orientation of the avenues derives from the central axes and the Golden Section relationship of the three underlying primary circles. Once the spatial requirements of its chief buildings are taken into consideration, the main avenues of the city derive from the *phi* ratio of the three underlying primary circles. These circles explain every major feature of the L'Enfant Plan. The creation of this diagram meant that I was arriving at the culmination of what was by now many months of work.

When I reached this point it was late fall in Washington. As the trees were being stripped bare of their leaves, I could at last draw the geometrical orientation of Pennsylvania Avenue on the L'Enfant Plan with confidence, using a line from point C4, west of the center of the Capitol, C, through P to the President's House, PH. If the radius of the first circle is 0.618 mile and the radius of the second circle is 1 mile, then the radius of the third circle is 1.618 of a mile. Figure 41 shows this geometry imposed upon the central portion of the L'Enfant Plan. Points C4, C3, C, C1 and C2 are really too close together to differentiate on this scale; but the point is clear: no matter how much the avenues appear to bend, they always fulfil the requirements of the underlying geometry.

In the same manner as the five-fold division of circle center D has established point P, so H is established by the same method in circle center E. A north–south line drawn through these points will also pass through points MV and I. MV, Mount Vernon Square, is located at the intersection of Massachusetts Avenue with circle center D. Point I is obtained by extending line A, E, – South Carolina Avenue – mirroring Massachusetts Avenue. This extremely consequential north–south line MV, P, H, I is 8th Street.

L'Enfant emphasised the significance of 8th Street by placing many squares with important monuments along its length. L'Enfant wanted P, for example, to be a large plaza with 'Grand Fountains'. H and MV were two of the squares to be adorned by the States. Point I, on the Potomac shore, was to feature a 'Naval itinerary Column'. And halfway between MV and P was the location of the 'Church intended for national purposes',

The Secret Geometry of Washington, D.C.

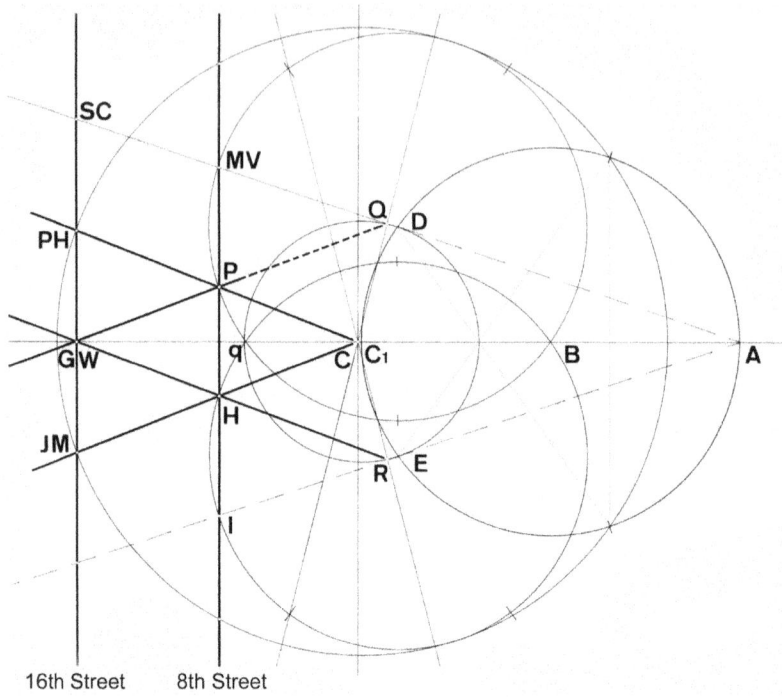

Figure 40. The Avenues: Pennsylvania Avenue is laid out by constructing a line from the Capitol through P to the point PH on the circumference of the large circle. (The pentagonal division of circle center D has already determined P.) Point PH is the President's House. C1, B (1760) + C1, q (1087) = C1, PH (2847). If C1, B is 1 then C1, F is $\Phi/1$ and C1, PH is $1/\Phi$. The White House and the Capitol are thus brought into a 'perfect' relationship through the Golden Section geometry of the original construction circles.

Maryland Avenue is laid out through points C, H and JM. An avenue was also to radiate from GW, the original site for the Washington Monument, to P and slightly beyond, as defined by point Q. This last section is now Indiana Avenue. Points GW, H and R (the west side of City Hall?) define Virginia Avenue. (On the L'Enfant Plan, the avenue continues at the same orientation south-eastward from point E.) H was to be a large square. The small area of the square that remains is now Hancock Park, behind the Smithsonian. Point I was to be a shore-side plaza with a monument to the Navy. P was originally to be another grand square with fountain. It is now the Navy Monument, beside the Archives Building. Point JM is now the Jefferson Memorial; in L'Enfant's time this land, now reclaimed, was in the Potomac. SC is Scott Circle. The significant north–south lines through the points of intersection of the circles and the radiating avenues are 8th and 16th Streets.

Here and in subsequent drawings, heavy lines show the location on the ground of the avenues that are under discussion. Light or serrated lines do not always show avenues. They reveal the underlying geometry.

The Golden Section

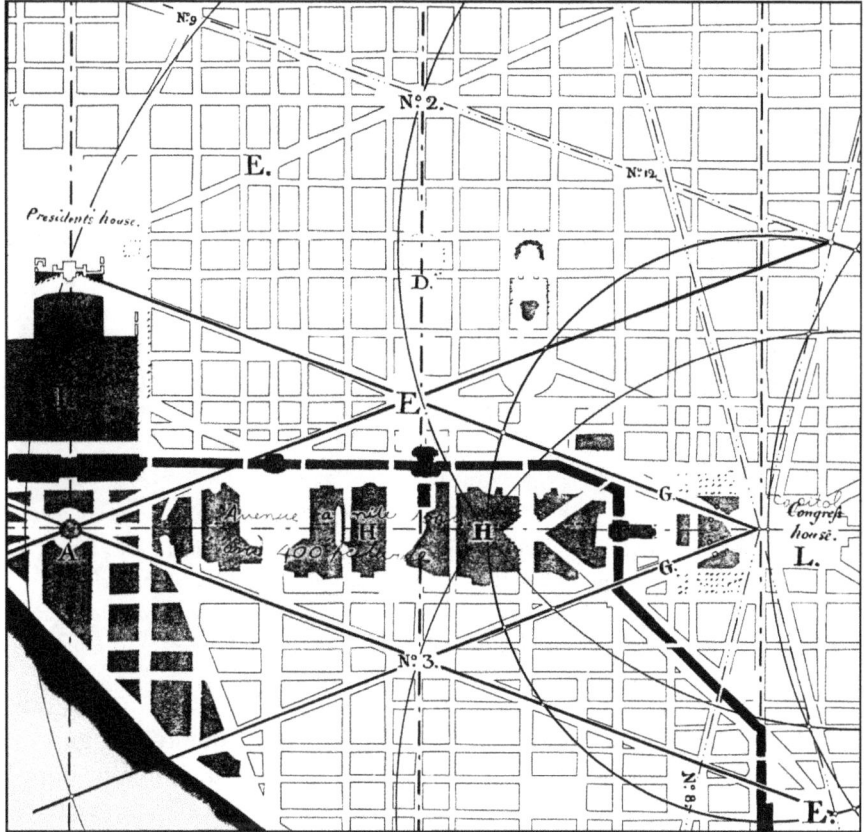

Figure 41. This shows a detail of the geometry of Figure 40 overlaid on the L'Enfant Plan. Note the Mall, L'Enfant's 'Grand Avenue', with the outlines of buildings along it, and the bends in Pennsylvania Avenue.

NC. All these squares were intended to be of great civic significance and their location is precisely determined by the pentagonal division of the underlying circles. 8th Street is approximately three-quarters of a mile from C1; the exact measure, given by multiplying the radius of the primary circle C1, q by *phi*, or 1087 by 0.618 to give 672 yards, then multiplying by 2 to give 1344 yards, will be discussed shortly.

The avenues can be extended and a second north–south line inserted at the intersection of point PH, the President's House, and point JM, the Jefferson Memorial, with the third circle. This is 16th Street. It is the next major axis of the city, aligned to the Potomac and centered upon the White House. A few years after L'Enfant's dismissal, Jefferson turned this line into the new zero meridian. Where 16th Street intersects the

The Secret Geometry of Washington, D.C.

Photo 6. This view north along Eighth Street, from the Archives Building past the fountains of the Navy Monument to the National Portrait Gallery, must come close to L'Enfant's original vision. He intended the site of the Gallery to be the location of a National Church, probably in the neoclassical style.

east–west axis of the Capitol on the Mall, a large 'equestrian figure of George Washington', GW, was intended to be located. L'Enfant hoped to design the monument himself, but he was never given the opportunity. Avenues running from points Q and R through P and H also locate this primary point. 16th Street is 1344 yards, approximately three-quarters of a mile, from 8th Street, placing the original site for the Washington Monument at just over one and a half miles from the Capitol. (2688 yards or $4 \times \Phi \times C1$, q.)

CITY HALL

Finally, it was obvious that the squares at D (and Q) and E (and R) were critical to the development of the diagonal pattern of avenues in the western half of L'Enfant's plan for the city. The two large squares lay on the intersections of the two primary circles. The division of both circles by their Golden Section relationship determined the location of both squares.

Like the Capitol and Square B, these squares were intended to be radiant centers that acted as generative or terminal points for the

The Golden Section

geometry of the avenues. It is these two squares and the Capitol that determine the matrix of diagonal avenues that lead to the west. Like the Capitol, no structures are marked on the plan within these squares; but also like the Capitol, the avenues converging upon them have more than one point of focus. Clearly, important buildings were intended

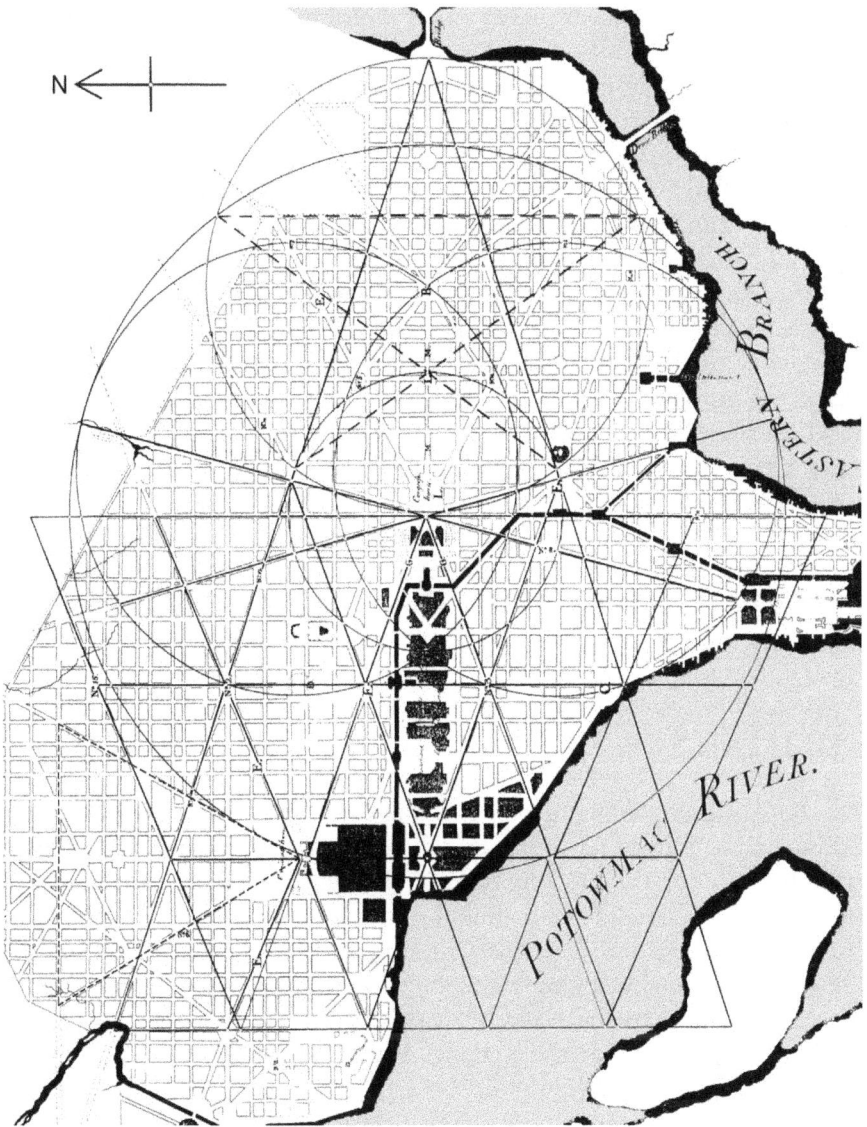

Figure 42. The L'Enfant Plan of 1791 laid over the geometric order derived from the ratios of the Golden Section.

for these squares; but L'Enfant does not say what they were to be. The Ellicott plan located the District Courts at D and the City Hall at the eastern end of square E, and I think this indicates the purpose that L'Enfant most likely had for them. But the Ellicott plan does not show City Hall in its correct location. The converging avenues show that L'Enfant envisaged City Hall positioned in the center of the square; the points at E and R marked the main western and eastern entrances of the building – or rather the complex of buildings. It was also likely that many other significant buildings were to have been located within and around this great square at E – a square that was approximately 700 yards long and 200 yards wide.

These two squares were intended to be important centers of public activity within the city. D, intended for the District of Columbia Courts, now serves as the site of Union Station. If the large commercial district intended for the eastern part of the city had developed, then City Hall and its square at E would also have been a busy location. A canal was to have crossed the western end of the square. A circular but unclear mark – almost 400 ft wide on the plan – suggests that a lake filled by local springs was intended for the eastern end. L'Enfant described 'grand fountains intended with a constant spout of water'. The great square, with the docks of the Anacostia just to the south, would have become the center of a vibrant city district. The area is now taken up by unsightly and sometimes overhead highways and railway lines, and by commercial buildings such as those of the Washington Post. One section of the square is preserved as Garfield Park.

SUMMARY

By the beginning of winter, when the ice had begun to form on the Susquehanna River, I felt I had sufficient evidence to conclude that it was the ratio of the Golden Section that underlay L'Enfant's original plan for the Federal City. L'Enfant's key sites – Congress House, the President's House and the Mile Column, and his intended locations for City Hall, the District Court and the Washington Monument – are all placed according to the Golden Section ratio. The ratio accounted for both the orientation of the main avenues and also the location of the key squares and other monuments.

What struck me the most was that the distance intended by L'Enfant between the Capitol and the White House, 1.618 of a mile, was in an absolutely explicit Golden Section relationship to the other primary distances. The radius of the first circle around the Capitol was 0.618 of a mile; the radius of the second circle around Lincoln Square, the Mile Column, was one mile; and the radius of the third circle – Capitol to the White House – was 1.618 of a mile. The Golden Section numbers could not have been stated more clearly. In other words, the Capitol to City Hall is to the Capitol to Lincoln Square as the Capitol to Lincoln Square is to the Capitol to the President's House.

Given that the L'Enfant Plan took the layout of the terrain and the existing roads into careful consideration, it is remarkable that this geometry emerged at all. Underscoring all the geometry was the pentacle, the five-pointed star, with its integral Golden Section ratios and 108-degree angles. I found the synchronicity between the 108-degree angles of the pentacle, the 1087 measures and the 108 degree orientation from north of the major avenues far too great to ignore. As L'Enfant was proceeding according to the proportions, measures, numbers and alignments established by this geometry, it is not surprising that he was adamant in his refusal to move either the President's House or Congress House when critics said they were too far apart or in the wrong location on their respective hills.

It seems indisputable that L'Enfant knew the three primary distances between the Capitol, the Mile Column, City Hall and the White House were in the relationship of *phi* to each other, but nowhere does he state this. Why not? Once the factor created by the depth of the buildings is taken into account, the avenues return to the underlying Golden Section geometry in a manner far too consistent to be accidental. It is the ability of these distances to determine the exact orientation of the avenues and the position of the squares that provides the principal evidence for the use of Golden Section geometry in the design of Washington, D.C.. I had to develop my analysis further, however, as there were certain aspects of the L'Enfant Plan that did not appear to derive from the geometry and seemed additional to it. Could they put my geometrical analysis at risk?

7

The Triangle and Other Avenues

> It is not only the heavens which declare the glory of God and the firmament which showeth his handiwork, but the humblest flower and the least shell which, together with the mightiest objects in the heavens, are all made and act by means of a curve developed from the Golden Section.
> William Preston, *Illustrations of Masonry*, 1772.

THE AVENUES AROUND THE WHITE HOUSE

Once I had discovered that the core of the L'Enfant Plan for Washington followed Golden Section geometry, I wondered if this applied to all the avenues in the city, especially as the avenues radiating out from around the White House and to the east of the Capitol appeared to have a geometry of their own. I began with an examination of the avenues around the White House.

Figure 43 was the next step in the development of the city's Golden Section geometry: the line of Virginia Avenue, from points R, to H, to GW, is extended to point S on what is now 23rd Street. 23rd Street to 16th Street is 1344 yards – the unit of measure established for the city grid west of the Capitol. Point S was originally intended to be the base of a large public square. It is now occupied by the Department of State. The line through S to the 'President's house', PH, and to Mount Vernon Square, MV, defines the orientation of New York Avenue according to the Golden Section geometry. But the actual orientation of the avenue differs from this because of the location of the White House.

As described earlier, the diagonal avenues deviate from the underlying geometry by the need for them to align to the entrances and not the centers of buildings. Both New York and Pennsylvania Avenues

The Triangle and Other Avenues

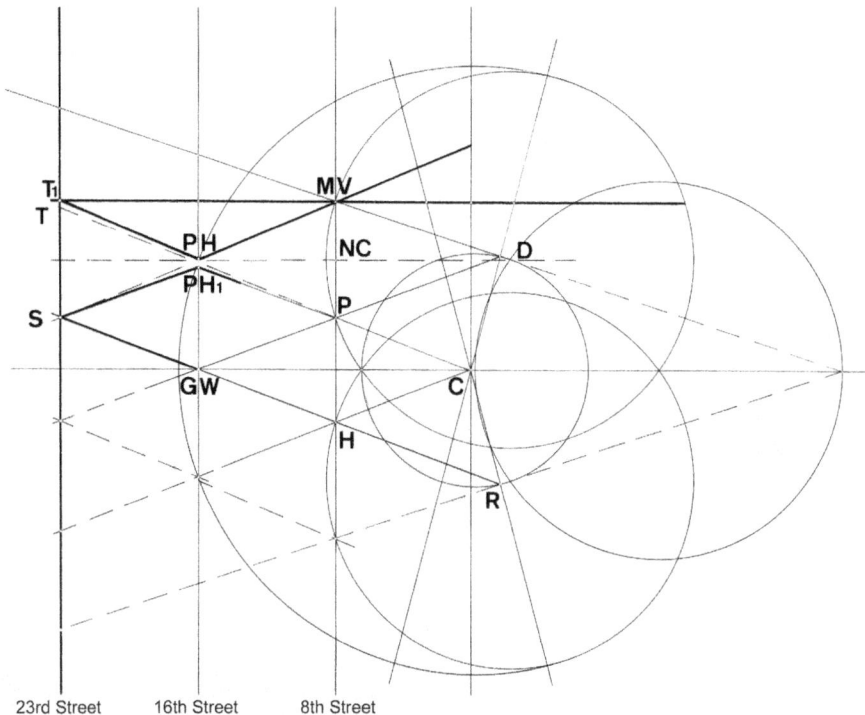

Figure 43. The Avenues around the White House: Extend Virginia Avenue from GW to S. Extend Pennsylvania Avenue, C, P to T. Draw in K Street by extending a line west from MV to T1. All points are determined by the north–south line of 23rd Street, 1344 yards from 16th Street. The orientation of New York Avenue is defined by line S, MV. However, the avenue is offset and aligned to the center of the sides of the White House, points PH1 and PH. The same is true for Pennsylvania Avenue. The avenues pick up from the north side of the building, point PH, and run to MV and T1. In this way, the avenues conform to the requirements of the underlining geometry while allowing for the depth of the White House. It is as though the width of the building has pushed the avenues out of an elastic band-like pattern to which they subsequently return. A line extended from point D runs due west through point PH. It bisects 8th Street at NC, the intended site for the National Church.

were altered from their true geometrical orientations and were aligned to the entrances on the northern and southern sides of the White House. The situation is made complicated by the fact that L'Enfant's exact location and design for the White House are unknown. An outline of the building is included on the map, but it is set so far south of most of the convergence points of the avenues that it cannot be in its correct location. L'Enfant may not have even drawn this building. An area to the north has been erased on the original plan and the words 'President's house' inserted.

The Secret Geometry of Washington, D.C.

Photo 7. The White House. View looking north from the Washington Monument. Connecticut Avenue, 16th Street and Vermont Avenue converge on a point to the north of the White House.

It is possible, however, to arrive at an idea of the size and location of an intended building by the avenues focused upon it. In this case, the avenues aligned to the White House present points of focus for a structure further north and possibly larger than that drawn on the map – a true 'Presidential Palace'. In Figure 45C on page 120, which shows the President's House not in the position on the L'Enfant Plan but in one possibly intended for it further north, there are in fact four convergence points: PH, PH1, PH2, and PH3. The Golden Section measure of 1.618 miles from the Capitol is to point PH, the second point from the top. It is highly likely that L'Enfant intended the main entrance to the building to be centered on this point; and the evidence supports this inference.

When James Hoban was hired in 1792 to design the White House, George Washington came to the city in August of that year to decide upon the site. Hoban's plan was enlarged to try to fill L'Enfant's huge outline (shown on a lost map) and to get the diagonal avenues to line up properly. But even though the President pushed the buildings further up the slope, they still did not reach the convergence points of the radiant avenues to the north. L'Enfant later complained that the White House was some 'twenty feet' lower in elevation than it should

The Triangle and Other Avenues

have been. Here, L'Enfant was making an important point. However, construction went ahead. On October 13, 1792, the cornerstone of the White House was laid in full accordance with Masonic ritual. James Hoban became the Worshipful Master of the first Masonic Lodge of the Federal District in 1793. In fact, it is interesting to note that all the members of this Lodge were operative Masons who worked either on the White House, or the Capitol, or both.

The lower section of New York Avenue on the L'Enfant Plan is aligned to point PH1, but Pennsylvania Avenue takes a bend along its length to align to the most southern point, PH3. The avenues should have mirrored each other; but L'Enfant was trying to accommodate a variety of options, including a lower position for the President's House. Pennsylvania Avenue departs from PH and runs to point T1. Point T1 is directly west of point MV on what is now K Street; conforming to the underlying grid pattern created by the geometry. New York Avenue departs from PH and runs to point MV. The original intention was for Pennsylvania Avenue and New York Avenue to mirror each other on the south side of the White House in the same way as they did on the north; but in order to do this, the White House was meant to be centered higher, on points PH and PH1, and Pennsylvania Avenue was to be straightened.

The bend in Pennsylvania Avenue between the Capitol and the White House demonstrated that the plan was a work in progress. Although there was lack of clarity on the plan – caused by erasing – L'Enfant knew it was important to have a clear view along what was to become one of the most famous avenues in the world. If Pennsylvania Avenue were bent, it would not have looked right. Bent avenues were exactly the kind of detail that critics of the plan took L'Enfant to task over. We know, however, that L'Enfant made several changes to a master plan – which has not survived – after the Plan of 1791 was presented to George Washington. As a preliminary draft, this sole surviving version of the L'Enfant plan was not intended to be accurate and adjustments were to be made to it. The bend in Pennsylvania Avenue was simply because the house in the only existing original plan was located too far south. When the President's House is moved north the bend in the avenue is easily removed, and all the avenues converge on the House in conformity with the underlying geometry. Figure 45C shows that the house outline marked on the L'Enfant Plan only has to come up one set of focal points for the avenues to come into alignment. Given that point PH3 was to the rear of the building, it was very likely intended to be the center of a feature, possibly low fountains, or a formal approach from a garden. PH1 may have been intended as some great room or colonnade with a view. PH was intended to be the main entrance to the building. I will mention PH2 in a moment.

I observed that the orientation of Rhode Island Avenue did not run from point T1, Pennsylvania and 23rd Street, as one would expect. As shown in Figures 44 and 44B, its orientation was from point T to LC. It has been adjusted to accommodate the different diagonals of the geometrical system created by the Golden Section template. To reconcile diagonals with different orientations, Rhode Island Avenue did not extend to 23rd Street; it began at the intersection with Connecticut Avenue. There was no deliberate intention to form a pentagon in another plane, as may at first appear. As is shown in Figures 14 and 52, a pure Golden Section geometry underlay the city; but L'Enfant had to fit important buildings and many focal points into the design. In fact, he allowed the anomalies introduced to the orientations of the avenues by the width of the primary buildings at C, D and E, to be resolved by the width of the President's House. The subtle adjustments to the plan required by these accommodations caused later engineers to shake their heads. Without recourse to L'Enfant's ideas, or even an accurate plan, they reoriented avenues to run to their logical, most obvious destinations.

Once I understood how the diamond pattern of the avenues generated by the Golden Section geometry of the primary circles was affected by the depth of buildings, it became easy to account for irregularities to the design. Indeed, I marvelled at the brilliance of L'Enfant; I could see how, by working out in his plan the requirements of buildings in real, three-dimensional space, he could place these structures inside the geometrical system. Figure 52 is a meditation on the interaction between a pure geometrical system and a set of actual diagonal avenues, squares and immense buildings on the ground.

Although the exact intention for point PH – now on the north side of the existing White House – is unknown, due to the uncertainties of the plan, I was convinced that it was an extremely important point in the geometry. It lies on the defining line of the western part of the city, 16th Street. When an east–west line is drawn from PH to point D, this bisects 8th Street at point NC – the intended site for the National Shrine or Church. L'Enfant also placed a prominent, but unknown, feature on this line just north of the Judiciary. I have no doubt that point PH, 1.618 miles from the Capitol, was intended to be the center of what L'Enfant conceived as a grand executive estate. As far as point PH2 – the focal point of the avenues radiating northward – is concerned, L'Enfant may have had in mind some kind of great entranceway, adorned

The Triangle and Other Avenues

with monumental statuary, perhaps a carriage circle. I think the present equestrian statue of General Lafayette, not far from PH2, would have met with his approval.

THE EQUILATERAL TRIANGLE

Although New York and Pennsylvania Avenues conform to the underlying Golden Section geometry, both Connecticut and Vermont Avenues appear to be quite independent of it. As shown in Figures 44 and 45, L'Enfant added an equilateral triangle to the pattern of avenues to the north of the White House. This is the only other geometrical figure in the plan of the city that stands outside of the Golden Section template.

Connecticut and Vermont Avenues were intended to depart from the White House at point PH2, at an angle of sixty degrees to each other and the east–west grid. These two avenues were to create two conspicuous squares at DC, Dupont Circle, and LC, Logan Circle; their intersections with Rhode Island and Massachusetts Avenues. As their sixty degree angle is that of an equal sided triangle, the third side of an equilateral triangle was to be formed by S Street (line k, l); 1344 yards from K Street. Further avenues, conforming to the underlying geometry, were to interconnect the various squares. Although when combined with the underlying pattern the triangle appears to create a pentacle, this was quite unintentional. This uneven pentacle – noticed by many observers – is formed by the intersection of the underlying Golden Section geometry with the equilateral triangle and no other geometry is required.

L'Enfant does not explain why he chose a sixty-degree angle for the two avenues radiating north from the White House. An equal-sided triangle, with sixty-degree angles, certainly presents a radical departure from the five-fold ratios of the fundamental Golden Section geometry of the city. (Yet I must emphasize that this angle is not preserved today. The angle was changed in the Ellicott Plan to fifty degrees.) The avenues could have been the same as those radiating eastward from the Capitol at fifty-five degrees, but L'Enfant deliberately chose not to do this. As L'Enfant had seen sixty-degree avenues radiating outward from the Chateau of Versailles in France, was he making a statement about the nature of the executive branch of government? Why were the sixty-degree angles of the equilateral triangle and its companion, the hexagram, to be around the President's House?

The Secret Geometry of Washington, D.C.

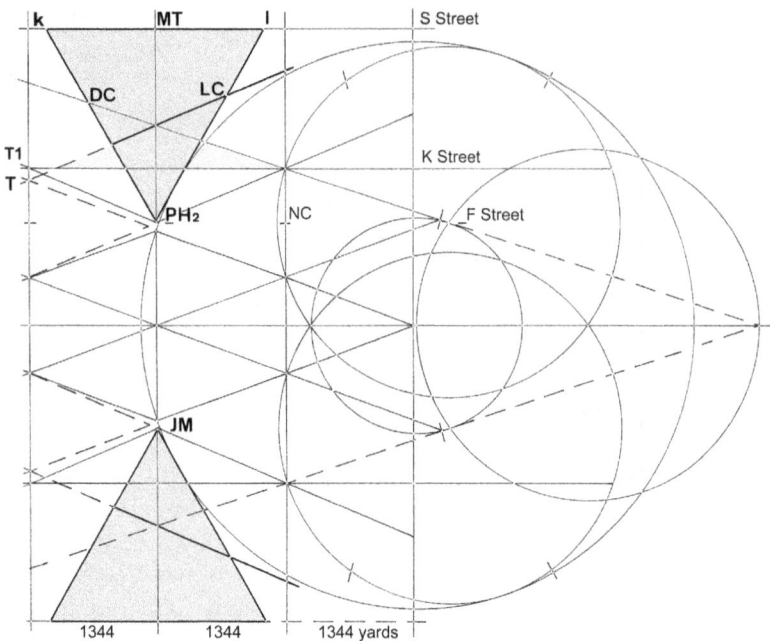

Figure 44A. The Equilateral Triangle beside the White House. From point PH2 north of the White House, Connecticut Avenue and Vermont Avenue radiate out at sixty degrees to pass through what is now Dupont Circle at DC and Logan Circle at LC. An equilateral triangle is completed by what is now S Street, k, l. Further diagonal avenues connect various squares. The temple and headquarters of the Scottish Rite of Freemasonry lies at point MT. For the sake of symmetry around the principal axis of the city, the triangle's counterpart to the south is included.

Two equilateral triangles can intersect to form a hexagram, a six-pointed star. In Figure 44, a second triangle, suggested by the symmetry of the plan, is shown. Three- and six-fold geometry is an essential component of traditional systems of number and measure; by selecting the sixty-degree angle for the two radiating avenues, was L'Enfant making the symbolism of 6 explicit? This symbolism does not occur anywhere else in the plan. In *gematria* or numerological symbolism, 60 has the same value as 6, as zero is not a number but just a marker. So what is the traditional meaning of 6, 60, and the triangle?

Whereas the number 5 is present in the structure of the forms of animate life and is associated with the earth, 6 is the number found in the structure of inanimate forms such as the hexagonal crystalline formation of water and many minerals. Whereas in traditional geometry the earthly and lunar number is 1080, corresponding to the 108-degree

The Triangle and Other Avenues

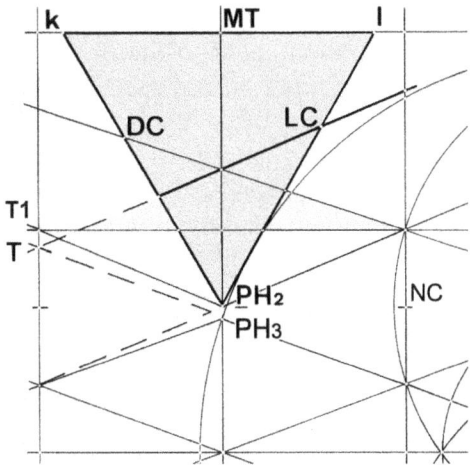

Figure 44B. The Equilateral Triangle beside the White House. Detail.

angle between the lines of a pentacle, the solar number is 6, or 60 and 666; its symbols are discs, triangles and hexagonal stars.

The reasons for these associations originate in the obvious ability of the radius of a circle to divide its circumference into six equal parts, or six equilateral triangles each with their three, sixty-degree angles. Similarly, using just a compass, it is possible to draw a circle with six circles around it – and then six circles around them and so on *ad infinitum* – to create the important geometrical figure described in Chapter 1 as the 'Flower of Life'. This figure generates not only triangular and hexagonal geometry but all the geometric forms, including the Platonic Solids. This feature identifies the circle and with it the number 6 with the creative circle of the heavens; the realm of spirit, authority and the sun. 6 traditionally represents the sun, 60 its measure and 666 its power. The Chateau of Versailles, with its sixty-degree avenues, was built as the residence of Louis XIV, the 'Sun King'. The number 6 has, of course, a close relationship with other numbers, especially 3 and 12. One of the challenges posed to geometers was to synthesize the earthly with the lunar and solar numbers – the 5 with the 6 – and thus reconcile the symbolism they represented.

I have never found any explicit evidence that L'Enfant was entertaining ideas like these. Yet six-fold geometry emerges here at the White House, and such ideas were certainly important to many of his contemporaries. It was a widely held belief, for example, that the ruler of a nation should be like the sun; identified with the number 6. There are also the following observations: Firstly, when the Washington Monument was built, the angle of 66 degrees 6 minutes was employed in the pyramidion

The Secret Geometry of Washington, D.C.

and almost 555.5 feet or 6666 inches was selected for its height. As described in detail in Chapter 9, the monument to the first President of the USA makes explicit use of solar symbolism and numerology.

Secondly, the extremely important mathematical value of *pi* or π, by which the diameter of a circle relates to its circumference, is in a 6 to 5 proportion to *phi*: $\pi^2 \times 6/5 = \Phi$ (or $2.618 \times 6/5 = 3.1416$). This property was explored in the dimensions of the Great Pyramid. As we shall see, through the introduction of a six-fold measure in the equilateral triangle L'Enfant reconciled 6 with 5 through the proportion of *pi* to the Golden Section. Again, although I have never read that this was a concern of L'Enfant, the resolution of the relationship of 6 to 5 is a perennial theme of sacred geometry and it is clearly in evidence in the L'Enfant Plan.

Thirdly, and perhaps most significantly, there is this: While the radius of the circle from the Capitol to the White House is 2847 yards, the radius of the circle around Lincoln Square is 1760 yards and the radius of the first circle around the Capitol is 1087 yards, there is as yet no appearance in the city plan of the proportionately smaller measure – according to the Golden Section – of 672 yards. If this was close enough numerologically to correspond to the solar number of 666, if it was to show up anywhere, surely it should be here in the geometry surrounding the President's House?

Indeed, there is such a 672 measure. It is half the distance of 1344 yards employed in the grid pattern of the western part of the city in which the President's House lies. The diamond plan that forms such a striking part of the geometry is based upon a grid of 672 or, twice that, 1344 yards. This distance is in the ratio of *phi* to all the other proportions. 672 is to 1087 as 1087 is to 1760, and 1087 is to 1760 as 1760 is to 2847. All these crucial distances of the city are in the proportion of the Golden Section: 1 to 1.618.

> So, 672 plus 1087 equals 1760, and $1087 + 1760 = 2847$, and $1760 + 2847 =$ etc., and 672 is to 1087 as 1 is to 1.618, 1087 is to 1760 as 1 is to 1.618, and so on.

Finally, the sides of the equilateral triangle itself are equal to the diameter of the primary circle surrounding the Capitol. That is, they are 2×1087 (or 1080) yards $= 2174$ yards; or the grid measure of 672 (or 666) yards $\times 2 \times \Phi$.

It could be said that in the original L'Enfant Plan, numerologically speaking, the number of the sun 666, focused around the President's House, was intended to meet with the number of the moon 1080, the radius of the circle around the Capitol, through the proportions of the triangle. They were tied into each other through the number of fusion 1760 or 1746, which is, of course, the radius of the second circle of the pentacle – associated with the people – that 'opened' the design of the main diagonal network of avenues in the first place.

It began to strike me that an equilateral triangle with its six-fold symbolism, reinforced by an underlying numerology of 666, but generated by a Golden Section matrix, would have explored the appropriate symbolic themes for the location of the house for the head of a republican and federal government. Could the geometry of the L'Enfant Plan around the White House be interpreted as an allegory in numbers concerning the delicate nature of leadership within a democratic and federal system? The Presidential triangle is 'embedded'; its three- and six-fold measures originate from an underlying five-fold structure uniting a balance of people, States, law and government. But it possesses its own powerful, solar character. Plato equated the triangular 'solid', the tetrahedron, with fire. The triangle, the hexagon and the pentacle explore the relationship between the sun, the earth and moon. The Executive, the People and the Representatives – or the regulators – of their laws, are geometrically conceived as standing to each other as sun to earth to moon.

These arcane ideas were all very well, but would L'Enfant have found them appealing? When L'Enfant attended the Académie Royale in Paris, he would have been exposed to ideas and symbols drawn from Egypt and the Old Testament. At that time, esoteric ideas were pouring into Europe as ancient texts were translated and, for the first time, travellers brought back accurate drawings of what they had seen abroad. When L'Enfant was in New York designing the 'Glory' over the altar of St. Paul's, he placed an equilateral triangle, symbolizing the Trinity, surrounded by solar rays, in the central position. In the center of the sixty-degree triangle was a Hebrew symbol for God. Similar designs are frequently found in the Masonic tradition. Finally, and perhaps most significantly, the palace of Louis XIV, the 'Sun King', at Versailles near L'Enfant's home, was developed from 1682 with the idea of the ruler, as the sun, at the head of the country. Among the most impressive features at Versailles are the avenues approaching the central chateau at the solar angle of sixty degrees. They form a partial equilateral triangle in relation to the chateau in the same way as the avenues of L'Enfant relate to the White House. L'Enfant, of course, was the son of an architect in service to the French king. On this evidence, several authorities have suggested that L'Enfant derived at least some of his inspiration for the federal capital from Versailles, and it is common to read in popular sources the mistaken idea that Versailles was the sole origin of the design for Washington, D.C.

How would the implicitly theistic and monarchic symbolism of the number 6 sit with a secular, democratic republic with a President at its head? Perhaps this was why L'Enfant had to carefully balance the American Executive with the Legislature and the People through his geometrical design. The solar qualities of leadership, the plan is saying, now derive from, and are voted for by the people, and are controlled by the regulating laws the people have chosen. Yet the leader is still empowered to act within the limits of the system. In numerological symbolism, the line between earth and heaven is precisely negotiated between 5 and 6, earth and sun, people and Head of State. In his design, L'Enfant is showing that the 6 is born out of the 5, not vice versa.

L'ENFANT'S SECRET

It is highly likely that L'Enfant's ideas came across as too elitist for the newly founded and populist United States. His courtly manners were certainly a factor in his final dismissal. Although he had politically sympathetic friends like Madison and Hamilton, any emphasis in his design upon the Executive would have been noticed and frowned upon. The States in general had to support the popular ideas of democracy. The liberty and equality of the Constitution was what the American people wanted to hear about, and to see in their national symbols.

Perhaps L'Enfant decided it was best if he kept all his efforts focused upon the Capitol area or on the region as a whole; in any event, this is what he did. He objected to all the available funds going toward the major buildings. But possibly he concluded it was best if he kept his guiding thoughts and ideas secret. He knew that sharing the details of the plan with anyone other than the President and his Secretary of State at this stage was inappropriate and had the potential to cause trouble. In the same way that he refused to show his maps until they could be revealed in their entirety, so he would not talk about his design until it was complete. He hoped that the design when presented as a whole could be better understood by all parties without the need for further explanation from him. Certainly Jefferson was watching him closely; even if there were others – more kindly disposed – who were not only concerned about giving the President more power but also about giving the people too much.

Although a grand executive estate with radiant avenues modelled after the absolute monarchy of the Sun King of France would never

The Triangle and Other Avenues

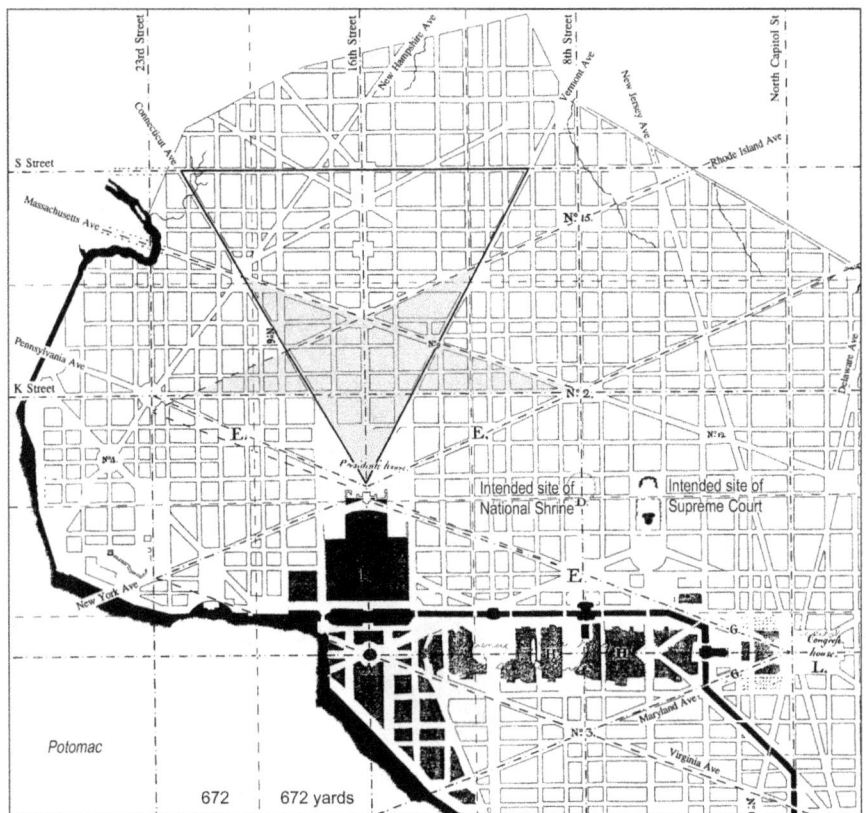

Figure 45A. The Equilateral Triangle and Grid around the White House. The uppermost line of the triangle lies on the basic grid of the western part of the city. The grid's measure is based upon 1344 yards. Half that measure is 672 yards. The sides of the triangle are 2 × 1087 yards. They are equal to the diameter of the first circle around the Capitol: $672 \times \Phi = 1087$. The shaded, uneven pentacle is incidental and was not intended by L'Enfant. It is formed by the intersection of the underlying Golden Section template with the triangle.

have suited the newly created democratic USA, the architect of the first occupant of the 'Presidential palace' probably secretly desired it. The axis through the President's House when combined with the equilateral triangle, as shown in Figures 44–45, had the potential to be greater than the first north–south axis through the Capitol. As we shall see, when he came to be President, even Jefferson took some dramatic measures to underscore the importance of this axis. The north–south 'Presidential axis' became extremely pronounced, relegating the one through the Capitol to second place. It was also quite possible that, in

The Secret Geometry of Washington, D.C.

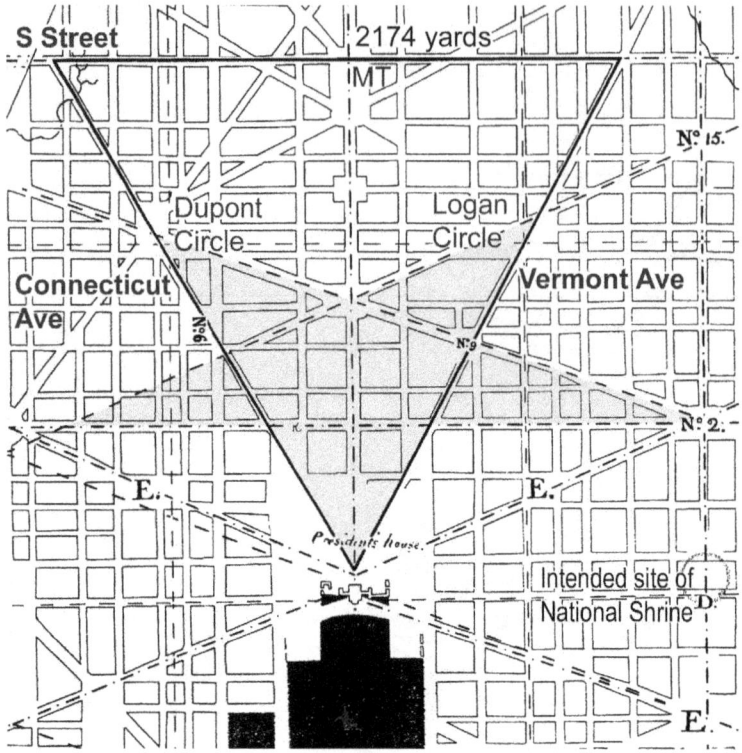

Figure 45B. Detail of the Equilateral Triangle.

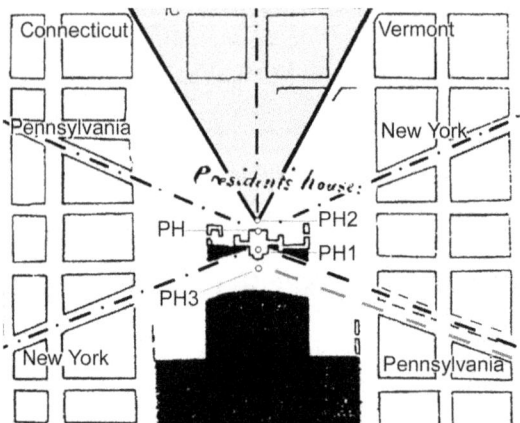

Figure 45C. This figure shows the President's house moved north into its correct position. The avenues now converge upon their proper centers. Only a small adjustment to the lower section of Pennsylvania Avenue is required; which, in fact, removes the anomalous bend along its length and brings it into harmony with the Golden Section geometry.

his creation of the solar equilateral triangle, L'Enfant was simply following the wishes of President Washington: his friend, old war comrade, employer and his patron.

THE EQUILATERAL TRIANGLE AND THE MASONS

One group of people to whom the symbolic associations of the triangle are known and who do keep them a secret are the Freemasons, who have made a notable contribution to the geometry of Washington through the careful placement of their lodges. The basic emblem that all Masonic lodges have in common is the dividers and set square. These dividers sometimes show a forty-five degree angle, but more frequently, a sixty-degree angle. The letter 'G' is customarily shown between the dividers; according to the Freemason Albert Pike, this does not stand for god as one might reasonably expect, but for 'geometry'. 'Geometry', Pike wrote, 'is the only science by which it is possible to measure and comprehend the universe'. If the dividers of the Masonic emblem are equated with the sixty-degree equilateral triangle emerging from the White House, some interesting items for consideration emerge.

The first point is that the upper left corner of the original triangle was close to the location of the Widow's Mite, where the Treaty Oak once stood. Even with the change in orientation of the two avenues from sixty- to fifty-degrees, Connecticut Avenue is still closely aligned to this point. This location is still called Temple Heights because in the 1920s and 30s several Masonic committees wished to build their lodges there. It seems the Masonic fraternity was strongly interested in placing a temple upon or near the site that claimed to be the mythic center for the area. But perhaps ironically, this is now the location of the Washington Hilton.

The second point is that the Washington temple of the Southern Jurisdiction of the Scottish Rite of Freemasonry was placed so that it lies in the very center of the upper line of the triangle. It is located midway between the points of the imaginary dividers, directly north of the White House, on the axis provided by 16th Street. The building, begun in 1911, was designed by John Russel Pope, who also designed the National Archives Building and the Jefferson Memorial. It was intended to be a symbol of the inner mysteries. Based upon a pyramid set on a cube, the temple was modelled after the tomb of Mausolus at

The Secret Geometry of Washington, D.C.

Photo 8. The lodge of the Southern Jurisdiction of the Scottish Rite of Freemasonry at 16th Street and S Street, Washington, D.C..

Halicarnassus in Asia Minor. It has thirty-three Ionic columns thirty-three feet tall, representing the thirty-three degrees of Masonry. It has four series of steps, one with three, one with five, one with seven and one with nine steps leading up to the entrance. There are ten columns on each side of the cube. The 'unfinished' or truncated pyramid on the summit has thirteen steps, the same number as the pyramid on the dollar bill. In this location, on the junction of 16th and S Streets – and later on the new zero meridian – this extraordinary temple forms a right-angle or square to the top line of the equilateral triangle, dividing it into two Pythagorean right-angle triangles. Some crucial Masonic symbols – the dividers, the square and the right-angled triangle – were thus incorporated, over a century after L'Enfant's dismissal, into the plan of the city of Washington.

The triangle and the number 3 occupy a highly important place in Freemasonry. Geometry literally means 'the measure of the earth'. And geometry itself traditionally began with trigonometry, 'the measure of triangles'. Trigonometry was fundamental to Egyptian thought – from where many Freemasons claim their traditions to have originated – since it allowed land to be accurately surveyed and re-allocated after

The Triangle and Other Avenues

the annual inundation of the Nile. It was probably the Egyptians who first determined the measures for *phi* and *pi* to several decimal places. The Great Pyramid, for example, built around 2500 BCE, incorporates both these and other 'transcendent' numbers into its design. The Greek mathematician, Pythagoras, reputed to have coined the term 'geometry', was said to have spent twenty-two years in Egypt being initiated into its science. Although he learnt it from the Egyptians, the theorem attributed to Pythagoras: 'the sum of the square of the hypotenuse of a right-angled triangle is equal to the sum of the squares of the other two sides', is probably the most important and most used of all geometrical theorems.

In Masonic allegory, the two sides of a triangle on either side of the right-angle represent the sun and the moon, the male and the female. They shed their light upon their union, the 'Blazing Star', that forms the hypotenuse. The hypotenuse is equated with the divine child, Horus. The same triad: sun, moon, star, is also represented by the Masonic 'Great Equilateral Triangle'. In the center of this triangle may be shown many things, such as the eye of Ra, the sun; or the Hebrew symbol of creative power, the *yod*, which L'Enfant had used in St. Paul's Chapel, New York.

Practical geomancy can be defined as the placement of objects and buildings in the landscape in order to control the most beneficent flow of subtle forces. One may be forgiven for wondering what influence Masons intended the location of the Temple of the Scottish Rite of Freemasonry to have had upon the federal city. Their temple sits in the center of the base of a triangle – whether equilateral or of fifty degrees – framed by two avenues radiating out from the White House. It creates two right-angle triangles. Whether the concept of subtle influence through geomantic placement and geometric relationship is credible or not, I asked the Washington Masons what they intended by the location of their temple in the geometric pattern of the city. Those whom I asked replied, perhaps understandably, that there was no plan. They dismissed the equilateral triangle along with all the other geometrical figures that they have been accused of adding to the design of the city. They also declined to speculate on what influence the Masonic tradition had upon L'Enfant.

I found it interesting to investigate what effect the changing of the angles of the triangle may have had upon the White House. A practitioner in the art of eastern geomancy told me that replacing the solar qualities of a sixty-degree equilateral triangle with a fifty-degree 'closed' triangle meant the flow of subtle forces through the triangle would become constricted and inward-focused rather than open and outward-flowing. At fifty-degrees or less, the *feng-shui* practitioner said, the angle is not considered expansive, but closed. It creates a figure known as the 'deadly arrow'. If this is true, then when combined with the intrusion of the Treasury Building into Pennsylvania Avenue and the blocking of the view of the Potomac, the 'closed' avenues to the north would mean a further loss of the outward-looking qualities that L'Enfant had built into his location for the White House. The Masons offered no comment on any of these speculations; and it is hard to assess the visual impact on the ground of the narrowing of the angle of the avenues due to the congestion caused by later building in the area.

In fact, due to security reasons, Pennsylvania Avenue and Lafayette Park to the north of the White House have become increasingly closed to public access in the last few decades. In terms of the geomantic analysis presented above, both the careful security measures and the tree-filled park would have the positive effect of buffering the 'deadly arrow'. Yet in terms of the Executive's need to look outwards and be open to the nation, short of changing the angles of Connecticut Avenue and Vermont Avenue, the area is now necessarily closed and there is little that can be done about it. I discuss in the final chapters whether I believe the changing of the White House triangle from sixty to fifty degrees had anything to do with the Masons.

THE CIRCLE OF THE PENTACLE (1)

At this stage in the analysis, I was satisfied that the origin of the main diagonal avenues in the western part of the L'Enfant Plan for Washington, D.C., derived from an underlying geometrical design based upon the Golden Section. Only the addition of the equilateral triangle was necessary to account for every significant factor. But I also had to examine whether Pennsylvania and Maryland Avenues, to the east of the Capitol, had similarly originated in the geometry established by the pentacle. At first glance, like the avenues north of the White House, they appeared not to.

Pennsylvania and Maryland Avenues radiate approximately southeast and northeast from the Capitol at an angle of fifty-five degrees between them. When these two avenues are combined with two radiating from Lincoln Square, they form a dramatic arrowhead that seems to have little to do with the underlying pentacle. However, the sixty-degree triangle had also appeared to have little relation to the pattern which determined the other avenues around the White House;

The Triangle and Other Avenues

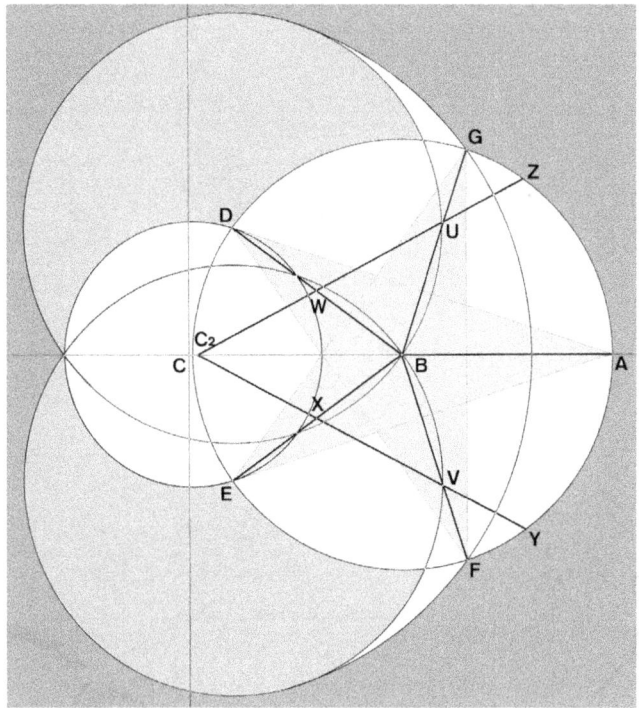

Figure 46. The Circle of the Pentacle (1): The pentacle A, F, E, D, G is defined by the primary circles proceeding in the proportion of the Golden Section from the Capitol and point B. Points U, V, W, X were to be squares. The location of the squares is determined by the centerlines of the arms of the pentacle and by Pennsylvania and Maryland Avenues, C2, Z and C2, Y. The angle of fifty-five degrees between these avenues brings them into relationship with the pentacle. W is now close to Stanton Park. X is now close to Seward Square. Y was the square before Sousa Bridge over the Anacostia. B to D (and beyond) is Massachusetts Avenue. B to X (and beyond) is North Carolina Avenue. A is now the RFK Stadium. E was probably to be the site of City Hall.

only through number was its secret revealed. So it was with the two avenues at fifty-five degrees to each other east of the Capitol. The number 55 was the clue.

55 cannot be directly linked to the pentacle through angles. But it is connected through mathematics and simple numerology. 5 is the number of points in the pentacle or sides in the pentagon. 5 plus 5 corresponds to the double pentacle or decagon. These figures divide their internal lines in the ratio of *phi*. (In the same way as mathematicians in the ancient world found that 22 over 7 gave a working definition for *pi*, they found that 55 over 34 or 89 over 55 gave an accurate figure for *phi*. 55 is the ninth number in a series, named after the Italian mathematician Fibonacci,

The Secret Geometry of Washington, D.C.

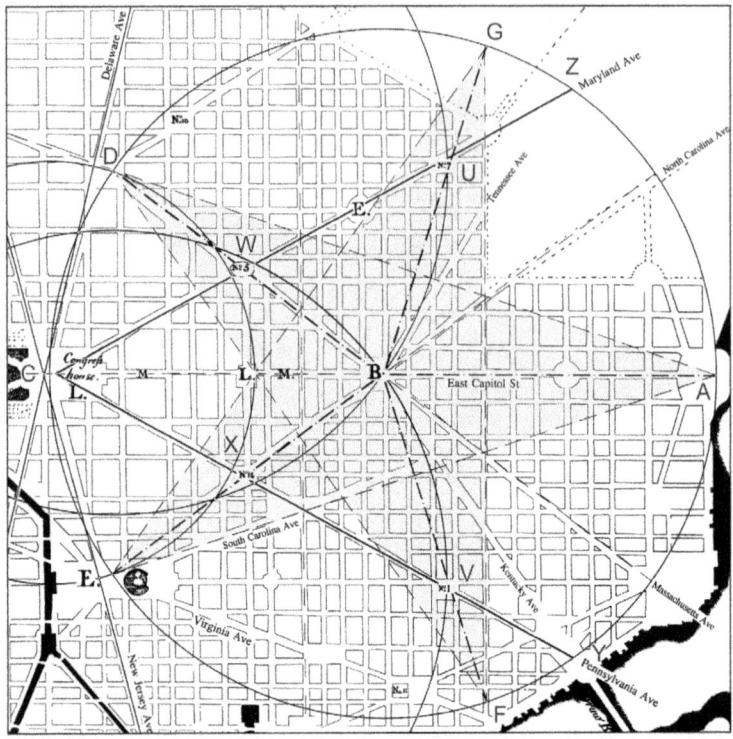

Figure 47. The L'Enfant Plan overlaid by the geometry of Figure 46. Pentagonal geometry determined the location of the pattern of the avenues and squares and does so to this day.

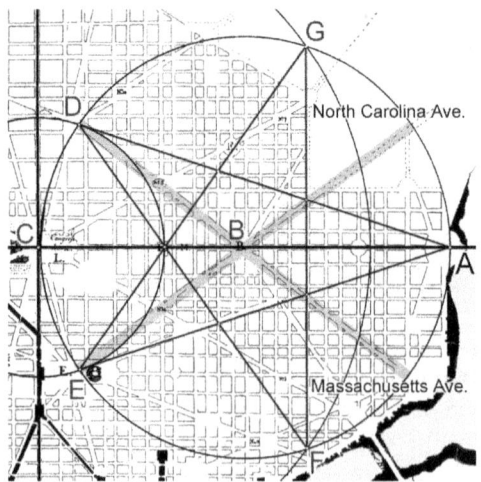

Figure 47 Detail. The orientations of Massachusetts Avenue and North Carolina Avenue in the eastern part of the city are clearly defined by the 'hidden' pentacle.

where each new number is the sum of the previous two: 1-2-3-5-8-13-21-34-55-89 etc.. As the series proceeds, the ratio between the numbers comes ever closer to *phi*. 55 plus 89 equals 144, the next number in the Fibonacci series; an angle of the pentacle.) The fifty-five degree angle selected for the avenues east of the Capitol underscored the importance of the five-fold Golden Section geometry in this part of the city. The avenues re-emphasised the union of the people and their representatives.

As shown in Figures 46 and 47, Maryland Avenue proceeds from the Capitol at C2 through points W and U to Z, Pennsylvania Avenue proceeds from the Capitol through points X and V to Y. According to the 1791 Hallet plan for the Capitol, thought to closely correspond to the ideas of L'Enfant, C2 is the main entrance to the Capitol complex. The four points, X, V, W and U were among the principal squares selected by L'Enfant to be adorned by the different States. As can be seen from the diagram, the underlying geometric circles, the central arms of the pentacle described by circle center B, and the two avenues at fifty-five degrees all pass through these squares. They combine to determine the size and shape of each square. The location of the squares and the fifty-five degree orientation of Pennsylvania and Maryland Avenues, in the area of the city to the east of the Capital, are precisely determined by the underlying pentagonal, Golden Section geometry.

THE CIRCLE OF THE PENTACLE (2)

As time went by, I became convinced that further streets and avenues in the eastern part of the city were all related to the defining geometry of the pentacle. I even found the hidden relationship between the geometry and the apparently irregular gridiron pattern for the streets. Figure 48, for example, shows that if D, B is extended to n it defines the completion of Massachusetts Avenue. When the sections of North Carolina Avenue that L'Enfant located on his plan are drawn in, e, B and carried by extension to m, then both lines n and m are midway between points of the pentacle.

Line B, L, now Kentucky Avenue, is laid out to point Y. But strangely, its equivalent, Tennessee Avenue, line B, j, does not run to point Z. It is slightly offset. There is some inconsistency in the angles of the avenues in L'Enfant's plan. This is usually explained by the need of each square to possess its own symmetry. Tennessee Avenue probably falls into this category. South Carolina Avenue, for example, does not follow line E, Λ as would be expected. But in order to appear

The Secret Geometry of Washington, D.C.

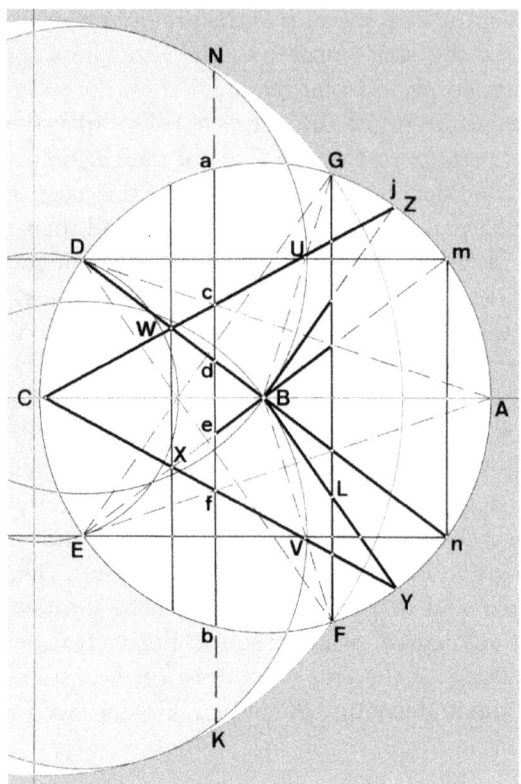

Figure 48. The Circle of the Pentacle (2): Further avenues and squares are defined by the internal geometry of the pentacle. Dark lines are avenues on the ground. Massachusetts Avenue bisects the five-pointed star with line D, B, n. Sections of North Carolina Avenue, E, B, m, do the same. Line N, K (from the five-fold division of circles center D and E) defines the position of squares c, d, e and f along what is now East 8th Street. Point F is the old ferry crossing. E, V, n is G Street. E, f, A is the orientation of L'Enfant's South Carolina Avenue but like North Carolina Avenue E, X, B, m it does not run the distance. G, F is East 15th Street. This kind of detail is likely to be of interest only to residents.

symmetrically balanced with the southeast section of Virginia Avenue, E, F, it was moved to lie a couple of degrees north. In turn, this section of Virginia Avenue, in order to satisfy the geometrical shift between the eastern and the western parts of the city, as well as the spatial requirements of the important building and plaza that was to be at E, ran at the same angle as before but was set slightly further to the north.

Although these asymmetries are confusing and might appear to lend credence to the argument that there was no geometric order in the L'Enfant Plan, I found that careful analysis of these diagrams proved the opposite. Deviations from the order appeared as deviations, dictated by the special circumstances of each site; yet throughout the whole there was a consistent order provided by the underlying geometry, which was always returned to as soon as possible.

This consistent order was provided by the pentacle. It clearly underlay the pattern of the city east of the Capitol. Beginning with the defining pentagonal angle E, A, D of thirty-six degrees, there was no mistaking the internal geometry of the pentacle. But although it defined the direction of every avenue in the area, it was hard to see. This raises the strong probability that L'Enfant deliberately concealed the five-pointed star as he did not wish to provoke a reaction to its obvious use. Certainly Christians have misunderstood the use of the pentacle by Freemasons. Indeed, in the 1820s there was a wave of anti-Freemasonry fervour in America, partly because of its employment of such mystical symbols. Whether or not this explains why L'Enfant decided to keep his use of the pentacle secret, the end result was the same.

From N and K, which are points of the pentacles in circles center D and E, a north–south line can be drawn. This intersects lines within the primary pentacle at points *a, c, d, e, f* and *b*. Most of these intersections were to be squares of greater or lesser degree. A similar north–south line through W and X also defined features of interest as can be seen from examination of Figure 47. Line G, F along one side of the pentacle is now East 15th Street.

Even though this is now going into very minor detail, east–west lines through the points established by the internal geometry of the pentacle are also of interest. Line E, V, n is now G Street. If extended it would go to the Jefferson Memorial. And corresponding to G Street in the upper part of the circle, line D, U, *m* when extended west is the alignment that passes through the center of the intended National Church and the north side of the White House.

THE GRIDIRON PATTERN OF STREETS

The streets that run north–south and east–west on the L'Enfant Plan appear to be irregularly spaced. To the bafflement of later utility companies, there was little uniform measure between the streets or larger blocks. Some uniformity was suggested by the 1344-yard grid at work between the main streets in the western part of the city, and by the employment of mile distances in the east, but it seems little more can be said than that. Yet

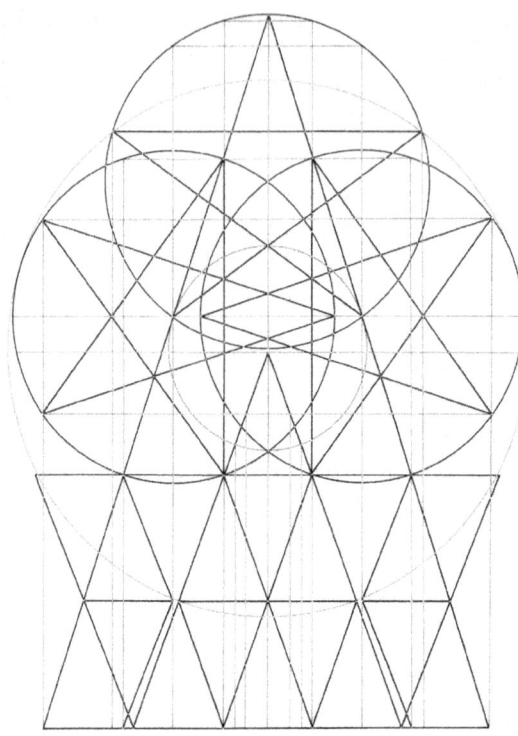

Figure 49. The Grid Pattern for the Streets: The pentacles are drawn in full to show how their Golden Section geometry governs the pattern of east–west and north–south streets. The grid shown is either comprised of streets, lines through centers of squares and places of significance, or a combination of both. From these lines – showing the Mall to be the main axis of symmetry – many other streets, not shown, can be drawn. Lines parallel to the Mall show the congruous positions of the canal (now Constitution Avenue), Independence Avenue and intervening streets. For the purpose of clarity, some details of the geometry have been removed, while the non-existent southwest corner has been drawn in for the sake of symmetry.

when I struck east–west and north–south lines through the key points in the defining Golden Section geometry of the city, a correspondence between the order created by the geometry and the gridiron pattern of the streets suddenly emerged.

Figure 49 shows the geometry of the city in dark lines, while a grid pattern of streets is drawn with the lighter line. To reveal the synchronicity of the two systems, or rather, the generation of the grid by the geometry, the three pentacles contained in the circles of one-mile radius are shown in full. In order not to overload the picture, other details of the geometric order are omitted.

The Triangle and Other Avenues

When the geometrical order of the city of Washington is applied to the irregular grid pattern of the streets, the method employed to lay them out becomes clear. The diagram creates a sense of symmetry and singularity out of the grid, when in fact, close examination reveals considerable complexity. Few distances are the same. It is a measure of the validity of the template that it is able to demonstrate any geometrical order at all. It makes especially clear the plane of symmetry around the primary east–west axis. However, it must be remembered that the southwest corner of the drawing did not exist in fact. At the time of L'Enfant, this area was under the Potomac. It testifies to the strength of the original design that what exists today as a result of land reclamation conforms to the pattern of the original plan – especially the placement of the Jefferson Memorial.

The east–west and north–south lines shown in Figure 49 were either streets or lines through centers of important squares or both. In many cases, intervening streets – not shown here – were arranged to be fractions of the distance between these lines, or placed to enhance or accommodate the squares and other places of significance. Between P and H, for example, the canal (now Constitution Avenue), Independence Avenue, and the other streets were arranged at fourths or eighths of the distance.

In the section describing the arrangement of the avenues around the White House, I discussed the precise distances underlying the basic grid pattern in that district of the city. I showed how they derived from the ratios of the Golden Section. I showed that the distance north–south from the canal (Constitution Avenue) to K Street, to the uppermost side of the equilateral triangle, and east–west between the Capitol, 8th, 16th and 23rd Streets, were based upon the measure of one mile $\times \Phi^2 = 672$ yards, (with *phi* as 0.618). See Figure 45. As the radius of the circle containing the pentacle in the eastern half of the city is one mile, and as the pentacle divides itself in the ratios of *phi*, it is not surprising these two parts of the city mesh together in an overall grid pattern based upon the Golden Section.

When laid over the template of the underlying geometry, I found L'Enfant's grid pattern for the streets, shown in Figure 49, particularly striking. It unified the city into a whole and developed the analogy between the city and a cathedral. It revealed the unity of the geometry that apparently divided the eastern part of the city from the western part, without reducing itself to an 'insipide' pattern of uniform blocks. Moreover, it demonstrated that the order of geometry upon which the city was built is ultimately traceable back to the Golden Section and its close companion, the pentacle.

The Secret Geometry of Washington, D.C.

SUMMARY

The proposal presented in the previous three chapters is that L'Enfant derived the location of the principal buildings, squares and monuments, as well as the pattern of the streets and avenues of the city, by combining central primary axes with the ratio of the Golden Section. The Capitol lay at the center of his plan; and Figure 47, for example, shows how definitively the Golden Section geometry of the one-mile-radius pentacle marked out the eastern half of the city.

The pentacle on the eastern side of the city was centered upon an area dedicated to the activities of the people; while the radiant avenues in the western part of the city were centered upon an axis through the house of the President. Five-fold geometry balanced six-fold geometry around a great central primary axis. See Figure 53 on page 170. Later developments pushed all the important buildings and monuments of the city into the section provided only by the Mall; but L'Enfant had intended them to be distributed throughout the city, which would therefore be balanced as a whole.

The equilateral triangle defined the orientation of Connecticut and Vermont Avenues north of the White House; as shown in Figure 42, no additional geometry needs to be introduced to explain any further feature of the plan. The triangle allowed L'Enfant to make a strong statement about Presidential power, which reflected the feelings of many but not all of his contemporaries. But – like the pentacle – he had to hide the triangle, to the point where its impact became lost. As we shall see in the following chapter, this did not stop an emphasis upon the Presidential axis from being developed further in subsequent plans.

(Note to the pedantic: In this description of the geometrical basis for the city found in the L'Enfant Plan of 1791, I have attempted to show how all main avenues and principal points describe and conform to the proposed geometric scheme. Where accuracy is critical, some detail has been explored. I estimate the overall accuracy of the analysis is ±1 percent, or about twenty yards in a mile. But comparison with modern surveys raises a question over the scale employed on the L'Enfant Plan. The distances given here are based upon L'Enfant's stated measure of one mile from Lincoln Square to the Capitol, and checked by comparison to accurate modern surveys. But if the 'scale of poles' on L'Enfant's plan is used, the distances come out too short, although the relative proportions are, of course, the same. There is no satisfactory answer to account for this discrepancy, unless the 'scale of poles' was inaccurately drawn. I believe this to be the case as L'Enfant's drawing was never intended for serious draftsmanship, only as a guide for the President.)

8
Washington after L'Enfant

THE DISMISSAL OF L'ENFANT

Many excellent books cover the dramatic dismissal of L'Enfant less than a year after he had begun his work on the plan for the Federal City. Here, it is only necessary to describe the episodes that throw light upon details of the L'Enfant Plan and upon the actions that subsequently affected the design of the City of Washington.

In the latter part of 1791, L'Enfant, for his own good reasons, was still reluctant to publish his map of the new city. This hampered the auctioning of city lots that was necessary to raise money for the public works. L'Enfant wished the public building works to continue so lots throughout the entire city could realize a higher price. He felt that speculators impeded the growth of the city by buying lots at the lowest price they could contrive and then doing nothing to develop them. But without auctions, there could be no money for the public works. This double bind frustrated the efforts of the three District Commissioners. They became increasingly irritated with the attitude of L'Enfant; his conduct seemed, to them, high-handed, secretive and expensive. And the Commissioners had the ear of the Secretary of State and the President.

L'Enfant's particular quarrel with the Commissioners was the constant diversion of funds to the building of the President's House and the Capitol. He wanted those funds to promote the growth of the infrastructure of the city as a whole, not just its main buildings, and so to encourage small-scale investment. L'Enfant wrote to George Washington in August:

> If we are to make of this city a fact it will be indispensable to consider every part of the proposed plan as essential ... and however unconnected they may appear at first every part should go forward with a proportional degree of despatch.

He asked the President to postpone the sale planned for October, as the lots around the key sites were obstructed by felled trees and thus unable to 'command the height price in a sale'. L'Enfant pleaded that it was 'essential to pursue with dignity the operation of an undertaking so worthy of the concern of a grand empire'. L'Enfant had vision; but the great undertaking – worthy as it might be – needed cash to become a reality, and it needed it immediately.

The President requested L'Enfant to produce a new copy of the plan for the city. L'Enfant engaged Stephen Hallet, later architect of the Capitol, to draw up the plan; but he then stopped its production. The auction went ahead without a map and the results were predictably disappointing; each side blamed the other. Finally, in exasperation, George Washington asked Andrew Ellicott to prepare an engraving for publication.

It appears that Ellicott had both the rough draft L'Enfant had presented to Washington in August and the unfinished copy prepared by Stephen Hallet to work from. L'Enfant gave the latter to Ellicott's brother, Benjamin Ellicott, on the understanding that the work would be returned to him for correction before engraving. In the Library of Congress is an unsigned map, known as the 'Line Drawing', that was probably drawn in December by Benjamin Ellicott to show the status of the surveys. Some time passed. Then L'Enfant heard through a third party that an engraver would soon be at work on production of a plan of the city. Having no idea what he would find, L'Enfant went to the Ellicott house and found a much altered plan in preparation. L'Enfant exploded and demanded the return of the plan and his originals. The senior Ellicott refused. The problem was compounded by the fact that immediately before this, L'Enfant's office had been burgled. His books, notes, sketches and plans for the city and for the public buildings were stolen. Some of these documents later showed up in circumstances that pointed the finger of suspicion at the Commissioners. It appeared that in order to have what they needed to finish the map the Ellicotts were supplied with drawings stolen from L'Enfant, although the Ellicotts themselves were unlikely to have known this.

The best evidence for this sorry state of affairs comes from a letter L'Enfant sent to Tobias Lear, Secretary to the President, dated February 17, 1792. After Andrew Ellicott was ordered by Thomas Jefferson to prepare a map, L'Enfant wrote:

> This determined me to concern myself no more about it being confident that the meaning of Mr. Jefferson's order to Mr. Ellicott could not be to publish the plan without my knowledge and concurrence, and convinced it would not be completely finished without recourse to the large map in my possession.

Then he added in pencil, 'but by the material stolen they got **all** that was wanted'. The word 'all' was heavily inscribed.

It seems that L'Enfant felt betrayed by Jefferson. He had been unaware that he could count on no favours from the Secretary of State. Indeed, Jefferson was sympathetic to the financial worries of the Commissioners and had no love for L'Enfant or his grand plan. Jefferson had some architectural plans of his own for Washington; when the opportunity came to apply some pressure on the impetuous architect, he did not hesitate to place some critical words in the President's ear.

In his letter to Lear, L'Enfant continued to complain that the plan was 'unmercifully spoiled and altered'. He added, by way of explanation, 'All the lineaments of the ground from which the whole direction of avenues can alone be perceived [have] been suppressed'. He went on to say, apparently trying to be as tactful as possible, that Andrew Ellicott's desire was:

> ... to suggest ideas of his own and gradually to deviate from the original plan [in a manner that] would tend to destroy that harmony and combination of the different parts with the whole, to effect which has been the chief object of my labor and concern.

L'Enfant made it clear that he was still willing to remedy the situation.

The Commissioners, meanwhile, were preparing their case. They were appalled by L'Enfant's latest estimate of a million dollars as the cost of work that did not coincide with their priorities. Commissioner Carroll was particularly upset that L'Enfant had ordered the foundations of a relative's new house to be removed because it intruded into the line of New Jersey Avenue. The Commissioner's relative, Daniel Carroll of Duddington, was told by Ellicott when he surveyed the avenue that the plan was 'mere fancy work, and would be very different when completed'. Jefferson had urged the President at the time to make it clear to L'Enfant that he was subordinate to the Commissioners.

The President was in a difficult position and prevaricated. On February 22, 1792, Jefferson wrote to L'Enfant that the President wished his appointment to continue, but that 'the law requires it should be in subordination to the Commissioners'. L'Enfant politely declined to concur with this situation, giving a long list of reasons why he should, in fact, remain subordinate to no one but the man who appointed him. As the terms of the Congressional Act of 1790 allowed the President to choose the federal site, appoint the Commissioners and the architects, L'Enfant was making a very good case. But it was not one that suited a democracy; nor did it

The Secret Geometry of Washington, D.C.

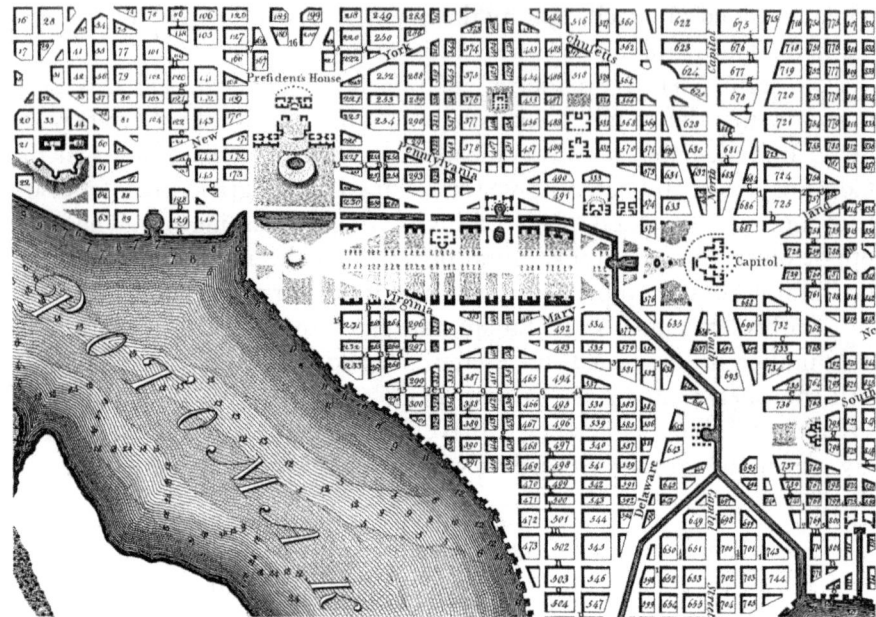

Figure 50. Central Portion of the Philadelphia Engraving of the Ellicott Plan of Washington, D.C., 1792. Although preserving the basic design of the L'Enfant Plan, squares are shifted, seeming irregularities are removed and the diagonal avenues are straightened and entirely or subtly reoriented. The Ellicott plan determined much of what exists today. It lacks the proportions found in traditional systems of geometry. However, the plan does provide an impression of how L'Enfant conceived the Mall and perhaps the shape and size of his intentions for the Capitol.

suit Jefferson. On February 26, Washington sent his personal secretary, Tobias Lear, to L'Enfant to make what turned out to be a final appeal. L'Enfant brusquely told Lear that 'he had already heard enough of this matter'. Washington took offense at this remark, and although the sources say he was later to have second thoughts, requested the resignation of L'Enfant. The next day, true to form, L'Enfant wrote to his patron, the President, 'I am now totally disengaged'.

Andrew Ellicott promptly provided a map, uninspected by L'Enfant and – despite a strong recommendation from Tobias Lear – without any credit to L'Enfant. Different companies made two engravings: Samuel Hill of Boston and Thackara and Vallance of Philadelphia. Although they are similar in substance, the engravings demonstrate that the landscape of Washington, D.C. was soon to be moulded by a plan that was critically different from the subtle 'lineaments' created by Major Pierre Charles L'Enfant.

'UNOFFENDING AS USUAL'

In March 1792, L'Enfant was sent a remuneration of $2,500 and an offer of one lot in the city. He refused to accept either. Many people still recognized him as being the most qualified person for this challenging project. His work crews strongly protested against his absence. The President expressed regret over L'Enfant's dismissal on several occasions. To the further distress of the Commissioners, it slowly dawned on those involved in construction that they now had to pick up exactly where L'Enfant had left off. Many proprietors collaborated to write a letter to the Commissioners lamenting L'Enfant's dismissal. They spoke of his 'great confidence ... mad zeal' and 'ungovernable temper' in one breath. Yet although L'Enfant had had the vision, it was the Commissioners who were responsible for the financial and legal affairs of the new federal city, and they possessed what L'Enfant had not – an accurate appraisal of the political and economic realities of the time.

A primary consideration of the Commissioners was that the members of Congress were reluctant to grant money to a grandiose scheme that took power and resources away from the states they represented. Although their voters liked the Constitution, they did not like the federal government and the taxes it demanded. At the time, there was little money for grand building schemes to be had. War debts were still being paid and construction of the federal capital was a very low priority. If Congress was beleaguered by constant requests for money, the whole question of the validity of this 'wilderness' site, still by no means settled in the public mind, might be opened again. Congress might choose to stay in established and civilized Philadelphia, or even New York. The Commissioners consequently needed ways of raising money without recourse to Congress.

If either the earlier Congressional schemes or Jefferson's own ideas had prevailed in 1791, there is little doubt that their small scale plans, which allowed room for later expansion, would have adequately fitted the practical requirements of the time. Jefferson's plans would have remained within the limits of the budget, and probably would have produced fine buildings for the President's House and Congress. But the urban settings would not have been as grand; above all, they would have entirely lacked magnificence, and the city would have been like any other – a grid, crowded and piecemeal.

To raise money, the Commissioners kept Ellicott constantly busy surveying individual public lots for auction. This prevented him from making precise surveys until 1793. As a result, inaccuracies crept into

The Secret Geometry of Washington, D.C.

Photo 9. The grave of L'Enfant in the Arlington National Cemetery.

his version of the plan. Early in 1794, Ellicott announced he would quit in May. He cited the 'extreme complexity' of the existing plan and the constant complaints by the Commissioners about the expense and slowness of the survey. Bickering and accusations of mistakes followed. In the end, Andrew and Benjamin Ellicott were dismissed in early 1794 and replaced by James Dermott. The Dermott Appropriation Map later became the legally recognized map of the city and was used throughout the nineteenth century, but again, the L'Enfant Plan was not substantially changed. Dermott was an ordinary draftsman in service to the Commissioners and without any sense of the vision which L'Enfant, Washington or even Ellicott had been trying to achieve.

L'Enfant went on to undertake several other projects, including the design of naval fortifications in Washington and the city of Paterson, New Jersey. He relied on his old war comrade, the President, to take care of his reputation and secure him suitable reimbursement for the task of designing the federal city. Washington died in 1799 before securing this remuneration, so L'Enfant prevailed on Congress to pay him his due. He claimed copyright and royalties on the fifteen to twenty thousand engravings sold by the city. But Congress did not pay him.

Finally, in 1810, a bill by Congress paid L'Enfant $666.66 for the design of the City of Washington. Why this figure was selected is unclear: a comment on L'Enfant's royal leanings? With interest, the amount became $1,394.20. L'Enfant's creditors took it all. In 1812, L'Enfant was offered a Professorship of Engineering, a paid post at the U.S. Military Academy, but he declined. By now he was largely ignored and even ridiculed in polite society for the pretentiousness of his fabled plan. It seems he was still hopelessly proud; but he was also broken by his ordeal. He remained loyal to the new state, but he was crushed by his betrayal by the two most powerful men in the country. It seems that from his neglect of all other concerns that he was only interested in preserving his honour and reputation. He became dependent upon the hospitality of friends, usually old war comrades. Thomas Digges of Warburton Manor, Maryland, wrote to Secretary of State James Monroe in 1816, 'The old major is still inmate with me – quiet, harmless, & unoffending as usual'. L'Enfant died, penniless, in 1825, at the age of 71.

DEPARTURES FROM THE L'ENFANT PLAN

Most writers on this topic have, it seems, compared the plans of L'Enfant and Ellicott and minimalized the differences between them. To be fair, a quick glance does not reveal much disparity. L'Enfant's design does appear to be preserved by Ellicott's plan. But a more thorough analysis, using the Golden Section template as its reference, shows the differences to be profound. As L'Enfant observed to Tobias Lear in February 1792, the Ellicott map meant that: 'all the lineaments of the ground from which the whole direction of avenues can alone be perceived [are] suppressed'. When the changes that happened immediately after L'Enfant's dismissal are supplemented by those that were introduced over succeeding decades, many departures from the original design emerge.

Massachusetts Avenue was straightened and reoriented, leaving only Mount Vernon Square (MV) and Lincoln Square (B) in their approximate original locations. This partly destroyed the Golden Section ratios through the removal of Square 'D' (now Union Station); and it also played havoc with the five-fold geometry of the pentacle in the eastern part of the city. The straightening of Massachusetts Avenue was already present in the Ellicott line drawing of December 1791. Once L'Enfant saw the drawings, this must have been a main cause of the fierce dispute between him and the Ellicott brothers.

The angle of orientation of Connecticut Avenue and Vermont Avenue radiating north from the White House was changed from sixty to fifty degrees. When this was combined with the change in location of Massachusetts Avenue, and thus of Dupont Circle (DC) and Logan Circle (LC), as well as other squares, the geometry of the equilateral triangle was lost. A sharper arrow now points at the White House.

New surveys of Pennsylvania Avenue, Maryland Avenue, New Jersey Avenue and Delaware Avenue meant that the correlation of these avenues to the Golden Section geometry was also diminished. Some squares and avenues were completely removed, any irregularities were straightened, and small changes were made to most avenues. Judiciary Square was made much smaller. The public land north of the President's House was halved. The squares were not dedicated to the States. Some of the changes were intentional; some were introduced by the exigencies of the situation. President Andrew Jackson (1829–1837), for example, supposedly obscured the view along Pennsylvania Avenue with an extension of the Treasury, as he did not want to see the Capitol.

Jefferson made sure that any references to the National Church site; the Mile Column; the grand fountains; the Grand Avenue; the cascade that was to flow before the Capitol; the arcaded streets and arched ways; and the meridian line through Congress; were either not put on the map or were not part of any building program. He was now firmly in control, and more especially so when he became President. Although public expense was also his concern, he removed anything that hinted of religion.

L'Enfant's conviction that the federal and civic buildings, the memorials and the national monuments must be distributed throughout the city, and interspersed by residential and commercial areas, was not understood and was forgotten. Most of the federal buildings were eventually located in the 'Federal Triangle' between Pennsylvania Avenue and the Mall. As a consequence, federal workers today endure serious traffic congestion in their commute. When they are not at work, and the museums and galleries close, the center of the city is strictly formal and effectively dead. Both the buildings and their daytime occupants have become isolated, referring only to themselves and the federal triangle, not to the wider city and the outside world.

The commercial plans for the eastern half of the city were never developed. The great designs for East Capitol Street, including the 'Mile Column' intended for what became Lincoln Square, were not realized. City Hall was not built at Square 'A'. The District Courts were not built at Square 'D'. The Supreme Court was not built in the location L'Enfant intended for it, but beside the Capitol on Jenkins Hill. With this, the symbolic independence of the court which L'Enfant had tried so hard to preserve was lost. As described below, a new Mile Stone was later placed beside the White House.

Finally, and perhaps most significantly, the development of the north–south axis through the White House, and the emphasis upon the Mall and the Washington Monument, took centrality away from the Capitol. The avenues of the city no longer radiated outward; they were turned around to look within.

'UNMERCIFULLY SPOILED'

In his letter of February 22, 1792, L'Enfant complained to Jefferson that sufficient evidence for the destruction of 'the harmony and combination of the different parts [of his plan] with the whole' could be seen by the 'ill-judged stand now of the Capitol and presidential [house]'. The geometrical study makes it possible to understand what L'Enfant meant by this.

The new White House was too small and located too far south, and so was unable to occupy the whole site L'Enfant had intended for it. The Capitol was also much smaller than he had wanted it to be. As a result, the points where the avenues converged upon these structures were altered, so that they and the measures between them were no longer in the geometrically harmonious relationship that L'Enfant had wished they should have to everything else.

Given that the ratios of the Golden Section are adjudged by architects to create the most harmonious and pleasing proportions, it is not surprising that L'Enfant singled out the altered stand of these buildings as the most compelling evidence for the destruction of 'the harmony and combination of the different parts with the whole'. The relationship that these buildings enjoyed to the whole was defined by the Golden Section proportions of the plan. When these changes, however small, are combined with the loss of Square 'D', the loss of the Mile Column, and the numerous adjustments to all the squares and avenues, the hidden ratios of the Golden Section in the plan were indeed, as L'Enfant protested to Jefferson, 'most unmercifully spoiled'.

From this perspective, it makes sense to say that although Ellicott appeared to most people to have made only minor changes, in a rationalization and simplification of the plan, to L'Enfant the changes that drew his most bitter complaints were those that distorted the geometrical ratios of the city as a whole. 'I cannot disguise to you', L'Enfant wrote on March 10, 1792 to the Proprietors of the territory within the Federal

City, 'that much has already been attempted by the contrivance of an erroneous map of the city about to be published, which partly copied from the original, has afterwards been mangled and altered in a shameful manner in its most essential parts'.

Essentially, the ever-practical Ellicotts, as well as Dermott after them, straightened streets into lines for convenient engineering. They were not concerned with the subtle diversity of the design, or the texture of the architectural fabric, that was to have created grand and interesting visual effects; they were only concerned with the straight cut. They made the public squares neat and symmetrical. None of these men had L'Enfant's experience of Europe, where architectural variety meant urban elegance, human involvement and intimate dimensions, and thus the creation of lively, warm, interesting and people-friendly spaces. No one, it seems, save L'Enfant, realized the planning wisdom of integrating civic, arts and commercial facilities with the federal and the residential areas so that each could serve as a catalyst for the continuing vitality of the other parts, and thus of the city as a whole. While L'Enfant saw his city as a vibrant architectural space in three and more dimensions, subsequent planners saw only a surveyor's city – two-dimensional and flat.

THE NEW MERIDIAN

I was particularly taken aback when I learnt that, in the winter of 1793, L'Enfant's intended zero meridian through the Capitol was abandoned and a new zero meridian was established through the White House, along 16th Street.

Thomas Jefferson personally surveyed and marked the new meridian with a wooden post at the point where it intersected the east–west axis of the city. He replaced this post in 1804, during his term as President, with a monument known as the Jefferson Pier – the axial crossing then being close to the Potomac River. At the same time, a stone was placed on the high ground about a mile and a half north of the White House, which became known as Meridian Hill. In effect, Jefferson removed the markers for the prime, zero-degree, north–south meridian from the Capitol and placed them on the new line of longitude through the White House.

In 1890 a stone called the 'Meridian Stone' was placed at the center of the Ellipse, just south of the White House. And then, curiously, the mile marker intended for Lincoln Square was also moved onto this meridian. In 1923, a 'Zero Milestone' was placed on the north side of the Ellipse. All distances from the capital were now to be measured from here. Expeditions across the continent would later set off in motor cars from this point. And in the same way as the prime meridian marking the center of the New World Order was moved from the Capitol, so the marker and measurer of all distances within the continent was moved from L'Enfant's Square 'B'. On the wintry day when I visited the Zero Milestone, I felt certain that this stone – the final result of the original intention to create a Mile Column – had ended up in the wrong place.

Both the placement of the Mile Stone here, rather than through the original Mile Column, and the definition of the zero-degree longitudinal meridian through the north–south Presidential axis, rather than through the Capitol, were part of the general shift of emphasis towards the Washington Monument. These acts accorded symbolic centrality in the city to the Presidency. Jefferson's actions in 1793 and 1804 were not just an affirmation of the view of sight along the Potomac from the White House. In spite of Jefferson's republican credentials, he knew exactly what he was doing. The relocation of the zero meridian through the White House was an astonishingly deliberate attempt to alter the symbolic balance of power between the Executive and the Legislature. Jefferson Pier, the monument at the new intersection of the axes, now marked the heart of the city, although it was soon to be replaced by the Washington Monument.

THE McMILLAN COMMISSION

Yet as Washington slowly expanded to fill the 'wilderness' and 'magnificent distances' of the L'Enfant Plan, an appreciation for the inaugural vision of the French architect grew with it. In 1909, the remains of L'Enfant were exhumed and reinterred, with full honors, at the Arlington National Cemetery. From there his grave commands a fine view over the city he did so much to create (see Photo 9). From careful study of his letters and documents it also became clear to many researchers that, however unbearable his temperament may have been to his contemporaries, the architect was single-mindedly devoted to the realization of his goal. That he was able to accomplish so much in the space of just over a year, in the creation of the nation's capital and not for personal gain, speaks volumes both for the essential integrity and strength of L'Enfant's character, and also for the power of his vision.

The eventual vindication of L'Enfant's reputation was partly occasioned by the realization, at the end of the nineteenth century, that the architectural character of the national capital was in crisis. A catalogue of disasters had befallen the city in the last one hundred years, including the burning of the Capitol and the White House by the British in 1814; the Civil War; neglect from unsympathetic legislatures; and the occupation of parts of the city by some of the most disenfranchised members of society. It was clear that mistakes had been made and that new guidelines were needed if these errors were not to be compounded. It was concluded that the best way to restore the city was to return to the plan originally conceived by the Frenchman. The L'Enfant Plan was revived in 1901–02 by the McMillan Commission and thereafter by the Senate Park Commission and the NCPC, the National Capital Planning Commission. Members of the Commission included the landscape architect Frederick Law Olmsted, Jr. and the architects Charles McKim and Daniel Burnham. The report of the members of the McMillan Commission declared that:

> The more they studied the first plan for the Federal City, the more they became convinced that the greatest service they could perform would be done by carrying to a legitimate conclusion the comprehensive, intelligent, and yet simple and straightforward scheme devised by L'Enfant under the direction of Washington and Jefferson.

The Commission's goals included the creation of a Mall whose character would go far beyond L'Enfant's design for a 'Grand Avenue ... bordered with gardens'. It would be a park, lined by rows of trees, museums and galleries, surrounded by great buildings and completed by monuments. Most visitors to Washington today would agree that the Mall serves as the formal, ceremonial and symbolic heart of the city. In fact, the Commission's plan for the Mall went through many stages of delay before it could be completed; only through the determination of generations of architects and politicians – including Presidents Theodore Roosevelt and William Taft – did it achieve its present magnificent form.

One insurmountable difficulty in furthering the restoration of the L'Enfant Plan was the unsightly projection of the Treasury Department Building into the line of Pennsylvania Avenue. Work on the Treasury had begun in 1836 and nothing could now be done about its obstruction of the avenue. But the problem of the mislocation of the Washington Monument was successfully resolved by realigning the entire Mall, and all subsequent buildings along it, to a new east–west axis. The Monument, begun in 1848, had to be moved to a location – 123 feet south and 372 feet east of the actual axial crossing, the Jefferson Pier – at a point where the ground could support its great weight. The visitor to Washington today is not aware, until they look closely at a map, that the Mall is oriented over a degree and a half from the true east–west axis of the city. Over time, the Mall was cleared of the railroad tracks, stations and other poorly located buildings that had filled the space, and was given a formal planting scheme.

The ideas of the Commission were furthered with the construction of the Lincoln Memorial to the west of the Mall, dedicated in 1922, and the Jefferson Memorial to the south of the Mall, dedicated in 1943. The construction of both these monuments was accompanied by considerable controversy. Yet tellingly, both are located on the L'Enfant Plan at coordinates that confirm and extend the geometry of the underlying Golden Section template. In L'Enfant's day they would have been in the Potomac River. (See Figures 42 and 53.) The McMillan Commission evidently followed L'Enfant's geometry where possible; however, criticism of these monuments included questions over the appropriateness of their neoclassical style and of the architectonic introspectiveness they created in their respective locations. The view along the Potomac from the White House, for example, which both L'Enfant and Washington had felt to be particularly important, was now obscured. The main north–south axis was now through the White House and the Jefferson Memorial instead of through the Capitol. The Lincoln Memorial extended the main east–west axis of the city only to the west. The two

Photo 10   *The Jefferson Memorial*

The Secret Geometry of Washington, D.C.

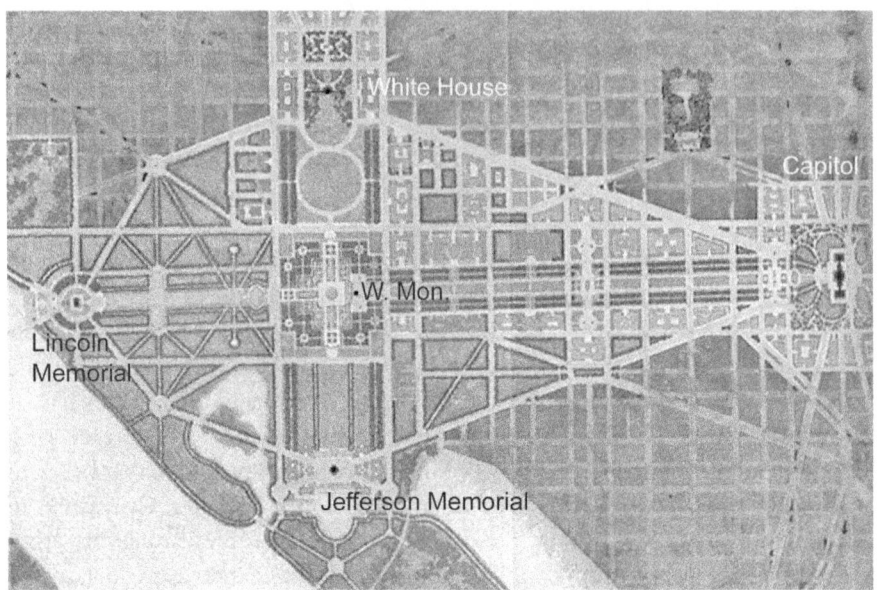

Figure 51. The proposals of the McMillan Commission made a great cross out of the Mall and centered the city upon the Washington Monument.

axes made a great cross through the Washington Monument, and this new focal point was enhanced by formal construction and planting schemes. Instead of being open to the natural features surrounding the city, the placing of the new memorials around the Mall increased the tendency of the center of government, and the city as a whole, to look inwards upon itself. The focus of visual attention in the city was now unmistakeably on the area designated for the Presidency.

It is often a surprise to visitors of the Federal Capital to discover that both the Capitol building and the White House actually look outwards. The assumption is usually made that the main facades of each of these buildings face the Mall. So strongly an emphasis has been placed upon the Mall as the city's center that it often comes as a shock to visitors when they realise that only small entrances open from these buildings onto the Mall, and that they were deliberately designed to open outwards, in L'Enfant's plan, to the rest of the city.

William T. Partridge, consulting architect of the National Capital Park and Planning Commission set up to continue the work of the McMillan Commission in the 1930s, studied the changes that had been made to the L'Enfant Plan over the last century and concluded: 'To an architectural mind the alterations in question destroyed the unity and symmetry of the whole'. Partridge was referring to the fact that the city L'Enfant had designed to look out over the surrounding landscape had now been turned to look in upon itself. Instead of its center being at the Capitol, the new center of Washington was now at the Washington Monument. The avenues that were originally intended to radiate outward and so connect the federal center to the people and the states of the Republic, had been symbolically turned inwards and their vistas had become closed. As other buildings went up, especially in the Federal Triangle, these either faced into the Mall or were erected to face each other. The outcome of the years of work carried out by the McMillan Commission meant the Mall became the central and the dominant feature of the city. See Figure 55 on page 180.

Henry Bacon, architect of the Lincoln Memorial, summarised the situation in 1911 when he proudly said the Lincoln Memorial, the Washington Monument and the Capitol, 'will lend, one to the others, the associations and memories connected with each, and each will have its value increased by being on the one axis and having visual relation to the other'.

After the efforts of restoration, however, and in spite of the McMillan Commission's misplaced emphasis on the federal triangle, the city of today is still fundamentally imprinted by the 'lineaments' of the original design. Washington is still, in many ways, the city of L'Enfant. Many different influences have created the character of the city which in 1791–92 was only a vision in the minds of a few far-seeing men. But it is still remarkable that so much of the geometrical order laid down by Pierre Charles L'Enfant has been maintained or restored despite contrary circumstances and deliberate opposition.

9

The Washington Monument

E PLURIBUS UNUM

This chapter argues that there is a close connection between the creation of the Washington Monument and the L'Enfant Plan for Washington, D.C. Designed within sixty years of each other, both employ the ancient symbolic principles of sacred geometry; yet whereas there is no positive proof of the deliberate use of these skills in the L'Enfant Plan, the Washington Monument contains symbolic measures that are far too explicit to be anything other than deliberately employed.

Congress authorized the monument in 1800–01 following an initial resolution of 1783 to erect 'an equestrian statue of George Washington'. At that time the Senate did not approve the $200,000 appropriation, so nothing further was done about it, perhaps because of some unease over the nature of the proposed designs. A proposal made in 1799, for example, called for a marble pyramid, one-hundred feet square at the base and this would have been entirely out of place. Other proposals included a 'mausoleum' modelled on the original at Halicarnassus, considered one of the Seven Wonders of the Ancient World. This was a huge square platform surmounted by a colonnade and then a pyramid with a quadriga – horses and chariot with king inside – on top. Mausolus had been a Hellenistic despot claiming divine legitimation, so it seems probable that this proposal was considered inappropriate. However, the Freemasons later based their Washington D.C. temple on this design, as I described in Chapter 7. L'Enfant himself had supported the original intent of Congress to erect an equestrian statue of the President. But by 1833 proposals were being made for an entirely different structure – an Egyptian-influenced obelisk. It is not entirely clear who thought of this first, but the architect Robert Mills is usually credited. His grand scheme of 1845 called for a six-hundred foot shaft surrounded by a one-hundred foot high circular colonnade, upon which could go a chariot and horses. Perhaps the President was to have been placed discreetly in the chariot, like a conquering emperor!

The Washington Monument

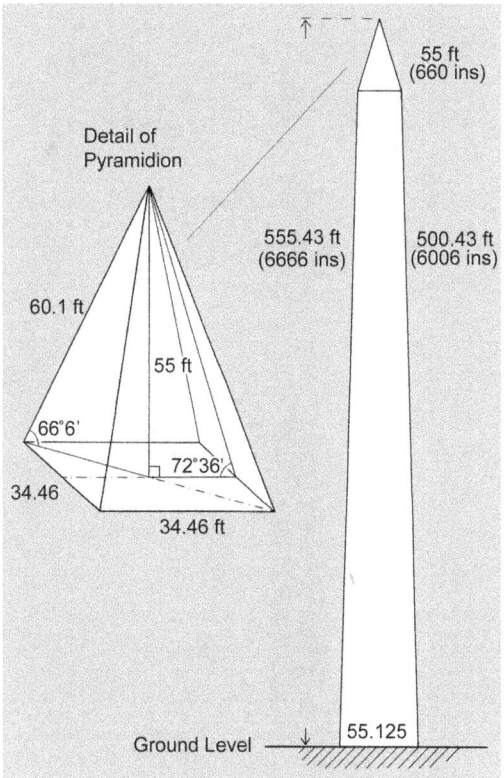

Figure 52. Monument Geometry.

In 1833 a group of private citizens, many of them Freemasons, had formed the Washington National Monument Association and solicited subscriptions. By 1848, there were sufficient funds to begin construction of the obelisk. The cornerstone was laid on July 4 of that year, with the Grand Master of the Grand Lodge of the District, Benjamin B. French, presiding, attended by large numbers of Masons. The available funds proved to be insufficient for the colonnade and quadriga, so they were – fortunately – abandoned, but the obelisk went ahead. However, the engineers in charge of the project found that the site that had been chosen, which was located on the intersection of the axes through the White House and the Capitol, was inadequate to provide a substantial foundation for this extremely heavy structure. So they moved the obelisk back from what was then the Potomac shore at the mouth of the Tiber to slightly higher and firmer ground. A smaller monument, commissioned by Thomas Jefferson and subsequently known as Jefferson

The Secret Geometry of Washington, D.C.

Photo 11. The Washington Monument.

Pier, was built to mark the actual point of intersection, but this is no longer in existence. The Mall was later realigned to the monument in a way that skewed it from the main east–west axis of the L'Enfant design.

The funds for this project continued to be limited, and after several long delays to construction, which included the Civil War, Congress finally stepped in and made an appropriation in 1876. The Washington Monument was finally dedicated in 1885 (Grand Master Benjamin B. French once again participated in the dedication ceremonies), and was opened to the public in 1888.

The Washington Monument is the tallest freestanding masonry structure in the world. Embedded in the internal walls of the shaft are ashlars — squared blocks — inscribed by the States of the Union who sent them. Ashlars from other sources also appear. There are many from the various Masonic lodges around the nation. One was even sent by the Pope, but this disappeared in 1855; it was probably stolen and smashed. A suspicion that this was done by anti-Catholic Freemasons contributed to the circumstances that caused work on the monument to be delayed, but the greatest factor in the delay of the construction was the Civil War. When work was resumed after the war, the stone used in construction was of a slightly different shade than that below, adding a discrete memorial of the effect of that conflict on the nation in the fabric of the monument.

The dimensions of the monument are as follows: The shaft has a height of 500.427 feet. The breadth of each side is 55.125 feet at the base, and 34.458 feet at the top. The pyramidion that forms the point of the obelisk has a height of 55 feet. This includes an aluminum pyramid on the tip that is 5.6 inches square and 8.9 inches high. The total height is therefore 555 feet 5.125 inches (although some sources say this should be 555 feet 6 inches), slightly more than ten times the breadth of the base.

The angle of slope of each face of the pyramidion is 72 degrees 36 seconds or 72.6 degrees. This is over half a degree more than the 72-degree angle present in the five-sided pentagon or pentacle. It seems curious that the 72.6-degree angle was chosen, when an angle of exactly 72 degrees would have placed the monument's pyramidion in the realm of the harmonious and 'perfect' proportions of Golden Section geometry. Certainly the fives in the measures of the monument appear to relate it to the pentacle and Golden Section geometry.

In the discussion of the pentacle in the L'Enfant Plan of the city, I suggested that aspects of *gematria*, or numerological symbolism, inform the design, above all, the selection of the angle of 55 degrees between certain avenues. The pentacle is the symbol, *phi* is the proportion and 5 or 55 is the number representing the elements, the senses, and the matrix of animate life. Although there is no direct evidence that the Freemasons, who would certainly have been aware of such things, were involved with the L'Enfant Plan, they were directly involved with commissioning the design of the Washington Monument. It seems very likely that the decision to make the monument 555 feet 5+ inches high was influenced by one or a number of the branches of Freemasonry that existed in the city at that time. These men would have had specific symbolism and meanings in mind that related to the number 5. Why the precise angle of the five-pointed pentacle or the pentalpha,

72 degrees, was not used for the crowning pyramidion seems therefore to pose us with something of a mystery.

Yet by considering the dimensions of the monument in inches we can solve the mystery. The obelisk's total height in inches is 6665.125+, which can be justifiably rounded up to 6666. The height of its pyramidion in inches is 660. The sides of its base in inches are 661.5. Then it is necessary to consider the angle of slope from the four corners of the base to the tip of the pyramidion. This is exactly 66 degrees 6 seconds, revealing the hidden number 666.

6666 and 666, like 66, 6, 660 and 60, are solar numbers and are connected with the circle and its six-fold geometry. In Islamic numerology, 66 is the numerical equivalent of Allah. In Judaism, the six-pointed star or hexagram is the 'Seal of Solomon'. It appears in every branch of Freemasonry. The associated 666 gains its notoriety in the West as the number of misused power and authority mentioned in the Book of Revelation; but more traditionally, 666 represents the solar principle. It is also a number of Christ. The sun, 666, shining from above, is the power that gives order to the chaos of earth. It is the masculine principle in action. Only if this power is misused will it lead to abuse. It was this unbalanced manifestation of 666 that the author of *Revelation* identified with the Antichrist or the 'Beast'. It is for this reason that 666 has come to be identified with concepts of the satanic, or extreme negativity, but this was emphatically not its original meaning.

As described in Chapter 7, L'Enfant appears to have favored six-fold geometry and 666 measures in his plan of the city around the White House. The monument to Washington was to be located 4 × 666 yards from the Capitol. An association with six – the number of the sun, action and authority – was most appropriate for the head of the hierarchy of government. And since towers have traditionally been associated with the sun, so the selection of an obelisk was also appropriate for this, the Executive section of the city. In Islamic architecture, the minaret – 'the place where light shines' – emphasizes the vertical, transcendent dimension of god. In ancient Egypt, the obelisk symbolised the rays of the sun.

The surprisingly exact manifestation of 6 or 666 in the various measures of the Washington Monument suggests these numbers were intentionally chosen by its architects and designers – men who either were themselves Freemasons or were influenced by this fraternity. Evidently, the numbers were seen as having greater primary significance in the monument of a President – who was himself a Freemason – than did Golden Section proportions and their accompanying measures. The highest initiation a Freemason can achieve is defined by half of sixty-

The Washington Monument

six, that is, the thirty-third degree. Furthermore, the lengths of the sides of the pyramidion, from the corners of the base to the tip are approximately 60 feet. This number, along with 666 and the other six-based numbers, was seemingly selected to emphasize the six-fold symbology of the monument.

In fact the Washington Monument is a complex allegory in numbers. Created under the influence of the self-proclaimed inheritors of the ancient architectural tradition, the Freemasons, it stands foursquare, the foundation of the temple. Any visible face of the pyramidion is a triangle, representing, among many things, the Trinity, or the dividers in the hand of the Supreme Architect. The Monument represents the single pillar of the nation, its lands and people, who are symbolised by the five-fold measures and the inscribed ashlars of each State in the shaft. It thus embodies in stone the national motto *E Pluribus Unum*, 'From Many, One'. Finally, the single pillar surmounted by the pyramidion has measures that fuse the numbers 5 and 555 with those of 6 and 666. 555 is the number of diversity and animate life. It is the earthly and lunar number. 666 is the authoritative and solar number of the head of the hierarchy, the President. It is particularly the number of the first, the founding President of the land.

666 and 1080

It is tempting to play with the numbers of the Washington Monument a little further. Some adjustment to the proportion seems to have been made to affect the numerical symbolism. For example, the height of the shaft is 500.427 feet. Why not exactly 500 feet or 6000 inches? If the object of the geometry was to reconcile 5 and 6, this would have seemed a good solution. However, to make the all important 66 degree 6 minute angles come out right, the designers needed that extra 0.427+ feet or $5\frac{1}{8}$ inches to add to the total height of the monument, and the pyramidion had to be precisely 55 feet in height, given a base of 34.458 feet. It is intriguing to note that the extra inches, when added to the length of a side at the base of the shaft, 55.125 feet, and the length of a side of the base of the pyramidion, 34.458 feet, add up to 90 feet.

$$55.125 + 34.458 + 0.427 = 90.01$$

Once again, these are strange numbers, as an even 55 feet for the base of the shaft would have yielded 660 inches. The intention of these minute adjustments is subtle however. For in the same way as the height of the Monument only reveals its meaning when given in inches, so the

90 feet measurement also reveals its full meaning when given in inches – 1080. This number is equal in importance to 666 in *gematria*. It is the feminine, lunar and earthly number, the polar opposite of the number of the sun. 1080 is a number found in the angles of the pentacle, and it is highly appropriate to the measures of the shaft, whose ashlars represent the unity of the American nation. By adjusting the measures of the monument by a tenth of one percent, the Freemasons who designed the Washington Monument imbued it with a profoundly rich numerical symbolism.

10

'... That harmony and combination of the different parts with the whole'

AN ARCHITECT'S IMAGINATION?

Throughout the years after I conducted my original research, both when I lived in the USA and after I returned to Britain, I thought long and hard about the striking commensurability of the L'Enfant Plan for Washington, D.C. with an ancient and universal system of geometric order. Many authorities have commented on L'Enfant's use of major avenues linking the different centers of American power in the city, seeing this as an appropriate pattern for a federalist system of government. But did the obvious features of the design point to an even more profound allegory in proportion, measure and number, hidden in the original dimensions of the American national capital? If so, what evidence was there of intentionality in the striking use of traditional symbolism and sacred geometry on the part of Washington's architect? What evidence was there for early Masonic involvement? And finally, what had the departures from the original plan meant for the city? These final chapters may raise more questions than they answer.

In the previous chapters, I have described how I became convinced that the proportions of the original L'Enfant Plan of 1791 were derived from the Golden Section – a principle employed in the ancient tradition of sacred geometry and architecture. In support of this, I could have argued that L'Enfant probably became familiar with these principles as a result of his early life and study in France. There, during the ascendancy of neoclassical aesthetics and the 'Age of Enlightenment', when writers such as Voltaire and Rousseau were stimulating democratic ideals and philosophical freethinking, there was an esoteric revival. L'Enfant revealed this influence – with its Masonic undertones – in his work in

New York. Yet during his work in the city of Washington, L'Enfant makes no mention, in any surviving written document, about traditional and geometric symbolism. Instead, he always insists upon the originality of his work. And, apart from his use of the sixty-degree equilateral triangle, he actually diverged significantly from any existing city plan in his use of the Golden Section. How can this be explained?

L'Enfant was conservative in his character, but he had a radical outlook. Born into a world of gentility and *noblesse oblige*, he was nonetheless deeply inspired by the ideals and the revolutionary spirit of his age. Throughout the eighteenth century many intellectuals and artists were abandoning established cultural and social values and looking to new sources of creative inspiration. Nowhere was this sea-change more keenly felt than in pre-republican France and in the emerging USA. L'Enfant had fought in the War of Independence, not because as a Frenchman he opposed the British, but because he passionately believed in the American cause and the possibilities it presented to him and many others. He wasn't interested in the prevailing artistic conventions that saw nature merely as the setting for biblical scenes or the palaces of monarchs. He wasn't interested in serving the existing status quo. He wanted to do something new, and America offered that chance to him. And when the time came to use his skills in the service of his new land, he rejected the imitation of traditional ideas. His plan for Washington, as he so significantly emphasised, was 'wholy new'. This was to be a plan appropriate to a *Novus Ordo Seclorum*; or, to mistranslate, a 'new and *secular* order of the ages'. Determined to reject European aesthetic and cultural patterns based upon imperialist doctrines and traditional religious values, L'Enfant infused and revitalized his architectural thinking with the increasingly republican and rational idealism of the new world, but also with an innovative relationship to nature, inspired by his and his contemporaries' deeply felt experience of the American landscape.

In a brief but highly significant comment, L'Enfant told George Washington that his goal was 'a sense of the real grand and truly beautiful only to be met with where nature contributes with art and diversify the objects'. Despite the incorrect use of his non-native language, this remark speaks volumes about L'Enfant's aesthetic intentions. Romantic ideas of nature as a sublime and powerful force, rather than the picturesque experience admired in the mid-eighteenth century, were coming into vogue at this time. Rousseau had pioneered the concept of the sublime in nature in France; in Britain, Wordsworth and Coleridge revealed a new creative power in nature in their *Lyrical Ballads*. Jefferson used

> '... That harmony and combination of the different parts with the whole'

similar terminology in his *Notes on the state of Virginia* of 1782. When combined with ideas bequeathed by the neoclassical tradition, such as that of the *genius loci* – the spirit of place – or the *anima mundi* – the world soul – a new sense of nature's power was beginning to provide a potent creative impetus for writers, artists and designers both in Europe and America. In the same year that L'Enfant prepared his design for the Federal City, 1791, American botanist William Bartram published his *Travels*, which introduced his countrymen to an entirely new aesthetic appreciation of the natural world. 'I approached a charming vale', wrote Bartram, 'amidst sublimely high forests, awful shades! darkness gathers round, far distant thunder rolls over the trembling hills; the black clouds with august majesty and power, move slowly forwards ...'. The architect Benjamin Latrobe would soon combine neoclassical forms with those drawn from the natural abundance of the American continent in his famous 'tobacco and corn cob' designs for the Capitol. This aesthetic impetus would peak in the middle of the nineteenth century with the American Romantic artists such as Thomas Cole, Thomas Moran and Albert Bierstadt, and in later American authors such as Thoreau and Whitman. Yet L'Enfant, the architect and visionary, appears to have anticipated these cultural changes. His philosophical and political radicalism respected the capacities of every individual, whatever their social status; it also re-evaluated and honoured the spiritual, ethical and aesthetic powers of nature. Freed from the mental shackles of church and state, each person in the new land was now at liberty to behave like a god in their personal world, capable of almost anything. The Romantics in general were finding a new aesthetic inspiration in the beauty of the untamed natural world; in America, however, nature was being identified as the powerful force that would shape the nation's destiny.

I have often thought it a shame that L'Enfant never had the opportunity to design the great public buildings, monuments, parks and statuary of Washington, D.C., since he might have introduced features that accurately captured the qualities of the newly-born American spirit of the age. It is hard to define this spirit; but it was acutely concerned both with the land or nature and also with the values of the individual: independence, equality, liberty and freedom. As described in Chapter 3, these values were central to the earliest mythos of the emerging country and had appeared early on in its symbols of self-definition. The goddess Columbia, as an embodiment of this national spirit, was seen as a force of nature emerging from the wilderness, striving for self-definition, freedom and living space in the new land. In her later, more sophisticated forms, Columbia became a neoclassical goddess of liberty, concord, peace and justice. If L'Enfant's intended parks, vistas and 'greenways', and his statuary for the Capitol: the 'Altar of Liberty' and his monumental cascade 'Liberty hailing Nature out of its slumber', had been realized, they would have made the French architect her champion.

Many late eighteenth-century Americans turned to the aesthetics of the sublime in their search for a language to comprehend and evoke the vast and majestic landscapes of their new continent. As a way of illustrating these nascent American values, there sometimes appear to be two prevailing views on how creative forces operate in the world. One, the transcendent view, sees creation from the top down; the other, the immanent view, sees it from the bottom up. The 'top down' view holds that God or a hierarchy of powers operating from some other realm emanates these principles and so creates and brings order to the world. A greater transcendent order is thus behind the physical world, which is just a 'shadow' of the divine world, and is therefore – according to Christianity and the other revealed religions – in a lesser or 'fallen' state. This worldview tends to be identified with oligarchies, monarchies and other forms of hierarchical power. The 'bottom up' view holds that the creation or life itself manifests these ordering principles. Molecules, cells, organisms, trees, rivers, hills, oceans, planets and galaxies – however chaotic they may appear – unfold themselves in accord with the ratios of the divine, and every individual enacts and expresses these principles in their actions. Here an immanent plurality of ordering principles coexist; one interpretation of them is no more correct than another. Diversity is the law when this worldview prevails; it therefore tends to develop participatory, egalitarian and democratic political forms.

These opposing – but not uncomplementary – views on the nature of life, order and government have profound implications for the way the world is seen: how it was thought to be created, how it should be governed, and how a scientist or an artist may work within it. In the late eighteenth century, the differences between these two worldviews came to a head on both sides of the Atlantic in the social struggle between evolving democratic forms and established systems of power. Did sovereignty reside in each individual person or was it concentrated in one divinely sanctioned ruler? The Americans had successfully fought their War of Independence to secure liberty from kingly rule and the French faced a painful revolution over the same issue.

From his ideas and writings, such as his reports to President Washington, it is evident that although L'Enfant was an idealist and a gentleman, he was also a soldier, an engineer and a man of action. He

> '... That harmony and combination of the different parts with the whole'

was also an individualist and an iconoclast in that he rejected the imperialist and religious values of old Europe. Nowhere in any of his writings does L'Enfant say he applied predetermined geometrical principles, or any religious, Masonic or neoclassical ideas, or that he ever favored any existing city plan, or any specific metaphysical point of view. On the contrary, the evidence suggests he took pains to reject such patterns; declaring for example that he did not need Jefferson's plans of European cities. He always insisted upon the originality of his views. Despite his innate aristocratic tendencies (tendencies that were ultimately to be his downfall), L'Enfant wanted no part of the religious, monarchic, imperialist and Old World values that his new nation had so recently liberated itself from. His sympathies entirely lay with American ideals of the new democratic Republic and also with the newly emerging sense of their national destiny being linked with the natural power of the vast landscape. He sought to express those ideals in a design for a new visionary city. When he found the basis for this design in the naturally occurring ratios of the Golden Section, true to his inflexible character, he would not tolerate any departure from the order that made the design a whole.

Sir Christopher Wren, working as an architect over a hundred years before L'Enfant, had no formal training or Masonic initiation. Wren is said to have drawn his plan for the rebuilding of London after the Great Fire from direct observation of the patterns of the natural world. It is my belief that L'Enfant, like Wren, found the inspiration for his architectural forms in nature. L'Enfant observed, surveyed, drew and lived with the landscape during his many years in the Revolutionary Army and he quickly took to the location that was to become the City of Washington. As many writers have remarked, in the 1790s L'Enfant was at the height of his physical powers – nature, perception, imagination, intuition, mind and body worked as one. He had fought in the war, received a wound, been imprisoned by the British, dined with the generals and been befriended by the powerful. By now his personal beliefs wholly conformed to his experience of the forming of the new American nation. He imposed no grid or preconceived mental order on the landscape, and he abandoned aesthetic conventions that narrowed artistic expression into the service of a monarchy, or class-conscious ideas such as the 'picturesque'. In his search for 'the real grand and truly beautiful' it seems that L'Enfant found in the landscape of Goose Creek and Jenkins Hill evocative, even sublime forms that were to shape a great, powerful and prosperous destiny for America. Thus L'Enfant appears to have incorporated the geometry of the forms of nature intuitively – if not entirely intentionally – into his grand design, which then displayed a fresh interpretation of the canonical proportions of the Golden Section found in sacred geometry and in the philosophical traditions of the world.

Today, many scientists consider that the universe does not conform to a hierarchy of laws which by definition become more causal as they become simpler. They prefer to avoid the ultimate equation, the unifying theory – 'God' or the 'Big Bang' – to which everything can be reduced. Instead, they now think the universe (and with it the world) is much better approximated by a model of constant enfoldment toward and unfoldment away from regions of complexity upon complexity. Chaos Theory, for example, demonstrates that while the world can be reduced to mathematical theorems, in every case a variable – a tiny 'interfering' factor – will set unpredictable chains of causality into motion. Fractal models and those of quantum physics infer that the archetypal forms of Plato, or the high geometric principles of a cathedral, mosque or temple, or the laws of Newton and Einstein, do not originate in a fixed divine source 'over and above' the world, but, equally wonderfully, emerge as immanent principles working in a multiplicity of centers within it.

Ultimately, the whole question of the primacy of nature or the primacy of order – of matter or spirit – is probably irresolvable. Like complementary polarities, the two are as necessary for each other as a river and its bed. Which makes the other? By the same token, evidence may never be found that can confirm the specific sources of L'Enfant's inspiration. A traditional geometrical order clearly informs his design for the city; but the way in which it was used indicates an original and open approach – the hallmark of a true artist. L'Enfant worked sensitively with the topography of the landscape, the consciousness of the American people, and his own creative genius. As the architect crossed and recrossed the landscape of the future city, its diverse forms inspired a new and compelling synthesis of politics and place.

OR MASONIC INTENT?

If L'Enfant, as claimed above, was proceeding intuitively for the most part – if he was either unwilling or really unable to explain the meaning of the geometric principles inherent within his plan – then surely the same was not true for the Freemasons. The intentional deployment of Golden Section ratios, of *gematria* (numerology), of the pentacle and the equilateral triangle – of geometrically ideal orders – was their bread and butter. So did Masons watch over the planning of the creation

'... That harmony and combination of the different parts with the whole'

of the cosmogonic center of their new world in America? The evidence shows that they most certainly did. In the same way as the boundaries of the Federal District were perceived by the Freemasons of the time as worthy of demarcation with suitable rites, so the city and its 'temples' were honoured with equivalent and even greater attention. Major Masonic rituals attended the laying of the cornerstone of the President's House in October 1792, and the laying of the cornerstone of the Capitol in September 1793. The latter event was a massive ceremony attended by all the dignitaries of the day. The Masons with their tools and regalia conspicuously presided over the ceremony as its 'high priests'.

The members of the Fraternity of Freemasonry were potentially the most qualified to undertake the creation of the sophisticated symbolic design outlined in this book. If they were responsible, then their traditions would reveal the meaning of the design. Yet my study of Freemasonry revealed few clues. Above all, I could find no evidence that showed the Freemasons were involved in anything other than the dedication ceremonies in the early history of the city. And nothing in the ample available evidence that showed there were Masons in the region with knowledge of the geometric systems employed by L'Enfant at the time he prepared his plan.

If I assumed, for the sake of argument, that their geometrical traditions were at hand, and that Freemasons were influential in the design of the city, then I had to ask myself what evidence for actions or influence on their part could be found in the designs of 1791–1792? As they understood it, were they satisfied with the message encoded in the L'Enfant Plan? Did it accord with the mandate placed upon every Freemason to recreate the dimensions of the Temple of Solomon – itself based upon the dimensions of the Ark of the Covenant – in their work on earth? The evidence suggests it did not.

Phi, the Golden Section, the pentacle and the number 5 provide the predominant symbology of the L'Enfant Plan. These emphasize the dimensions of the earth, nature, the body, and the moon as well as the secular, humanistic and natural sciences. The Golden Section played a role in the dimensions of the Masonic Temple – especially in the branches which claimed to originate in Egypt – but where in L'Enfant's plan were the other heavenly ratios they esteemed so highly? Where were *pi*, the 6, the 8, the 12, and the other prescribed orders, measures and dimensions of heaven? Where were the square, the hexagram and the octagon? These were the familiar forms of the Temple: the cube of the New Jerusalem and of the Ark. Where too was the classic architectural resolution of the circle and the square? These were the predominant forms used by

Islamic and Jewish architects, the Freemasons, and their cousins the Rosicrucians and the Knights Templar, for their template for the heavenly city on earth. L'Enfant had no interest in any of them.

Admittedly, L'Enfant did place a triangle in his avenues, so moving toward the 6 in the measures around the White House. The Freemasons were attracted to the area of this numerical symbolism in many of their later designs. They made a long and concerted attempt to construct a huge Grand Lodge on one corner of the triangle. Eventually they placed a lodge in a position that bisected the triangle into two right-angled triangles – thereby approaching a fundamental Pythagorean Theorem through the geometry of the city. But I found no evidence that this temple – a truncated pyramid upon a cube – was intentionally related to the design of the city. What was more, it was built long after L'Enfant's work with the equilateral triangle had already been destroyed. In the measures of the Washington Monument the Masons undoubtedly elevated the number 6 and reconciled it with 5; but then again, the Washington Monument was designed long after L'Enfant.

Again, for the sake of argument, some members of the Masonic fraternity may have felt that the single downward-pointing, sixty-degree triangle formed by the radiating avenues of the L'Enfant Plan north of the White House focused too much power on the Presidency. Perhaps they thought that L'Enfant – under the influence of the hierarchical Alexander Hamilton – desired overly strong, monarchic powers for the Executive. After all, L'Enfant did call the original White House the 'Presidential Palace' on his map. If Thomas Jefferson was alert to and wanted to eliminate any monarchic pretensions such as these, then why did not any jealous Masons?

After L'Enfant's departure, it is just about conceivable that some Freemasons – perhaps even the District Commissioners – influenced Ellicott to alter L'Enfant's equilateral triangle. In his adjusted plan, Ellicott's avenues radiate at a rather less-than-imperial fifty degrees. In architectural tradition, when a sharp triangle points at a building in this manner it is considered to exert a limiting influence rather than an expansive one. In other words, Connecticut and Vermont Avenues depart from the original design to radiate out from the north of the White House in a manner calculated to limit Presidential power rather than enhance it. But once again, I could find no evidence that this change was intentional. Ellicott appears to have made his decision to alter the angle of the avenues on engineering grounds alone.

Perhaps there were Freemasons behind the mysterious removal of L'Enfant's papers early in 1792? Could it have been they who supplied

'... That harmony and combination of the different parts with the whole'

them to Ellicott with the instructions to alter the geometrical dimensions of the city? If so, this would have provided me with the necessary evidence. Yet Ellicott did not only alter the angle of the White House triangle, his work after L'Enfant's dismissal also damaged the *phi* proportions of the city. The triangle and the suggestion of the 6 completely disappear in his plan, and the pentacles are diminished. The Ellicott Plan, although on the surface more precise, does not contain any of the proportions of traditional geometry; nor does it advance any metaphysical symbolism. The introduction of the narrow triangle pointing at the White House seems therefore to reveal more ignorance than malignant intent. If any Masons were behind the change, they were more likely acting from material self-interest as landowners or property developers rather than from the wish to manipulate symbols.

Any suggestion that Ellicott and the Freemasons might have opposed L'Enfant on the grounds of conflicting symbolism, and stole his papers to further their ends, is therefore most unlikely. Ellicott was not a Freemason but a Quaker; presumably his brother Benjamin was one also. However, Ellicott did do one unusual thing for a Quaker, by accepting the military rank of Major. He also attended the Masonic dedication ceremonies, and his directors, George Washington and two of the District Commissioners, were Freemasons. Yet the changes made by Ellicott to the plan of the city are those of a pragmatic engineer. If it were true that the Commissioners ordered the theft of the papers, it was not with the intent of altering the plan, but to get around the delay in publication so that lots could be sold and money generated to further the construction of the city. Furthermore, as a hugely powerful politician and popular Mason, George Washington had the near unanimous support of the Masonic fraternity. If they supported him, then just as he supported L'Enfant, he supported all his brothers in the Lodges with numerous appointments and contracts. There was, after all, a great deal of money to be made in the development of the Federal City.

To give the Washington Freemasons their due, perhaps they did not know how to interpret the L'Enfant Plan. Possibly there was conflict or confusion among them over its interpretation. The District Commissioners interpreted it one way, the Grand Masters – if any were available – another. Perhaps, in contrast to L'Enfant's fluid, intuitive 'lineaments', they had expected something more easily recognizable, more formulaic. If they had noticed it, L'Enfant's emphasis on the Golden Section would have probably seemed too humanistic, and his recourse to the *phi* proportions of nature far too secular and democratic. It is important to note here that the emphasis of L'Enfant's plan was on the creation rather than on the creator – it was 'bottom up' rather than 'top down' in its inspiration. The Masons would have favored an emphasis on the primacy of the metaphysical, hierarchical and unchanging order of the heavenly spheres. They had little interest in the Golden Section and its earthly pentacles; this is still true of Masonic geometry today. The Masons would have preferred the triangle, with its implicit solar 6, if they had given any thought to L'Enfant's design. They would have wanted its emphasis to be on the power of the *logos* and on the active masculine principle of leadership, not on nature. Yet the Masons seem to have missed their opportunity to introduce a vision of their own symbolism into the design of the city; although they were able to make their mark on the Federal District – in a scheme that was approved, ironically, by Jefferson – and with initiatives such as the Washington Monument.

So were there likely to have been any Freemasons in the area at the time who understood the symbolism in L'Enfant's plan, even if it was not intentionally Masonic? A Grand Master would probably have had the skill to see what L'Enfant was doing, even if he lacked the communicative ability or inclination to explain it. The draftsman of L'Enfant's plan for publication and a future architect of the Capitol, the Frenchman Stephen Hallet, was just such a Freemason. Hallet had the necessary technical knowledge to understand the plan and he was in a position to know it intimately. Hallet also had the skill to explain it. Washington historian Pamela Scott thinks it was Hallet who wrote – in French – the anonymous tract of 1795, *Essay on the City of Washington*, which explained and defended the L'Enfant Plan, although – and this is highly relevant – not in any Masonic terms. In fact, Hallet soon came into conflict both with the Masons and with Congress, and was also dismissed from his role. There was also the architect of the White House, James Hoban. But Hoban, a knowledgeable Freemason, also did not appear until after L'Enfant's dismissal in 1792.

Does L'Enfant's background and his role in the creation of the Society of the Cincinnati suggest he had Masonic connections? This society took its name from the Roman Consul Cincinnatus, who led the army of Republican Rome to victory, then retired to his farm. A deliberate analogy was being drawn between the Roman Republic, America and George Washington. But while the Society of the Cincinnati had all the characteristics of a Military Lodge in the tradition of the Knights Templar, and some of its members were also Masons, it was not a Masonic order. The Society was an aristocratic fraternity based upon its former military role and was concerned with protecting and promoting the interests of its members. I could find no evidence of its having architectural concerns. Furthermore, neither the Society, nor the Grand Masters of the Masonic lodges, were based in Washington. They were based in Boston, New York and Philadelphia. Consequently, they had little or no influence on L'Enfant when he made his plan. Indeed, it is well known that President Washington eventually had to distance himself from the Society of the Cincinnati because of its elitist tendencies.

Membership of the local Masonic lodges in Maryland and Virginia rarely amounted to more than a dozen. The local Maryland lodge, Georgetown Lodge No. 9 (later the first District of Columbia Lodge), had only nine members. None of them was likely to have had anything more than rudimentary geometrical knowledge. The records show the membership to have comprised bankers, merchants, farmers and land-owners, not scholars. The Alexandria Lodge No. 22 was not founded until 1788, with Washington as its first Master, although he rarely attended meetings. As Commissioner Johnson complained to the President about new candidates for the Commission, 'I wish there was a greater quantity of Men for choice who could and would do better'. Apart from Hallet, who arrived in Washington late in 1791 – and several subsequent architects and workers on the White House and Capitol – few qualified, or 'operative', Freemasons were present in the area at this time.

It is also important to note that American Freemasons at the time of L'Enfant's design were already under suspicion by those who resented their power and influence. The Church opposed Masonry, as it believed it should have sole control over all matters, religious, mystical or otherwise spiritual. It could not tolerate a symbolic system – however complementary – that claimed earlier origins than its own. Founding father John Adams wrote against Masonry, believing it to be a conspiracy in favour of the wealthy against the poor. This widely held view was not helped by frequent Masonic displays of conspicuous consumption. In his book *Revolutionary Brotherhood*, Steven Bullock provides many descriptions of the fraternity parading, sometimes drunkenly, in their wigs, aprons, jewellery, fine clothes and other eighteenth-century regalia down American main streets. To Bullock, as to Adams, Masonry was all about wealth and social class. It may have been simpler to conceal Masonic ideas than it was to display them in the late eighteenth century. This was definitely the case thirty years later. American anti-Masonic feelings in the 1790s may explain why Hallet wrote his defence of L'Enfant's plan anonymously and omitted any reference to Masonic ideas.

However slight was Freemasonry's actual involvement in the original design of the city, it seems obvious that both the Masons and other influential persons in the area were not so much unhappy with the design as with the temperamental architect. It is probable that the President's change of heart was directly caused by those who wanted L'Enfant's dismissal. The Commissioners could not allow one high-handed architect to control not only the design of the new city but also the rate of growth, the deployment of money, the employment of workers, the issuing of contracts and the sale of lots. And while L'Enfant demanded skilled labour and paid his workers well, this inevitably brought him into conflict with local landowners who saw slave labour as the best means of securing their economic goals. At this point it is entirely reasonable to assume that the Commissioners, their fellow slave owners, businessmen and their brothers in the Lodges prevailed upon the President to do something about L'Enfant. The President, in the end, upheld their views. L'Enfant was relieved of his duties. In the chaos that ensued, the L'Enfant template for the city – rich in the proportions of the ancient and sacred order of traditional geometry – was not improved but badly damaged.

L'Enfant was distraught when he saw what Ellicott had done to his plan. His main argument against it was 'disproportion'. If L'Enfant had been working with principles derived from a Masonic background and if he was influenced by contemporary Masonic contacts, then why did he not explain his work to them in his letters? L'Enfant was perfectly capable of speaking and writing about everything else. Given that his patron, George Washington, was a Mason, surely L'Enfant could have explained his ideas in Masonic terms. Instead, he failed to explain them in any terms. The only clues to a geometric system to be found in all his letters and texts are vague references to the 'lineaments of the ground from which the whole direction of avenues can alone be perceived', or remarks of the kind that his design for the city had subsequently 'been mangled and altered ... in its most essential parts'. These references may be suggestive, but they are not enough to clarify and describe the intentional use of traditional sacred geometry.

I had to conclude that L'Enfant was working partly intuitively and partly secretly. His plan was a wholly new interpretation of the Golden Section ratio. I believe he was aware of this canonical tradition of sacred geometry and that informed his actions, but that he was reluctant for whatever reasons to make its use explicit. Nowhere could I find evidence that he discussed geometry with anyone, although he met and spoke with many – such as Alexander Hamilton and George Washington

'... That harmony and combination of the different parts with the whole'

– who understood the significance of his task in highly symbolic and idealistic terms. It is very likely that L'Enfant had read William Preston's influential *Illustrations of Masonry*, and had been exposed to the 'perfect' proportion of the Golden Section in his early training; but I do not think he was using it explicitly in his design for Washington. I think L'Enfant knew that if he made this feature explicit then he would antagonise Thomas Jefferson even further than he already had. Instead, his plan was achieved through a highly individualistic, naturalistic and intuitive interpretation of the Golden Section ratios. L'Enfant never went into details, but he declared that Ellicott's alterations would 'deviate from the original plan [in a manner that] would tend to destroy that harmony and combination of the different parts with the whole, to effect which has been the chief object of my labor and concern'. In the context of the loss of the geometric ratios, I don't think the meaning of this statement could be any clearer.

The Freemasons, meanwhile, had become almost conspicuous by their absence. Until Stephen Hallet's writings in 1795, no Mason showed any understanding of L'Enfant's work or came to his defense. Neither Jefferson, Washington, Carroll nor Stuart make any reference to Masonic principles whatsoever in their correspondence. All the support came down in favour of the pragmatic and non-esoteric Ellicott. After that, development of the city limped along in the hands of business-minded superintendents such as Samuel Blodget and James Dermott, whose efforts were directed into raising loans and attracting investment, rather than retracing any grand esoteric symbolism.

Yet there is no doubt that the contribution of Freemasonry to eighteenth-century American society was extensive. It provided an important pillar of the social order, helping to define its conduct and ideas. The fraternity played a vital role in the War of Independence and in the development of the young nation state. Perhaps, as several historians have pointed out, the most significant contribution of Freemasonry to American development was in the idea that authority lay within the offices of the order, not in the individuals who held them. This idea finds its earliest recorded expression in ancient Egypt. Here, power lay in the office of the Pharaoh, not in the individual who occupied it. Freemasonry insisted upon the election of its members to the offices of the order and on the independence of its lodges. In the same way as power was invested in the office of the Grand Master of the Lodge, and between the Grand Lodge and the Lodges, so power was invested in the office of the President and between the different branches of the American government.

I had no choice but to conclude from the available evidence that direct Masonic involvement in the early design of the city was non-existent. Any influence that Masonic symbolism and ideas could have had upon L'Enfant's design was indirect. Whatever ideas he picked up from the Masons as an independent architect were freely interpreted in his own, often idiosyncratic, terms. I also became convinced that at the time, the involvement of Masons in the city was mostly practical, mundane and concerned with business interests. Even the most highly placed Mason of them all, the President, limited his contribution to his driving vision. The Washington Masons of the late eighteenth century appear to have placed practicalities before esoteric and symbolic ideas. It seems likely that they contributed less to L'Enfant's design than they did to his eventual downfall and dismissal.

11

Avenues to the Stars

At the heart of [the plan of Washington, D.C.] is a new definition of the Monumental Core that includes not only the Mall and the traditional ceremonial spaces, but also North and South Capital Streets, the Anacostia River and adjacent areas. The Capitol once again becomes the symbolic center of the city, as L'Enfant intended, with its power radiating outward in all directions.
    Extending the Legacy, the *National Capital Planning Commission*, 1997.

CONCLUSIONS

Once I became certain that the plan for Washington had been designed without direct Masonic involvement and with only brief suggestions by the definitely non-Masonic Thomas Jefferson, I could rely upon the few references made by L'Enfant concerning his symbolic intentions in the federal city. The only indisputable evidence of L'Enfant's objectives is to be found in his reports to George Washington and in the single surviving original plan of 1791. It is this original plan, restored and published by the Library of Congress in 1991, that provides the basis of this analysis.

    The argument presented in this book shows that the geometry and dimensions employed by L'Enfant in his design for the city created a profound as well as fitting architectural representation of the democratic, republican and federal character of the emerging United States. The design of their new capital city suited the social, commercial and political character of Americans and the forms of government they were creating for themselves. The vitally important distribution and balance of political and economic power between the People, the States, the Legislature, the President, and also between the courts and the market place as upheld in

The Secret Geometry of Washington, D.C.

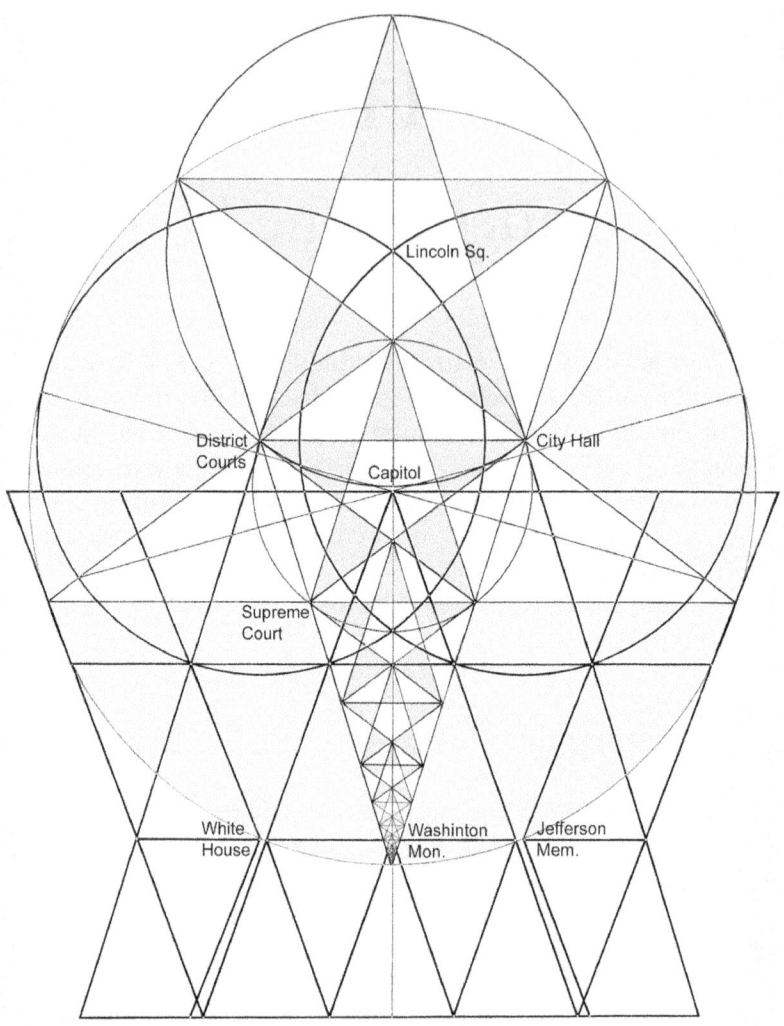

Figure 53. The L'Enfant Template, the geometry revealed by the main diagonal avenues and squares of the Federal City, is here overlaid by the template of archetypal or 'perfect' Golden Section ratios – the sequence of five-pointed stars. Not all avenues are shown.

the Articles of the Constitution – was perfectly expressed by L'Enfant's use of Golden Section ratios between their respective symbols and locations in the city. This Golden Section geometry initially defined each part of the city, and placed it among ratios that kept it, L'Enfant wrote, in a 'harmony and combination of the different parts with the whole'. His plan was thus an inspired interpretation in symbolic geometry of the newly forming character of late eighteenth-century America.

By placing the Capitol on primary axes in the center of the plan, and relating all the other key buildings to this site in a ratio that is fundamental to the structures of the natural world, L'Enfant gave formal, visible expression to the all-powerful, central and representative qualities of the Legislature and its generative position in the New World order. The law of the new nation was to be centered and built upon those powers of nature that had, since their ancestors' arrival, ordered the affairs of the colonists and the prosperity of their lives in the new continent. Through their representatives who would assemble and hold office in its new federal center, the people and the States were intended to collaborate in defining the laws and guiding principles of America. By placing the President's House on a secondary axis, amid ratios and measures that evoked hierarchical and solar principles – wisdom and authority – L'Enfant acknowledged the need for the President to bow to Congress; but he also affirmed the qualities traditionally essential to leadership. It is clear from his letters that he greatly admired the indomitable will of the first person to occupy the post of President.

The diagonal avenues radiating outward from each 'house' were intended to represent the balanced relationship between the Executive and the Legislature; as well as their openness to and connectedness with the federal government, the people, and the States of the Union. The precisely measured spatial relationship between the two houses was calculated to reconcile and harmonise their distinctive qualities; while the third major branch of central government, the Judiciary, was kept distinct from both of them. Yet although all three buildings were integrated within the Golden Section geometry, no avenue was to run from the Supreme Court to either house. This underlined its intended independence from any excessive influence by the people, the Legislature or the President.

The Itinerary Column, one mile east of Congress, from which all the distances on the continent were to be measured was to be located at the center of the district of the people. This site is now Lincoln Square. Here squares and streets were intended to provide the equivalent of the Greek *agora* and Roman *forum,* the place for commerce and all the affairs of life. L'Enfant and his contemporaries held that it was the energy and activities of the people that would run the new country like a machine that needed only a gentle touch from central government now and then to regulate it. Americans had the historic opportunity to realise this republican outlook through the bounty and the challenges of their new land. Freedom, independence, self-definition, commercial opportunity, and as little interference in the life of the individual from

The Secret Geometry of Washington, D.C.

Photo 12. The Emancipation Monument in Lincoln Square, 1876.

central authority as possible, were ideals as characteristic of American society at that time as they are today. The people were seen as equals – at least more so than in the Old World – and the sovereignty of the new nation was vested in them: 'We the People ...'. opens the text of the Constitution, accurately capturing the political spirit of the time. Therefore, the centers of the people in their capital city were intended to symbolise that political sovereignty resided ultimately in them: that it was they who were to be the driving force of the nation. Not only were the District Courts and City Hall located on fundamental points of the geometry to the north and south of the center; but L'Enfant also applied this republican ideal on the west side of Congress in the Mall, where the people were to gather in this 'place of general resort'. He made it clear that the people's 'play houses, rooms of assembly, and academies' were to complete the configuration of the center of the federal city.

Figure 54 provides a schematic view of L'Enfant's primary axes, and shows the centrality of the Capitol, the radiant center provided by the President's House, and the center provided by the Mile Column at 'B', now Lincoln Square.

Reinforcing the democratic and republican message of the original geometry was the subtlety of L'Enfant's creation of distinctive axes, figures and ratios around the President's House. Traditional concepts of authority and power were encoded both in the Sixteenth Street axis and in the numbers 6, 60 and 666 – which invoke the solar qualities of the six-fold hexagram – but such values were carefully limited by the avenues of the equilateral triangle. In L'Enfant's original design, the symbolic influence of the Presidential axis and the triangle were always referred back to their source in the Golden Section ratios of the

Avenues to the Stars

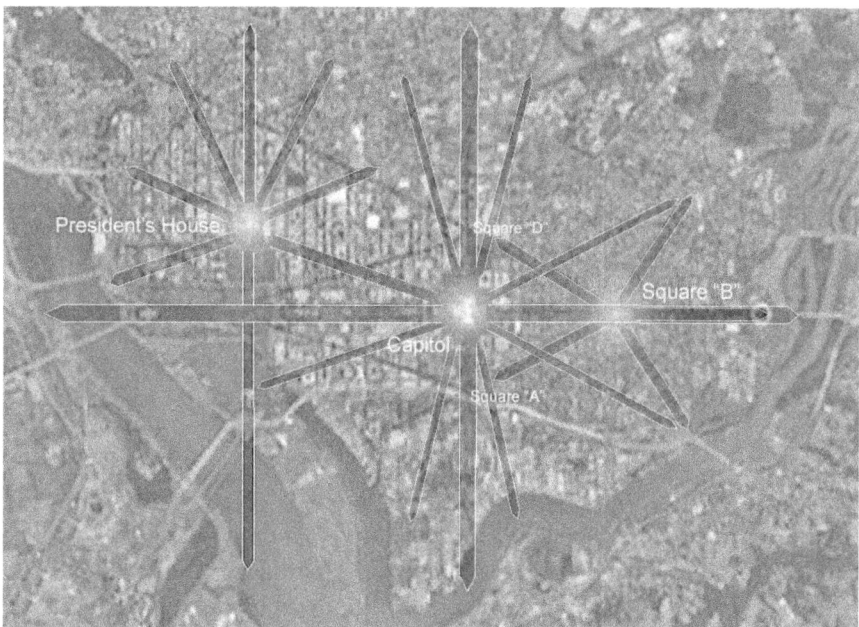

Figure 54. The L'Enfant Plan of 1791. Two primary axes radiate outward from the Capitol, defining it as the center of the city. The Golden Section geometry of a five-pointed star radiates outward from Square B, now Lincoln Square, in the east. The avenues of the White House radiate outward in the west. The pair of avenues, set at sixty-degrees, north of the White House, is the only figure not generated by the underlying Golden Section geometry. The first stage of the diagonal matrix of avenues generated by the geometry is marked in a finer line.

underlying geometry. Both the axis and the triangle were, in fact, embedded in a more fundamental matrix whose source was the Capitol. In other words, no overt statement of absolute power for the ruler was being made in the design of Washington, D.C., as it had been at Versailles or the Chinese Imperial City, although the need for vision and ultimate authority was certainly being recognised and granted to the Executive. Only much later were stronger messages about the power of the President encoded in the relocation of the north–south 'global' meridian through the White House, and in the striking proportions of the Washington Monument. As described in Chapter 9, the Monument was a Masonic allegory, in solar numerology, of the quasi-monarchic power of the President. It is above all the Washington Monument, together with the increasingly enclosed and formal emphasis upon the Mall, and the transfer of key symbolic elements in L'Enfant's design such as the Zero Milestone and the Zero Meridian to the Ellipse and Sixteenth Street, which has shifted Washington's symbolic balance of power in the direction of the Presidency.

L'Enfant's original geometrical image was of a five-fold – *phi*-fold – Golden Section matrix that generated a diagonal grid of avenues opening out to the landscape around the city. The architect had created a hidden symbolism whereby the people, the States and the branches of the federal government – the Legislature, the Executive and the Judiciary – could relate to each other through multiple and independent centers in an open, balanced and constantly self-referencing system. Although the diagonal matrix within which the Executive is set visually appears to hold and contain the system, in fact, it is generated by it. L'Enfant's message appears to be that however much power is given to the Executive, sovereignty must ultimately lie with the American people, since it is they who will elect their leaders. The White House, the Washington Monument, the secondary north–south axis and the sixty-degree radiant avenues: all these details made strong statements about the especial powers of executive leadership, even though the subsequent closing of the angle of the avenues to fifty degrees – for whatever reason – limited their symbolic effect.

Nor did L'Enfant entirely subscribe to the increasing secularism of the times. He intended there to be a non-sectarian national church and a great ceremonial center in the new city. Yet while the locations of these formal sites were to be defined by the geometry, these were not to be linked by the matrix of avenues to the centers of power. L'Enfant wanted each of the squares on the intersections of the underlying geometry to be dedicated to a State of the Union – linking them directly to power. But these proposals were not adopted. Jefferson made sure any religious or esoteric implications in the design were immediately removed. L'Enfant's proposed 'altar of liberty' at the heart of the Capitol, and numerous other monumental sites evenly distributed throughout the city were all struck from the design. The cemetery at Arlington across the river, the National Cathedral, the Mellon Auditorium, and especially the Mall came to provide Washington's only formal and ceremonial sites. These are clear indicators that L'Enfant could never have made his use of the Golden Section explicit, given its symbolic and mystical connotations, because of Jefferson's desire to strengthen the rational and secular inclinations of the new country. The representative message was only partly achieved – probably after L'Enfant's suggestion – by the naming of the avenues after the States.

THE PENTACLE

The dominant symbol that emerges from the underlying geometry of the L'Enfant Plan is the pentacle. The pentacle is a harmonious, integrative and balanced symbol whose Golden Section proportions are found throughout the natural world. The Pythagoreans and Neo-Platonists saw it as the symbol that integrated multiple sources – the one with the many, the above and the below – and preferred it over other symbols that emphasized only a single transcendent source. In a republic of political checks and balances, it was possibly for this reason that Americans favoured the five-pointed star as a recurring national motif. As a 'five-fold triangle whose lines reproduce to infinity' wrote Freemason William Preston in the late eighteenth century, the pentacle represented many things: the 'light of dawn', eternity, and divine providence. The pentacle is also a symbol of material wealth in esoteric lore. It was used on the national flag, on the Great Seal, for the badges of law officers and on the currency as a symbol of the autonomy of the individual States. The pentacle was also used in the dimensions of the Headquarters of the US Department of Defense, the Pentagon, begun in 1941. (Although the Pentagon is situated so that its axes are oriented on the White House and on the Capitol, and the building itself may be an acknowledgement of the Golden Section ratios of L'Enfant's original design, its location has no direct relationship to the geometry of the original plan of the city. However, the Pentagon's shape arose from its original intended location three-quarters of a mile further north. This location would have placed it in a commanding relationship to the L'Enfant Plan, but would have reinforced the Washington Monument and not the Capitol as the center of the city.) The pentacle appeared in Washington to crown the brow and shield of the 'Lady of Freedom' positioned over the Capitol in 1876. L'Enfant had already employed the pentacle at least twice in his career: once in his design of the eagle medallion for the Society of the Cincinnati and again as a motif in the ornamentation of Federal Hall in New York.

Although L'Enfant must have been aware of its meaning – it suited the requirements of the time and once drawn it subsequently measured all aspects of the design – for his own reasons, he kept his use of the pentacle and the Golden Section ratio concealed. Yet the Golden Section ratio that is present in the precise distances between the Capitol, the mile column and the White House stands out above all the symbolic features which L'Enfant employed to express the appropriate balance between the centers of power in the city. The ratio was used in its most explicit formulation (0.618:1:1.618 miles) to determine the location of and the relationships between all the most important sites.

The first pentacle, centered on the Capitol, linked the Supreme Court, the District Courts and City Hall. This pentacle truly was a star of the people. Yet it was the second pentacle that was especially significant for the deeper symbolism of the city. This second pentacle was centered on the Mile Column and therefore had a radius of one mile. It surrounded the proposed commercial district, and, above all, it was aligned to the main axes of the city and pointed to the east. Its arms, set at 108 degrees from north, may also have pointed to the heliacal rising of certain first magnitude stars. In St. Paul's Chapel, New York, L'Enfant had depicted an American eagle flying from east to west bearing a curtain of stars. I contend that his second pentacle, which structured the eastern avenues of the Federal City (shown in Figures 10 and 47), was conceived in the same manner. As an 'Eastern Star', this pentacle can be seen in diverse ways: as the star of a newly free and independent people rising in the east; as ushering in of a new era of human idealism designed to transform the old world order; and also as promoting the economic growth of the nation, in anticipation of numerous settlers moving west to exploit the abundant resources of the continent. Yet the Eastern Star was seemingly also intended to represent the equal distribution of those resources among the people as a whole. The people now looked to the government to support their new found sovereignty, equality and economic freedom through articles of law, multiple investment opportunities and low taxation in their new land.

If the Golden Section template of the city was to be extended, it is easy to imagine its sequence of five-pointed stars expanding and progressing ever westwards to cover larger and larger areas of territory in the North American continent. In one sense, these pentacles are a potent symbol of late eighteenth-century commercial expansionism writ large upon the earth. But L'Enfant also wished to emphasise the equilibrium and reciprocation that was necessary between all the different parts of the nation. His geometric succession of pentacles expands through their natural ratio, yet at each expansion it refers back to the original source: the expansion is to the original as the original is to the whole. As the continent that lay to the west was settled by the colonists, through the newly won independent and acquisitive spirit of the people, its development was carefully regulated by its elected leaders and the law. In ancient architectural symbolism, the activities of the people had always occurred under the eye of heaven – the temple stood over the market place. Although such religious imagery was marginalised in the new American republic, it was ideas like these that contributed to the creation of such symbols as the eye upon a pyramid, still found upon the American dollar bill.

It was partly due to the wish he shared with his political allies, such as Thomas Madison and his friend Alexander Hamilton, to uphold a strong centrist Executive; partly because of the personal respect and admiration he had for his patron Washington, that L'Enfant consistently referred all the different parts of the nation back to the whole in his design for the national capital. The whole, in this instance, was represented for L'Enfant by the office of the President. In that office – or in the ancient traditions of sovereignty and kingship, in the ruler's actual physical body – all became one: *E Pluribus Unum*. The implicit idea, derived from L'Enfant's origins in pre-republican France, saw the leader not as a part but as a symbolic representative of the body politic as a whole; it survives to this day in the unacknowledged cult of the American Presidency. Although Jefferson had firmly deleted L'Enfant's designation of 'Presidential Palace' for the house of the President, once he was himself elected to that office Jefferson introduced far-reaching architectural measures, such as the shifting of the zero meridian, to symbolically strengthen the quasi-royal associations of the White House. Even recent developments to improve and landscape Pennsylvania Avenue to the north of the White House, in 2004, have made comparisons to and borrowed ideas from Buckingham Palace, the royal residence in London.

It is obviously significant that the center of L'Enfant's second pentacle, the square marked 'B' on the L'Enfant Plan, originally intended to be the heart of a thriving commercial district and now the center of a leafy but sadly neglected residential neighborhood, features the Emancipation Monument – Lincoln freeing the slaves. The enfranchisement of the people of the United States held exactly the kind of symbolic meaning that L'Enfant originally intended for the center of his 'Eastern Star'. Like the opponents of slavery among the group that framed the American Constitution, he saw the possibilities which the continent offered as only being realised through the full enfranchisement, education and abilities of its entire people. Moreover, L'Enfant may have heard that this area on the summit of Jenkins Hill had once been the site of Native American councils and commerce; how suggestive, then, that it was from here that L'Enfant intended all the distances to the corners of the nation be measured. Yet sadly, for the native peoples, their omission from the civic rights and ideals instituted by these eighteenth-century developments was to usher in two centuries of persecution and pain. The neglect of this spot on the plan reflects this continuing imbalance in American society.

Yet this second pentacle, or 'Eastern Star', rooted on the Anacostia shore, can be understood in esoteric and spiritual terms as intended to open the city to the influence of powerful celestial and sublime forces as well as natural ones. The emerging star of the new nation – complete with its recent Constitution and Bill of Rights (just passed in 1791) – rising like all new beginnings in the east, was intended to align the city to the heavens. This second pentacle of one-mile radius was to throw its rays over the city from the place of sunrise, imprinting it and the continent that lay beyond, not only with the pattern of its many avenues but also with the new republican and revolutionary values that had originally come from Europe. Like a heliacal rising star, it is likely that the 108 degree angle of the pentacle aligned the primary avenues of the city to the rising in the east of such first-magnitude stars as Regulus and Sirius. The astronomer Benjamin Banneker may have provided L'Enfant with such details based on his observations. Regulus is one of the four royal stars of the Persians. It is the 'princely' star influencing leaders and so regulating the affairs of the nations of earth. Sirius marked the coming of the annual inundation for the Egyptians and thus the miraculous renewal of their land's fertility. As a future almanac writer, Banneker would have been well aware of the prominence of Sirius in the astrological chart of the US, in a position that signified the amassing of wealth and the acquiring of fame. The one mile radius of the second pentacle would also have set it within a system of terrestrial and numerological harmony. Finally, this second pentacle refers the whole design back to the source as it generates the third circle and the third pentacle in harmonic ratio with the first. The third pentacle in the design of the city makes the connection with the White House and the 'Presidential estate'.

To summarise in the simplest of Golden Section terms: the first pentacle, the star of the Capitol, is to the second, the star of the people, as both are to the third, the star of the President. The Legislature is to the People as they are to the Executive – from one, to two, to three to one.

THE 'MONUMENTAL CORE'

The contribution of the McMillan Commission of 1901 to the restoration of the L'Enfant Plan of Washington was extensive. The Commission picked up where L'Enfant had left off over a hundred years before. It restored many important areas of green space in the Federal District as a whole and cleared up excessive and ugly urban development. But although restoration of the original vision of L'Enfant was foremost in the minds of the members of the Commission, who included several pioneers of the 'city beautiful' concept, the steps which they took to develop the Mall seriously affected the symbolic balance of values in the city. The Commission's introduction to the Mall of additional major buildings, museums, sharply prescribed spaces and inward-looking monuments and memorials resulted in the accentuation of its introspection, coldness and formality. Above all, the Capitol's north–south axis was replaced by the 'Presidential axis', and the centrality of the Capitol was replaced by that of the Washington Monument. The Mall now became more of a 'monumental core' that contrasted significantly with L'Enfant's 'place of general resort'. The development by the McMillan Commission of the Federal Triangle, the Washington Monument, the north–south axis through the White House and the Lincoln and the Jefferson Memorials, also greatly increased the focus of the city upon the Executive branch of government. At the same time, the long-standing lack of attention to the city east of the Capitol by the Commission has resulted in a further neglect of the vital qualities which this part of the city was intended to represent and nurture. A schematic representation of these developments is shown overpage in Figure 55.

It is unlikely that the McMillan Commission deliberately intended to remove centrality from the Capitol, or to reinforce the existing over-emphasis upon the Washington Monument and the Presidential axis. The Commissioners were responding to over a hundred years of financial neglect and piecemeal development that had diminished the power and beauty of the original design. They saw the Mall as a vital part of a larger plan of restoration of the city as a whole and apparently did not understand the dangers implicit in their one-sided improvements. It is widely felt that with the recent completion of the Museum of the Native American, all space for further development in the Mall has been filled. But as it is not understood that the capital city facilities were originally meant to be extended throughout the entire city, there seems to be a feeling of resentment that no new monuments and memorials can now be included in the Mall. To summarise: the overall result of the Commission's work was to subdue the influence both of the Capitol and of the eastern half of the city as a whole, while it elevated the importance of the city's western, 'Presidential axis'.

The overall symbolic implication of all the changes made to the L'Enfant Plan points to the increasing isolation of the federal government and the leadership from the country. By implication, these institutions

The Secret Geometry of Washington, D.C.

Figure 55. The McMillan Plan of 1901. Although following and restoring the L'Enfant Plan, the Commission contributed to the emphasis on a third 'Presidential axis' with developments such as the Lincoln and the Jefferson Memorials. The original east–west axis is now defined only in the western half of the city and the primary north–south axis now passes through the White House. All buildings look inward to the Monumental Core. At the intersection of the new axes, the Washington Monument is now the center of the city. This situation still prevails today.

have become separated from the qualities of the law; in structural terms, they have lost a relationship of mutual reciprocity with the sovereign powers of the States and the people. They have also lost their intended connection to the sublime idealism represented by the Eastern Star. L'Enfant's multiple and generative pentacles, instead of working in a balanced dynamic, are now set in a pattern that concentrates power in one part of the city – at the top. This over-developed Executive symbolism in the city plan is not only indicative of an increasing predominance of Executive and federal authority over State authority and individual rights. It also points to another, equally valid reading, of materialistic and self-centred ambitions running unchecked and beyond the law on the continent. By the middle of the twentieth century, the symbolic configuration of Washington revealed a nation not only out of touch with each of its parts, but also out of touch with the greater world outside of its borders. Lacking the wider idealism that could have connected the new nation through the development of the eastern half of the capital city to the greater world, America was now turned to look within itself.

MUD AND STARS

It is not hard to understand the events that led up to L'Enfant's dismissal during the foggy, muddy and leaf-strewn days of autumn 1791–92. The members of Congress and the Commissioners were by now increasingly agitated about rising costs. They felt L'Enfant was withholding valuable information from them that could have generated the income they needed. To them, L'Enfant's scheme was too extravagant, ridiculously pretentious. Even the American public was becoming increasingly skeptical about the 'city of roads but no houses'. Jefferson, although interested in geometry and ancient traditions, preferred the mellow architectural order of his rural residence at Monticello. He wrote about the degenerative effects of city life and was rarely in town. The Masons were more interested in pursuing mutually supportive business interests than in pursuing esoteric architectural symbolism. Americans in general were becoming bored with the federal city. At this point, even the President's dynamic vision seemed to falter under the pressure of other, more immediate, priorities. Both the city and payment for his architect would have to wait, so that the Union could be held together, national security maintained, the 'Patowmack' canal built, agriculture and industry developed and commerce encouraged. After L'Enfant's departure, the implementation of a botched plan had more to do with expediency, profit, efficiency and pragmatism than an idealistic and imaginative interpretation of ancient and universal truth.

Yet it is still true that the City of Washington was planned according to the traditions of sacred geometry; thankfully, much of the original design can be seen there today. The Golden Section ratios between the Capitol, the Mile Column, the terminal squares and the White House survive. They are in clear accordance with traditions of ratio, number and measure that had been sanctified by usage in the temples of the Old World and described by ancient philosophers and visionaries. The placing of the Capitol upon an astronomically located, central axial crossing; both the diamond shape and precise orientation of the Federal District of Columbia; the five-fold measures of the pentacles: all these details can be found in ancient and classical traditions of ordering the world. The orientations of the diagonal avenues, with their thirty-six, fifty-five, sixty and 108 degree angles, leave little room for doubt that a highly symbolic system of geometrical order was originally employed by L'Enfant, even if its content was neither explained nor fully developed, and was subsequently seriously departed from.

Sacred geometry was first developed to ensure that human affairs were ordered in accordance with the divine order. The classical worldview held that this order originated in the patterns of earth and sky. It was given to mankind by the great powers that inhabited these regions. The patterns and ratios that came from direct observation of nature and the heavens allowed humanity to create systems of geometry, number and measure that emulated the cosmic order. Gradually, these systems became highly conceptualised, to allow human activities to be regulated by this order and, in turn, to help humans to follow and even anticipate the motions that ordered the heavens. Through measure, people could know when the sun, moon and stars would rise and when the seasons would begin. Through number and measure they could understand and be in harmony with the tides of life. But it was considered especially important to use geometry, mathematics and astronomy to align the orientation and the forms of a national center with the heavens. Palaces, temples, shrines, monuments, memorials, parliaments and city designs everywhere expressed a people's strong desire for their national center to be in harmony with the highest expression of the divine. Because of L'Enfant, Washington is almost unique among modern cities in conforming to this traditional practice.

The legend of the Widow's Mite reveals some of the complex symbolic notions that were running in the popular American imagination at the time of the city's foundation. A rich vein of mythic and political allegory was explored in the imagery of the native, then classical, Goddess Columbia and in the stories of the Washington Treaty Oak. The later works of the Freemasons Hallet, Hoban and Preston; the development of the idea and iconography of the 'Lady of Freedom'; the Masonic dedication of the 'temple' of the Capitol; the striking dimensions of both the District of Columbia and of the Washington Monument; all these developments show that profoundly symbolic concepts continued to be in circulation in Washington over later decades. But above all, it was L'Enfant's own genius, and his all-consuming dedication to originality, art and excellence, that created in the City of Washington an urban ideal that is free from any hint of pedantic imitation or mere pretentiousness. L'Enfant's geometry gave

America's capital a powerful symbolic foundation which could fully justify its self-description as the capital of a *Novus Ordo Seclorum*.

THE FUTURE

When I came, in recent years, to complete the research I had undertaken for this book in the early 1990s, I found myself imagining a future renaissance of the ideals that had prevailed at the time of the foundation of the American Republic. I found myself asking, if there could be a re-imagining of the original ideal order of the founders – in something like a return to Eliade's 'cosmogonic' time of origin – then how would those principles find symbolic expression in the impressive capital city of today?

It seems too late to restore the informal nature of the Mall; too late to move the Treasury out of Pennsylvania Avenue, or the Supreme Court out of the shadow of the Hill. Likewise, it seems impossible to reinstate the angles of Massachusetts, Vermont and Connecticut Avenues, or to restore the district diamond, Lincoln Square, the Mile Column or the Zero Meridian. The avenues continue to turn the city within; they no longer connect the city to the nation without. The key federal buildings, the Capitol, the Lincoln Memorial, the Jefferson Memorial and the White House seem forever destined to refer only to themselves and to the obelisk in their midst. The city's symbolic center of power has shifted away from the Capitol to the 'Presidential axis'. The Washington Monument stands as a monolithic emblem of the power of the Presidency at the city's heart. It seems this pattern cannot be changed. Or can it?

What would be the ideal symbolic template for the American capital of the future? If L'Enfant was sensitive to the generative pattern prevalent in the forms of the natural world, with its roots deep in ancient tradition and in the patterns of earth and sky; if he was attuned to the idealism of the newly emerging nation and to the vision of its founders for truly enlightened government; and if he intuitively expressed all this in a profound geometrical 'plan wholy new'; then is it possible for his template to be restored or redeveloped in a pattern appropriate to a new era? And if so, would the geometrical and symbolic qualities of the original template still express the values of a nation that has changed so much, has faced considerable adversity, has adapted and grown so enormously, and is now holding such extensive global responsibility and power?

It is unlikely, given their anti-colonial ideology, that Jefferson and Washington ever anticipated the extent that their nation was to become a world power. But had they imagined the logical conclusion of their own policies – after all, Jefferson was soon to make the Louisiana Purchase – would their architect have included that empire building into the capital city? If so, where were California Square and Alaska Square to go? Where would the avenues leading to the Caribbean, the Pacific and Asia be? Could Jefferson and Washington have envisaged a response to a national security program that required a building the size and shape of the Pentagon? Could they have imagined the need for a United Nations or an International Court of Justice, to be sited if not in their capital city, then at least in the USA? How, in other words, would their architect have integrated a new wave of humanitarian ideals into his design?

In the late eighteenth century a group of uniquely gifted men formulated an inspired vision for their nation. If they were alive today, and had the opportunity to plan their capital city once again, it seems certain that they would now adjust its design to make it ever more inclusive – to allow the net of their democratic and humanitarian ideals to be more widely cast. How might they have wanted their ideals of liberty, justice, equality and democracy – defined by the Articles of the Constitution and the Bill of Rights – to be further developed in the architecture of their foundation, to symbolically include any whom, at the time, they were excluding? How might they have honoured and represented the integration of North and South, of slaves, of women, of many different ethnicities, including the native peoples, in the architecture of their city? How might they have represented their relationship to the world beyond their borders in the face of events in the twentieth- and twenty-first centuries? How would they have symbolically resolved the perennial American tension between its internal liberal, democratic character and its need for strong external security? How might the pattern of the city change to describe America's new balance between its heart and its boundaries?

At the beginning of the twentieth century, the members of the McMillan Commission realised the integrity of L'Enfant's design when they were charged with the task of restoring the city of Washington. Today, the changing needs of the city still exercise the minds of many. Plans are now being made to expand and renew the spatial dynamics and symbolic values of the capital city in a twenty-first century redevelopment scheme. It seems reasonable to hope that this debate will lead to a close examination of L'Enfant's underlying geometry, if America is to create a renewed civic order worthy of the concerns of a new age.

At a Senate Subcommittee meeting in April 2005, John V. Cogbill III, Chairman of the National Capital Planning Commission (the NCPC), spoke of establishing a '21st-century vision for the National

Avenues to the Stars

Capital Region and the National Mall'. The proposed Legacy Plan of the NCPC called for an expansion of 'Washington's monumental core'. It defined this monumental core as the Mall. Mr Cogbill acknowledged the admirable role of the McMillan Commission in returning to and 'reinforcing L'Enfant's themes', but he believed that the Mall should not be overwhelmed by any further 'monumental or commemorative buildings'. Instead he argued the monumental core of the city should now be expanded to other areas of the city, so that – and this was surely the point – 'the Capitol would truly become the center of the city, with symbols of the nation radiating out in all directions'. Mr Cogbill also claimed, controversially, that the Legacy Plan considered 'the Mall a finished work of art', and specifically mentioned 'North and South Capital Streets, the Anacostia River, and adjacent areas' as the prime targets for development. A quotation from the Legacy Plan is given at the beginning of this chapter. Its proposals are still under review at the time of going to press. Figure 56 shows the key conceptual 'Framework Diagram' of the NCPC's proposals.

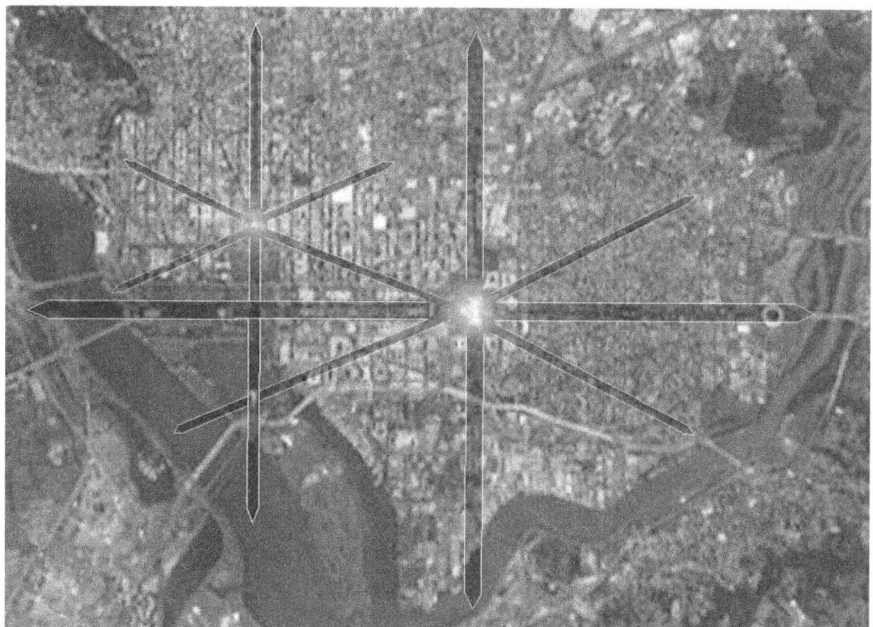

Figure 56. The 'Framework Diagram' of the Legacy Plan of the NCPC, 2004. Centrality is restored to the Capitol. Avenues radiate outward from the Capitol and the White House. The introspection of the Mall has been broken. The plan is elegant and simple, but it overlooks the eastern part of the city.

The Secret Geometry of Washington, D.C.

This is extremely promising. Americans are now contemplating the renewal of their capital in spatial and symbolic terms. The more fundamental a capital city's symbolic pattern, the more creative and beautiful it is, the more authority and power it has, the more it affects us, and the more its people instinctively feel it to be representative of the ideal principles of their nation. But as yet, it is unclear in its reports whether the proposed renewal that the NCPC has in mind will be one that looks further than its local and continental environment – as far afield as its global neighbors. Through its Golden Section geometry, the City of Washington has been from its foundation symbolically attuned to a fundamental pattern of strong democratic values – and also to the creation of tremendous economic power and wealth. Can it now review and revise its symbolism to harmonise with the other geometric systems and foundation patterns that exist in the world?

The articulation of American ideals through the Golden Section symbolism of its capital foundation automatically sets Washington in resonance with all similar forms, many of them ancient, across the world. The city is in harmony with all '*phi*-fold' Golden Section geometric systems because the Golden Section and its associated pentacle resonates with the fundamental geometry of nature, of organic life and of humanity. As I have repeatedly emphasised, Golden Section principles are at the core of DNA and of natural design. They are also – as everyone who experiences the tremendous power of the American landscape can sense – central to the subtle energies of the *anima mundi*, the world soul or spirit. But there is much more to Washington's Golden Section geometry than that. Washington's *phi*-fold order has the potential to harmonise with **all** expressions of fundamental geometric or archetypal order, whether in three-, four-, six-, seven-, eight- or twelve-fold forms. As I showed in Chapter 1, the Golden Section is also in accord with many different forms and geometries, such as the Platonic Solids. The conceptualization and application of these systems around the world has allowed humanity to understand and attune to the many dimensions and principles – lunar, planetary, solar, cellular, molecular and stellar – that exist alongside the Golden Section and which, in their totality, order life on Earth. Through the universality of their symbolic orders, our ancient civilisations became part of a participatory, creative and responsive global network. They had engineered a greater attunement between human life and life as a whole: in its elements and forces, in the energy of the earth and in the order of the heavens.

My hope is that through this analysis of the original design of Washington, D.C., the available vocabulary for understanding and articulating the profound symbolism of the American capital can be extended and deepened. In imagining a renewed design for the city, I suggest that the place to begin is with the original multi-centered Golden Section Template that L'Enfant intended for the city. My interpretation of the embedded symbolism of his geometric design points to several possible lines of action that could help the city at a time when there is pressure upon it to revitalise and redevelop.

Reinstating the Capitol as the symbolic center of the city is the foremost priority – one that I share with the National Capital Planning Commission and, I am sure, with many others. The Capitol, L'Enfant's 'Congress House', was always intended to be the center of the city. Moving the city's current structural emphasis away from the Mall and onto the further development of North, South and East Capitol Streets, and also toward the eastern half of the original city in general, can help to restore this centrality. Any new monuments and memorials should be given appropriate locations throughout the entire city. I would re-emphasise that the main entrances of both the White House and the Capitol do not themselves look inwards, to the center of the city, but north and east, outwards towards the nation. But in order to reveal and emphasise these alignments, both Sixteenth Street, north of the White House, and East Capitol Street, east of the Capitol, will need some kind of symbolic re-opening. Some of this work, however security-conscious its motivation may have been, has already been achieved by the 2004 Pennsylvania Avenue project on the north side of the White House.

I would also support any measures, however symbolic these may appear, to re-establish the Zero Meridian through Congress; for the sake of political balance, it should no longer pass through the White House. The proposed development by the NCPC's Legacy Plan of the South Capitol Street Corridor, with parks, spaces for memorials and new public buildings, would support this goal. The projected seven-acre 'commons' to be sited north of a new Frederick Douglass Bridge, complete with a grand formal entrance into the city, would also reemphasize the Capitol Meridian and go some way towards reinstating the intentions that L'Enfant had for the great square he located at point 'A'. At the same time, it would be highly desirable to mark in some monumental form Ellicott and Banneker's new world Meridian, established by 'celestial observation', through North and South Capitol Streets. I also warmly support the current proposals for the development of Eighth Street. A glance at Figure 40 will show how fundamental Eighth Street is to the geometry of the city.

I urge the removal of the Zero Milestone from its current location at the Ellipse and its relocation to Lincoln Square, where L'Enfant had intended it to be. Additional monumental and memorial sites located around Lincoln Square, and from there throughout the city's eastern quarter down to the Anacostia waterfront, will help revive and democratize this neglected area and allow many more people from across the nation to participate in the feeling of being represented in the national capital. A renovation of Lincoln Square might also valuably include some initiatives to honour the importance of Jenkins Hill as a historic meeting place for the indigenous native people. But what is needed, above all, is the encouragement of architectural projects and ideas that can engage with and come from the people themselves – new schemes which can represent all colors and classes of Americans in their diverse experiences of life.

L'Enfant envisaged the area around and to the east of the Capitol as having an unobtrusive monumentality that could integrate comfortably with the people dwelling in and moving through it. The parks and squares in this part of the city were intended to cater for the people's different needs in commerce, housing and leisure. Here, the humble was intended to coexist alongside the great in a marriage of citizen and nation. The development of Lincoln Square and South Capitol Street (together with the addition of the Legacy Plan's proposed new memorial locations, parks, urban facilities and marinas near the RFK stadium and alongside the Anacostia River) will be crucial in countering the formal over-emphasis upon the Executive in the western half of the city. These projects can help to honor L'Enfant's original intention of symbolically incorporating the people with the central Legislature and the Legislature with the people in the eastern part of the city.

The key to the proposed NCPC's Legacy Plan lies in its dispersal of 'national capital activities throughout the city and the region'. This plan aims to integrate mixed use of urban spaces with the expansion of federal facilities and room for future economic development. A chief goal is 'pedestrian-oriented development' that, after L'Enfant, would make the whole city a more exciting place to visit and to live. The plan calls for new entrances to the city at the bridges and approaches to South, North and East Capitol Streets. These will help to re-emphasize the Capitol's centrality, and will bring life to urban areas that have been harmed as much by long-standing environmental neglect and commercial expediency as they have by class and ethnic divisions. Development of the area at the end of East Capitol Street, around the RFK stadium, the Anacostia waterfront and Kingman Island, will, I believe, prove particularly auspicious. As the reinstatement of point 'A', the tip of L'Enfant's Eastern Star, the NCPC's proposals will symbolically re-open the Federal City to the influence of a new era of national vision and idealism.

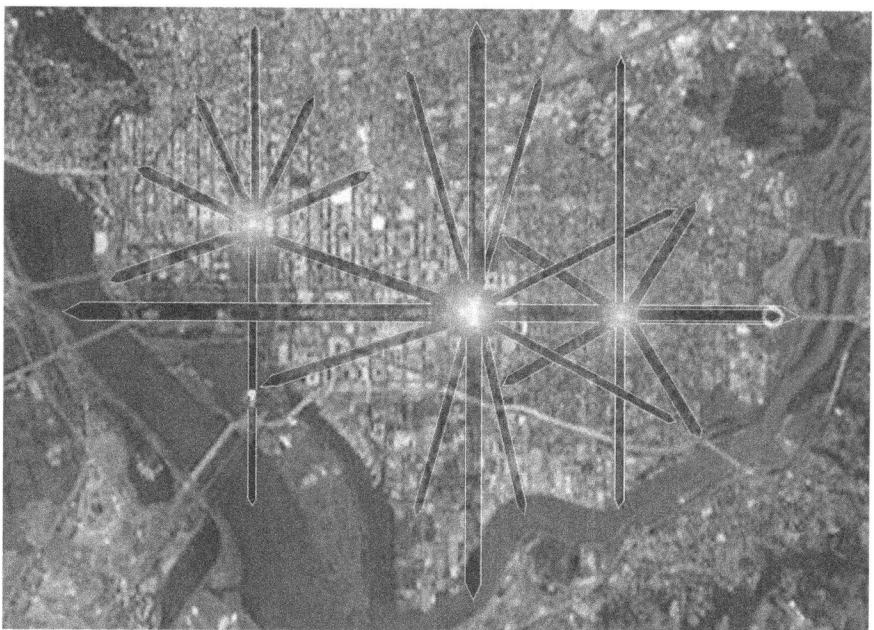

Figure 57. The Golden Section Template, 2006. Centrality is restored to the Capitol and all avenues radiate outwards. The five-pointed pentacle in the east balances the radiant avenues of the Presidency in the west. As the angles of avenues were irreparably altered, the original pentacle and the original six-fold geometry around the White House cannot be precisely restored but the essential geometry remains the same.

Figure 57 shows how my proposal for the development of the eastern part of the city can restore the original L'Enfant design, and symbolically balance people with Legislature and Executive.

A CITY RESTORED

Another interpretation of the template may lead one to conclude that the city has been dominated by qualities and forms often characterised as 'masculine': linearity, formality, rationality, objectivity, high centralization, high technology, war memorials, and so on, with all the coldness and distance that accompanies them. However, the original template also honoured the more fundamentally 'feminine' principles. The Golden Section ratio is, above all, the ratio of life, of nature, of the 'Great Mother', of Gaia, the Earth. It was also closely associated with the qualities of the goddess and the planet Venus. It seems L'Enfant wanted to imprint the city with these architectural forms. If L'Enfant had had a wholly free hand, architects like Sibley-Jennings have suggested that his radiant, axial avenues would have had a less linear and a more fluid, flowing character. The city could have looked more like a Paris or a Rome. Today, perhaps only Dupont and Logan Circles can give us some idea of what L'Enfant had in mind for his 'lived-in, architectonic' spaces.

The foundation legend of the City of Washington concerns a captive woman, a local native chief and an oak tree. The symbolic effects of the eventual liberation of this woman – as described by her release from the different boundaries that contained her – extended beyond the tree, beyond the district, and even beyond the political and cultural boundaries of the nation, out into the entire world. It is the figure of a woman – the 'Lady of Freedom' described in Chapter 3 – representing freedom, liberty, truth and justice, that looks out eastwards from the summit of the dome of the Capitol. Neither her gender, nor the direction of her gaze, is an accident. Nor is Brumidi's fresco on the interior of the Capitol dome. Here a group of women proudly represents the original States, Liberty, and other national qualities, each in the style of the irrepressible and much earlier American Goddess Columbia.

Photo 13. The 'Lady of Freedom'.

Over the course of my research, I became aware that the figures of Freedom and Liberty, long used in the iconography of the American national capital and present in American legends and popular consciousness, have much in common with those from other traditions around the world. Above all, I noticed that they closely paralleled the idea of Ma'at from the ancient Egyptian tradition. Ma'at, usually represented as a female deity crowned with a feather, sometimes represented by a pair of scales, is the Egyptian principle of Truth and Universal Justice; she represents one cosmos under one law. Like so many other ancient peoples, the Egyptians conceived of law as a 'feminine' principle, and the Pharaohs had to uphold Ma'at – often depicted as a seated figure resting in the palm of their hands – as a symbol of their adherence to divine law. America's native Lady of Freedom, with her feather headdress, sword and shield, looking eastwards from the summit of the Capitol dome, is an appropriate and evocative symbol of the American aim of adherence to the divine order.

As I reflect on the completion of this work in the war-torn years of the early twenty-first century, I have become convinced that those responsible for the redevelopment of the symbolism of the capital city of the USA face a challenge that goes much deeper than clearing urban blight and providing civic amenities. They will have to find ways to make it clear that the laws, rights and principles expressed in the American Constitution – which were only slowly extended to include all its citizens – are now considered to extend to all peoples, not just within the nation, but throughout the world. They have the challenge to ensure that the icons, symbolic motifs and values of the city are strong, broad and deep enough to allow Americans to extend their fraternal identification with one another to all of humanity, and also to all life on earth. The struggle to include all Americans in the founding principles of the nation has been enormously costly and is still incomplete. But to extend those principles, without the use of force, on a global scale, will inevitably demand an even greater price from America.

If it can now be re-evaluated and deepened, the idealism at the heart of American identity and consciousness can honor the self-determination of all peoples. Together with the democratic principles of equality, justice and liberty, the symbols which underlie its capital remind us of the reciprocity not only of all human life, but of all beings in the interdependent harmony of life on Earth. These are principles whose importance our generation – unfortunately at the eleventh hour – is only just beginning to realize. It has taken humanity a painfully long time to grasp its complete dependency upon the natural environment, and to understand that nature cannot long support an ever-increasing global human population, all now aspiring to live first world lifestyles. If America is to work in closer co-operation with the other peoples of the world in the challenging times ahead, then it will need to broaden its political ideals to include the honouring of all life on earth. At the risk of a tremendous tautology, I have attempted to show in this book that, however abstract the founding principles of a nation may appear to be when these are expressed as abstract symbols, it is precisely when they are communicated in this way that they can have a uniquely powerful effect upon our lives.

Despite the commercial priorities or lack of imagination of some who had a hand in Washington's historical development, the symbolism of the capital city of the American nation still approximates to the idealistic character of its founding vision. The original geometric design of L'Enfant for what the NCPC calls 'the symbolic heart of America' is now being reconceived and will soon be renewed. But can it be reconceived to include not only all Americans, but also all peoples, throughout the world? As the symbols of their primary central foundation are being redeveloped and enhanced through public and private initiative, Americans are being offered a reconnection with their most deeply held ideals. The naturally resonant and life-affirming Golden Section ratio that underlies the American capital, and integrates all the parts of the nation into a productive balanced whole, has the potential also to harmonise America's destiny within a truly universal geometric network. In the same way as the circles and pentacles that symbolised this harmony in the original design of its capital city could be imagined extending westwards, and over time as including vast numbers of people across its continent, so those ideals can also be imagined as extending outwards, to create a new level of international unity between the American nation and the entire world.

The challenge is to find the will and imagination to restore and expand the pattern of the original vision. Yet who today has anything like the vision that Pierre L'Enfant experienced in the spring of 1791, when he imagined Washington in relation to the 'celestial axis', and began to imprint upon the American landscape a geometric pattern that could perfectly represent the revolutionary principles of a new nation? The city L'Enfant dreamt, designed and passionately believed in was to surpass anything that anyone else could imagine at the time – even the vision of George Washington. Its first architect was misunderstood and rejected; but L'Enfant has been proved right, of course, in the extent of his belief: this embryonic city was to become so great and powerful that it exceeded even the grandness of his dreams. America was fortunate indeed to have its capital designed by a man courageous enough to look beyond the obvious, by combining the pragmatic concerns of urban planners everywhere with the partial manifestation of an extraordinary dream – a dream of perfectly balanced government. Yet if Washington is to be renewed in a manner that truly accords with the idealistic principles of America's founders, it needs to dream again, and this time on a global scale, and once again infuse solutions to pragmatic urban concerns with far-seeing idealism. At this time, the stakes in Washington are very high indeed. They go to the heart of America's relationship with the world.

References

Chapter 1

All overlays of the L'Enfant Plan throughout this book are based upon *L'Enfant's 1791 Manuscript Plan for the City of Washington*, full-color facsimile and computer-assisted reproduction, courtesy of the Library of Congress, Washington, 1991.

Mircea Eliade, *Cosmos and History: The Myth of the Eternal Return*, trans. W. Trask, Princeton, NJ: Princeton University Press, 1954.

Robert Lawlor, *Sacred Geometry: Philosophy and Practice*, Thames and Hudson, 1982.

A. Coomaraswamy, *The Transformation of Nature in Art*, Dover Publications, New York, 1956.

Tons Brunés, *The Secrets of Ancient Geometry and its Use*, two volumes, trans. Charles M. Napier, Rhodos, Copenhagen, 1967.

R. A. Schwaller de Lubicz, *The Temple of Man: Apet of the South at Luxor*, two volumes, trans. Deborah and Robert Lawlor, Inner Traditions International, Rochester, Vermont, 1998.

Chapter 2

Kenneth R. Bowling, *The Creation of Washington, D.C. The Idea and Location of the American Capital*, George Mason University Press, Fairfax VA, 1991.

Bob Arnebeck, *Through a Fiery Trial: Building Washington 1790–1800*, Madison Books, 1991.

Don Alexander Hawkins, 'The Landscape of the Federal City', *Washington History*, Volume 3, 1, 1991, 10–33. For a description of the District Commissioners, see William C. di Giacomantonio, 'All the President's Men', in the same volume, 52–75.

Silvio A. Bedini, (1) 'Benjamin Banneker and the Survey of the District of Columbia 1791', *Records* of the Columbia Historical Society, 1969–70. (2) 'The Survey of the Federal Territory', in *Washington History*, Volume 3, 1, 1991, pp. 76–95.

Sally Kennedy Alexander, 'A Sketch of the Life of Major Andrew Ellicott', *Records* of the Columbia Historical Society, 2, 1896.

Chapter 3

Records of the Columbia Historical Society, 11, p. 139.

John Claggart Proctor, 'Indian Lore – The Legend of the Widow's Mite', *Washington Sunday Star*, March 18, 1928. See also February 18, 1934.

Erle Kauffman, *Trees of Washington – The Man – The City*, The Outdoor Press, Washington, 1932.

Pamela Scott, 'L'Enfant's Washington Described: The City in the Public Press, 1791–1795', *Washington History*, 3, 1991.

Ernest B. Furguson, *Freedom Rising: Washington in the Civil War*, Knopf, Random House, 2004.

Phyllis Wheatley's poem was first published in the *Pennsylvania Magazine*, 1776.

For more on neoclassicism, Columbia and the American relationship to nature, visit: http://www.learner.org/amerpass/unit04/ or: http://xroads.virginia.edu/~CAP/Nature/cap2.html

Chapter 4

'L'Enfant's Reports to President Washington', *Records of the Columbia Historical Society*, 1899.

Hans Paul Caemmerer, *The Life of Pierre Charles L'Enfant*, National Republic Publishing Co., Washington, 1950.

Elisabeth S. Kite, *L'Enfant and Washington 1791–1792*, Johns Hopkins Press, Baltimore, 1929.

L'Enfant-Digges-Morgan Collection, Manuscript Division, Library of Congress.

J. L. Sibley Jennings Jr., 'Artistry as Design: L'Enfant's Extraordinary City', *Quarterly Journal of the Library of Congress*, Volume 36, 3, 1979.

Ralph E. Ehrenberg, 'Mapping the Nation's Capital: The Surveyor's Office, 1791–1818', *Quarterly Journal of the Library of Congress*, Volume 36, 3, 1979.

Richard W. Stephenson, *A Plan Whol [l]y New: Pierre Charles L'Enfant's Plan of the City of Washington*, Library of Congress, Washington, 1993.

John W. Reps, *Monumental Washington: The Planning and Development of the Capital Center*, Princeton University Press, 1967.

Pamela Scott, ' "This Vast Empire": The Iconography of the Mall, 1791–1848', in *The Washington Mall 1791–1991* edited by Richard Longstreth, 1991.

J. J. Jusserand, introduction to *L'Enfant and Washington 1791–1792*, Elisabeth S. Kite, Johns Hopkins Press, Baltimore, 1929.

Chapter 5

Albert Pike, *Morals and Dogma (of the Ancient and Accepted Scottish Rite of Freemasonry)*, Southern Jurisdiction of the United States, 1925.

Robert Lawlor, op. cit., 1982.

References

R. A. Schwaller de Lubicz, op. cit., 1977.
Mircea Eliade, 1954 and *Patterns in Comparative Religion,* trans. R. Sheed, London: Sheed and Ward, 1958.

Chapter 6

David Ovason, *The Secret Zodiacs of Washington, D.C.,* Century, London, 1999.
Robert Lawlor, op. cit., 1982.
John Michell, *The New View Over Atlantis,* Thames & Hudson, London, 1969, p. 156.

Chapter 7

William Preston, *Illustrations of Masonry,* 1772.
John Michell, *The Dimensions of Paradise,* Thames and Hudson, London, 1988.
Robert Lawlor, op. cit., 1982.
Albert Pike, op. cit., 1925.
Robert Macoy, 1869, *A Dictionary of Freemasonry,* Gramercy Books, New York, 2000.
H. P. H. Bromwell, *Restorations of Masonic Geometry and Symbolry.*
David Stevenson, *The Origins of Freemasonry: Scotland's Century 1590–1710,* Cambridge University Press, Cambridge, 1988.

Chapter 8

Ellicott Plan of 1792, courtesy of the Library of Congress.
Elisabeth S. Kite, op. cit., 1929.
L'Enfant-Digges-Morgan Collection, Manuscript Division, Library of Congress.
The L'Enfant *Memorials,* transcribed in the *Records* of the Columbia Historical Society, Volume 2, 1899.
For an analysis of the problems between L'Enfant and the District Commissioners see Daniel D. Reiff, *Washington Architecture 1791–1861: Problems in Development,* U.S. Commission of Fine Arts, Washington, 1971.
William T. Partridge is quoted in H. Paul Caemmerer, *A Manual on the Origin and Development of Washington,* U.S. Government Printing Office, Washington, 1939, pp. 28–9. Partridge also drew a comparative map of the L'Enfant and Ellicott plans. This appears in 'L'Enfant's Vision', *The Federal Architect,* April 1937.
John W. Reps, op. cit., 1967.
Richard Longstreth, Editor, *The Mall in Washington 1791–1991,* Washington, 1991.
Development of the United States Capital, U.S. Government Printing Office, Washington, 1930.

Chapter 9

F. L. Harvey, Jr., 'Washington National Monument, Washington, D.C., Concise Description – Details in the Construction. From Annual Reports of Col. Thos. Lincoln Casey, Corps of Engineers, Engineer in Charge'. *Monograph of the Washington National Monument: Dedicatory Ceremonies, February 21, 1885.*

John Michell, op. cit., 1988.

Albert Pike, op. cit., 1925.

Chapter 10

William Bartram, 1791, *Travels through North and South Carolina, Georgia, East and West Florida*... New York, Penguin, 1996.

Thomas Jefferson, *Notes on the State of Virginia*, 1782.

Steven Bullock, *Revolutionary Brotherhood: Freemasonry and the Transformation of the American Social Order, 1730–1840*, University of North Carolina Press, Chapel Hill, 1996.

Margaret Jacob, *Living the Enlightenment: Freemasonry and Politics on Eighteenth-Century Europe*, Oxford University Press, Oxford, 1991.

Pamela Scott, op. cit., 1991.

Bob Arnebeck, 'Divided City: A Short History of Washington, D.C.', *www.geocities.com/bobarnebeck/*, 2004.

Robert Macoy, op. cit., 1869.

David Stevenson, op. cit., 1988.

Chapter 11

Elisabeth S. Kite, op. cit., 1929.

'L'Enfant's Reports to President Washington', *Records of the Columbia Historical Society 2*, 30, 32, 1899.

John V. Cogbill, III, Chairman, National Capital Planning Commission, *Testimony before the Senate Subcommittee on National Parks*, April 12, 2005.

For the National Capital Planning Commission's Legacy Plan and related proposals visit: http://www.npc.gov./

Index

Abydos, Egypt 21–2, 91
Académie Royale de Peinture et de Sculpture, Paris 51–2, 117
Adams, President John 2, 72, 73, 165
Age of Enlightenment 63, 76, 82–3, 155–6
agora, Athens 83
Algonquin, language 27–8
Alexandria, Virginia 26, 27, 30, 33, 35, 72, 165
American sublime 156–60, 176, 180
Anacostia, River 33, 50, 56, 62, 95, 106, 169, 178, 185, 188, 189; *see also* Eastern Branch
Anacostia, tribe 38
Annapolis 57
anima mundi 157, 186
Angkor Wat, Cambodia 19, *21*
Ark of the Covenant 71, 72, 161
Arlington National Cemetery 143, 174
Arnebeck, Bob, author 25, 55
ashlar *78*, 79–80, 151, 154
axis mundi 2, 42, 68–9

Bacon, Henry 147
Banneker, Benjamin, mathematician 4, 34–5, 51, 74, 75, 86, 95, 178, 187
baroque 60, 91
Bartram, William, author 157
bazaar 81, 83, 84
Beall, Ninian, landowner 30
Bedini, Silvio, author 34
Bierstadt, Albert, artist 157
Bill of Rights vi, 45, 178, 184
Blazing Star, *see* Eastern Star
Blodget, Samuel, surveyor 167
Bowling, Kenneth, author 25, 26
Brumidi, artist 190
Brunés, Tons, Mason 18
Bullock, Steven, author 165

Caemmerer, Hans Paul, L'Enfant biographer 52
cathedral 80–1, 83, 84, 91–2, 131, 160
Capitol 2, 3–4, 6, 8, 12, 17, 30, 32, 39, *46*, 47, 56, 58, 68–75, 82–6, 87, *90*, 96–8, 101, 104–5, 106–7, 111, 115, 116, 118, 124–5, 127, 132, 140–7, 152, 157, 169, 171–3, *173*, 175–9, 181, 183, 185, *185*, 187–9, *189*, 190; as temple 2, 46, 72–3, 182; location 59–62, 65, 68, 73, dedication 72, 161

Capitol City, *see* City of Washington
Capitoline Hill, Rome 84
Cahokia, Mound City 25
Cayuga, tribe 29
Carroll, Daniel, District Commissioner 33, 35, 135, 167
City Hall 2, 4, 6, 61, *89*, *97*, 104–7, 140, 172, 176
City of Washington 2, 10, 14, 23, 83; geometry 25–33, 65–132, 55, *102*, *125*, *126*, 146; design 56–63, 117–8, 142, 159–160, 166; symbolism of vii–viii, 17–8, 41, 44, 61, 66, 86, 122, 143, 169–78, 180–92, *189*
Civil War 26, 144, 150, 151
Clark, Grand Master Joseph 72
Cogbill III, John V., Chairman of NCPC 184–5
Columbia, Goddess 36–7, 43, 46–50, 157–8, 182, 190; *see also* Federal District
Congress House, *see* Capitol
Connecticut Avenue 39, *110*, 112–5, *114*, 121, 124, 132, 139–40, 162, 183
Constitution, American vi, 45, 75, 82, 86, 118, 137, 169, 172, 177, 178, 184, 191
Constitution Avenue *130*, 131
Crawford, Thomas, sculptor 47
Cuzco, Peru 68

Da Vinci, Leonardo 16
Delaware Avenue 96, *97*, 140
Delaware, tribe 29
Dermott, James, surveyor 138, 142, 167
diamond, 35, 37, 181, 183; pattern 112; *see also* Federal District;
Dickens, Charles, novelist 67
Digges, Thomas, friend of L'Enfant 139
District Courts 2, 4, 6, 61, *89*, *97*, 106–7, 140, 172, 176
District of Columbia, *see* Federal District
District Commissioners 32–3, 51, 64, 67, 133–8, 162–3
Dupont Circle 113, *114*, 140, 190

E Pluribus Unum, national motto 13, 17, 47, 153, 177
East Capitol Street 2, 66–7, 73–4, 82–4, 86, *89*, 140, 171–2, 187–9

197

The Secret Geometry of Washington, D.C.

Eastern Branch 27, 28, 33, *54*, 56, 62; *see also* Anacostia
Eastern Star 95, 98, 100, 123, 176–8, 180; *see also* pentacle
Egypt, Egyptian tradition v, 1, 13, 15, 16, 18, 20, 21, 47, 68, 70–1, 77, 79, 90–1,100, *99*, 117, 122–3, 152, 161, 167, 178, 190
Eighth Street 101–4, *104, 109*, 112, 131, 187
Eliade, Mircea, anthropologist 1, 70–1
Ellicott, Andrew, surveyor 4, 33–5, 51, 55, 59, 74–5, 86, 134–8, 141, 142, 162–3, 166–7, 187
Ellicott, Benjamin, surveyor 134, 138, 142, 163
Ellicott Plan 88, 106, 113, *136*, 139, 162–3
Emancipation Monument, *see* Lincoln Park
Executive 12, 17, 117, 118, 143, 173, 174, 178, 179–180; *see also* White House

Fairfax, Virginia family 30
Federal City, *see* City of Washington
Federal Congress, First 26
Federal District, 27, 32–7, *34*, *37*, 49, 53, 64, 79, 84, 161, 183; geometry of 75–80, 86, 164, 178, 181, 182; *see also* Columbia
Federal Hall, New York 52
Federal Triangle 140, 147, 179
Fibonacci, mathematician 15, 125
Flower of Life 20–4, 115
forum 86, 171; at Rome 83–4, 86
Franklin, Benjamin 29, 52
Freemasonry vi, 1, 2, 18, 35, 39, 53, 76–80, 91, 95, 99, 100, 121–4, 148–54, 159 160–8, 173, 181; anti-Freemasonry 65, 76, 129, 151, 165; ritual 35, 37, 111, 149, 161; Washington Masons 64, 72, 76, 110–1, 121–2, 149, 150, 163, 165, 168; Washington lodges: Alexandria No. 22 35, 165; Georgetown Lodge No. 9 165; Grand Lodge 39, Maryland No.16 35, Scottish Order 76, *114*, 121, *122*, 123, 148
French, Benjamin B., Grand Master 149, 150

Gaia, goddess 189
geomythics 50
gematria 100, 114, 151, 154, 160
genius loci 44, 49–50, 71, 157
geomancy 66, 123, 162
geometry, five-fold, *see* pentacle; sacred 1, 15, 18–24, 121, 182; six-fold 20–3, 99, 115, 117, 121, 152, 172; of temples 2, 70, 77–81, 182
Georgetown, Maryland 26, 27, 30, 31, 32, 56, 165
gnomon 15, 42
Golden Milestone, *see* Zero Milestone
Golden Section 1–2, 8, 13, 14–6, 19, 23–4, 88–93, *88, 89, 93*, 99–100, 106–7, 108, 110, 112, 113, 116–7, *119*, 123, 125–7, 130–2, 139, 140, 141, 145, 151, 155, 159–164, 167, 170, 172–8, 181, 186, *189*, 189, 192
Goose Creek 30, 33, *54*, 159; as Tiber 57, 58, 59, 60, 66, 84, 149
Great Falls 28–31

Great Pyramid 1, 16, 91, *99*, 116, 123
Great Seal vi 25, 53, 175; *see also* Novus Ordo Seclorum
Greenleaf Point 28, 44
Gutheim, Frederick, author 28

Hallet, Stephen or Etienne, architect 87–8, *90*, 127, 134, 164–5, 167, 182
Hamilton, Alexander, Treasurer, statesman 27, 52, 56, 118, 166, 177
Hilton Hotel, Washington 40, 121
Hiram of Tyre, architect to Solomon 18
Hoban, James, architect, Mason 110–1, 164, 182
Hopewell, culture 18
Horus, god 123
House of Congress, *see* Capitol
Humanism 16

Imhotep, Egyptian architect 18
Immunis Columbia, coin 46
Imperial City v, 68, 75, 173
Independence Avenue *130*, 131
Indiana Avenue *102*
Iroquois Confederacy 29, 42
Islamic tradition 1, 80, 81, 83, 84, 99, 152, 162

Jackson, President Andrew 140
Jefferson Memorial 14, 85, *102*, 103, 121, 129, 131, 145–7, *145*, 179–81, *180*, 183
Jefferson Pier 142, 145, 149–50
Jefferson, Thomas vi, 26, 27, 32, 33, 35, 51, 52, 56, 57, 60, 63, 64, 75, 99, 103, 118, 119, 134–5, 137, 139–43, 144, 149, 156–7, 159, 162, 164, 167, 169, 174, 177, 181, 183–4; *Notes on the state of Virginia* 156–7
Jenkins Hill 33, 44, *54*, 59, 61, 66, 73–4, 140, 159, 177, 188
Johnson, Thomas, District Commissioner 33, 165
Jones Point 35, 75
Judiciary 61, 112, 140, 171, 174, 178; *see also* Supreme Court
Jupiter, god 84
Justice, goddess 36; *see also* Ma'at
Jusserand J.J. author, ambassador 58

Kentucky Avenue 127, *128*
Knights Templar 76, 99, 162, 164
Kremlin 25

Lady of Freedom, 'Lady Liberty' 36, 47, *48*, 175, 182, 190–1
Lafayette, General 51, 113
Langworth, John, landowner 30, 39
Latrobe, Benjamin, architect 157
Lawlor, Robert, author, mathematician 75, 88
Lear, Tobias, secretary to George Washington 134–6, 139
Lee, Thomas, land agent 30–1
Legacy Plan, *see* NCPC

Index

Legislature 13, 17, 86, 143, 169, 171, 174, 178, 188; *see also* Capitol
L'Enfant, Pierre Charles 2, 46, 51–64, 118, 133–9, 143–4, 155–60, 169–83; army career 52, 156; boyhood 51, 117; character 53, 55, 143, 156–9; conflict with Commissioners 64, 67, 133–7, 162, 166, 181; grave *138,* 143; and Masonry 80, 91, 117, 121–4, 151, 160–8; and George Washington 17, 55, 58–9, 63–4, 82, 111, 121, 133–9, 156, 166, 169, 177
L'Enfant Plan viii, 2–13, 55, *57, 58,* 57–63, 65–8, 82–6, 118, 148, 155, 169–78, *173,* 178; versions 63, 134; accuracy 107, 124, 129, 131, 132; 'Template' 3, 145, *170,* 187, *189;* geometry 6–15, 19, 23–4, 87–107, *102,* 108–17, 124–8, *125, 126,* 132, 145, 161, 174, 175–8, 181–3; avenues 14, 59, 60–3, 65, 82, *90,* 95, 96–105, *105,* 108, *170,* 171, 174, 182; grid 59–61, 66, 129–31, *130;* alterations 134–6, *136,* 139–44, 146–7, 166–7, 179–81
Leonardo da Vinci, artist 16, 69
Liberty, *see* Columbia, Goddess
liberty cap, pole etc., 36, 45–6
Library of Congress 35, 56, *57,* 63, 134, 169
Lincoln Memorial 14, 85, 145–7, 179–181, *180,* 183
Lincoln Park/Square 67, 74–5, 87, *89,* 98, 104–7, 116, 124, 139, 140, 142–3, 171–2, *172, 173,* 176–7, 183, 187–9, *189*
Logan Circle 113, *114,* 140, 190
London 25, 159
Louis XIV 115, 117, 118
Louis XV 52, 64
Luxor, temple 15, 19, *20,* 91
Lyrical Ballads 156

Ma'at, Egyptian goddess, as justice 36, 47, 190–1
Madison, James, statesman 27, 32, 118, 177
Magnesia, Plato's city of v, 75, 83
Mall, 'Grand Avenue' 2, *58,* 60, 84–5, 86, *103, 130,* 132, 140–1, 144–7, 172, 174, 179–180, 183, 185
Manahoac, tribe 29
Mannacasset, native chief 38–9, 42, 45, 190
Maryland Avenue 33, 96, 100, *102,* 124–9, *125,* 140
Masonic Temple 71, 72, 76–80, *114,* 121–2, *122*
Masons, *see* Freemasonry
Massachusetts Avenue 10, 94, *94,* 100, 101, 113, *125, 126,* 139, 140, 183
Mausolus, Halicarnassus 121–2, 148, 162
McMillan Commission 14, 143–7, *146,* 178–81, *180,* 184–5
Mecca 1
Medina 1, 68, 75
Mellon Auditorium 174
Metatron 21, Metatron's Cube 21–3, *22*
Merkabah 80, *81*
Meridian Hill 142
Meridian Stone, *see* Zero Milestone
Michell, John, author, mathematician 84, 100
Mile or 'itinerary column' 6, 66–7, 74–5, 82–4, *89,* 98, 106–7, 140–1, 171–2, 175–6, 181

Mills, Robert, architect 148
Minerva, Goddess 36, 46
Mohawk, tribe 29
Monacan, tribe 29
Montgomery, General, monument to 53
Mound City, Illinois 25
Mount Vernon 26, 27, 30, 51
Mount Vernon Square 94, 101, 108, 139

Nacotchant, tribe 29, 33, 84
National Church *58,* 62, 101, *104, 109,* 112, 129, 140, 174
Native Americans 28–30, 37, 38–9, 42–5, 47, 50, 84, 177, 188
Navy Monument 101, *102, 104*
NCPC, National Capital Planning Commission 144, 146, 169, 184–9, *185,* 192
neoclassicism 53, 58, 145, 155, 157–8
neo-Platonism 77, 79, 175
Netr/w v, 71
New Jersey Avenue 96, *97,* 135, 140
New Jerusalem v, 1
New York 26, 52, 53, 55, 123, 137, 156, 165; Federal Hall 52, 175; St Paul's Chapel 53, 117, 123, 176
New York Avenue 108–110, *109,* 117
North Carolina Avenue *125, 126*
North Capitol Street 2, 73–4, 86, 96, 169, 185, 187–9
Novus Ordo Seclorum vi, 2, 156, 183
Noyes, Magadalena 44
number 84; three 115, 117, 122; four 77, 80, 94; five 94, 114–6, 151, 153, 161; six 77, 80, 94, 114–8, 152–4, 161, 164, 172; twelve 80, 115, 140, 172; thirteen 122; thirty-three 122; thirty-six 182; fifty-five 124–7, 151, 182; sixty 114–6, 152–3, 172, 182; one hundred and eight 95, 100, 107, 114–6, 182; six hundred and sixty-six 100, 114–7, 152–4, 172; one thousand one hundred and eighty 100, 114–6, 153–4; one thousand seven hundred and forty-six 100, *116*–7

obelisk 85, 148–152, 183; *see also* Washington Monument
Old Testament 117
Olmsted, Frederick Law, Jr., architect 144
omphalos 68, 71
Onondaga, tribe 29
Oneida, tribe 29
Ovason, David, author 95

Paris 25, 51, 52, 57, 60, 190
Parthenon, Athens 15
Partridge, William T., architect 146–7
Pennsylvania Avenue 29, 33, 39, 56, 62, 96, 100, 101, *102, 103, 109,* 111–2, 120, 124–9, *125,* 140, 144, 177, 183, 187
Pentalpha, *see* Eastern Star, pentacle
pentacle 93–101, *99, 125, 126,* 129, 131, 151–2, 175–8

Pentagon, The 175, 184
phi, *see* Golden Section
Philadelphia 26, 56, 63, 137, 165
Pike, Albert, Freemason, author 80, 121
Piscataway, tribe 29–30
Plato v, 75, 77, 83, 90, 117, 160; *Laws* 83; *Republic* 84; *see also* Magnesia
Platonic Solids 19, 23, *23*, 79, 92, *92*, 115, 186
Potomac River 26–33, *34*, 50, 59, 60, 61, 67, 124, 142, 143, 145, 149
Potowomek, tribe 29
Polaris, star 79
Powhatan, tribe 29, Confederacy 30
President's House, *see* White House
Preston, William, Freemason, author 108, 167, 175, 182
Proctor, John Claggart, author, journalist 41, 44
pyramid 18, 53, 122, 148, 151–3; *see also* Great Pyramid
Pythagoras, Pythagorean tradition v, 19, 69, 77, 91, 100, 122–3, 162, 175

Ra, god 123
Regulus, star 95, 178
Republic, American vii–viii, 63, 64, 164, ideals 49, 82–3, 86, 156–160, 171–2, 175–8, 183–4, 191–2
Revelation 152
Rhode Island Avenue 112, 113
Rock Creek 29, 39, 56
Romantics 156–7
Rome 68, 83–4, 86, 164, 171, 190
Roosevelt, President Theodore 144
Rosicrucians 162
Rousseau, Jean-Jacques, philosopher 155, 156
Russel Pope, John, architect 121

Savannah, siege of 52
Schwaller de Lubicz, R.A., geometrician 69, 75
Scott Circle 102
Scott, Pamela, historian and author 164
Senate Park Commission 144, *see* McMillan Commission
Seneca, tribe 29
Shawnee, tribe 29
Sibley Jennings Jr., J.L., architect 63, 190
Sirius, star 95, 178
Sixteenth Street *102*, 103–4, 108, *109*, 112, 121–2, 131, 142, 172–4, 187
Smith, Captain John 29
Society of the Cincinnati 53, 164–5, 175
Solomon, as Grand Master 72, seal of 80, 152, signet of 100
Solomon's Temple, *see* Temple of Jerusalem
South Capitol Street 2, 73–4, 86, 96, 169, 185, 187–9
South Carolina Avenue 94, 100, 101, 127, *128*
St. Paul's Chapel, *see* New York
Statue of Freedom, *see* Lady of Freedom
Statue of Liberty 36, 47
Stephenson, Richard, author 63
Steuben, General 52

Stonehenge 19
Stuart, David, District Commissioner 33, 35, 51, 167
Supreme Court 2, 4, *5*, 10, 17, 51, *58*, 61, 96, 140–1, 171, 183
Susquehannoc, tribe 30

Taft, President William 144
temenos 75, 78–9
Temple, of Solomon in Jerusalem v, 70–1, 72, 76, 80, 161
Temple Heights 39, 121
Tennessee Avenue 127, *128*
Thoth, god *99*, 100
Tiber, *see* Goose Creek
Treasury 140, 144, 183
tree, *see axis mundi*, Treaty Oak
Treaty Oak 30, 39–45, *40*, 121, 182, 190
triangle, 122; equilateral 113–24, *119*, *120*, 123, 132, 140, 156, 160, 162–4, 172–4; 'Federal Triangle' 140, 179; right-angled 122–3, 162; uneven 113, 117, 121, 123–4, 162–3, 174
Tuscarora, tribe 29

Venus, planet and goddess 88, 189
Vermont Avenue *110*, 113–5, 114, *114*, 124, 132, 139–40, 162, 183
Versailles 25, 51, 60, 113, 115, 117–8, 173
vesica piscis 6, 23, 91–3, *92*, *93*
Virginia Avenue *102*, 108, 128

Washington, D.C., *see* City of Washington
Washington, President George vi, 25, 26–7, 28, 31–3, 36, 39, 41, 51, 52, 55, 56, 58–9, 60, 63–5, 67, 72, 75, 82, 83, 110, 118, 119, 121, 133–9, 144, 145, 148, 152–3, 163, 165–8, 177, 181, 183–4, 192
Washington, Lawrence 26, 30, 31
War of Independence 25, 26, 52, 158, 167
Washington Monument 11, 12–3, 16, 17, 59, 85, *102*, 104, 106, *110*, 115–6, 141, 143, 144–154, *150*, 162, 164, 173–4, 179–181, 182, 183
Wheatley, Phillis, poet 36
White House viii, 2, 12, 13, 17, 25, 32, 39, 51, 56, 58–61, 65, 85, 97, 101, 106–24, *109*, *110*, *120*, 132, 139–47, 152, 161–4, 171–5, 178, *180*, 181, 183, 187
Widow's Mite 30, 38–45, 121, 182, 190
Williamsburg 57
Wordsworth, William, poet 156
Wren, Sir Christopher, architect 159
Wright, Frank Lloyd, architect 40, 66

Xochipilli, Toltec/Aztec god *37*

Yggdrasil, world tree 42
yod 123

zero-degree meridian 2, 73–4, 86, 103, 140, 142–3, 173, 177, 179, 183, 187
Zero Milestone 67, 83–4, 86, *89*, 141–3, 173–4, 177, 183, 187–8

www.ingramcontent.com/pod-product-compliance
Lightning Source LLC
Chambersburg PA
CBHW061302110426
42742CB00012BA/2025